Model Company Files

A guide to preparing audit

and non-audit files

Model Company Files

A guide to preparing audit and non-audit files

Published by

Accountancy Books

Accountancy Books
Gloucester House
399 Silbury Boulevard
Central Milton Keynes
MK9 2HL

Tel: 01908 248000

ISBN 85355 658 0

Typeset by Datix International Limited, Bungay, Suffolk
Printed in Great Britain by Bell and Bain Ltd, Glasgow

Contents

Introduction

The Practitioner's Audit Service is a comprehensive audit service for small and large companies alike. The *Compilation Reports Manual* provides a system for dealing with independent accountants' assignments for audit-exempt companies. This book has been produced in response to requests for practical guidance on the use of these two systems. The *Model Company Files* contains three complete current files, each designed to illustrate a different approach to companies. The files are based on real files from real clients, although clearly some details have been amended to protect confidentiality. Whilst this book is called *Model Company Files*, the principle objective is to produce realistic example files that could be achieved in practice, rather than theoretically perfect files. The key objective is to show what a good file should look like.

The first file, Collins Park Management Co Ltd, would normally be a totally exempt company requiring neither an independent accountants' report, nor an audit report, However, some of the members have insisted on an audit. This file has been completed using *The Practitioner's Audit Service.* The file has taken advantage of the 'opt-out' option under the system. It does not therefore, use the standard audit programmes, but uses the planning documentation to specify the audit approach to be adopted.

The second file, Roberts Design Limited, requires an independent accountants' report. This uses the documentation in the *Compilation Reports Manual* and demonstrates the difference between an audit assignment and a 'compilation'.

The third file, Bright-a-Light Ltd, is also produced using *The Practitioner's Audit Service.* This is a larger client, and uses the full standard audit programmes as the basis of the audit.

Content of the files

This book only includes the current audit files. It does not include any of the normal information schedules or letters that you would expect to find on the permanent, tax or correspondence files. The files do not therefore, include letters of engagement, any details relating to the directors' personal tax work, nor annual returns. The files also exclude the various draft stages of the accounts, in order to keep the book to a manageable size.

The files incorporate checklists from Volume III of *The Practitioner's Audit Service.* All three files use the simplified checklists for small companies that are not part of a group. The main checklist is used in Bright-a-Light Ltd. The annual review of changes is used in Collins Park Management Co Ltd and the checklist for abbreviated accounts is used in Roberts Design Ltd. Being the first year of incorporation, Roberts Design Ltd should also use the main checklist. However, again with a view to controlling the size of the book this checklist has been omitted from Roberts Design Ltd. Reference should be made to Bright-a-Light Ltd for guidance on how the main checklist should be used.

Similarly, the accountants' computerised nominal ledger printouts for Bright-a-Light have not been included.

Collins Park Management Co Ltd

This is a flat management company. Contributions are made to the company from owners of the 32 flats. These contributions are used to pay for the grassed area outside the flats to be cut, and to pay for the street lighting on the unadopted road.

With a turnover of just £1,600, this would normally be a total exemption company, requiring neither an audit nor a 'compilation report'. However, in the past, disputes have arisen over whether or not children should be allowed to play football on the grassed area outside the flats. Some of the tenants who wish to prohibit the playing of football in this area stood for election to the management committee, but were not appointed. There is now an element of distrust between these tenants and the management committee. They have therefore requested that an audit be undertaken.

The company has virtually no assets and liabilities, and only minimal income and expenditure. The planning forms therefore opt out of using the standard programmes. Instead, the majority of the audit work revolves around a 'rental' control account.

Roberts Design Ltd

Roberts Design Ltd is a consultancy company which provides services exclusively for one company which it invoices weekly. Its only fixed asset is a car. It carries no stock and its trade debtor represents the invoice for the last week of the year, which should be paid the following week. Creditors consist mainly of the various taxes due and the accountancy and audit fee.

The only employees of the company are Mr and Mrs Roberts. The professional work is carried out by Mr Roberts, whilst his wife acts as company secretary and deals with the administration of the company. Mrs Roberts also writes up the cash book and operates the payroll.

This is an assignment which requires an independent accountant's report. However, it is also an accounts preparation assignment, and therefore illustrates how the accounts preparation work can be used on 'compilations'.

Bright-a-Light Ltd

This company is a much larger entity. It wholesales and retails coal and bottled gas, together with a large amount of associated products such as barbecues. The company is again controlled by husband and wife directors, but also employs other staff. The systems are fairly straightforward, but include computerised sales, purchase and stock ledgers and computerised payroll.

Although the audit is generally a low risk audit, the file treats trade debtors as a high risk. This illustrates how the sampling for a file is affected by the differing risk factors.

This file also introduces two independence problems, with a close personal friendship existing between the directors and the auditor. The audit partner has also been involved in the audit for over seven years. The file therefore demonstrates how to deal with problems such as these.

Although the client has better accounting systems than many clients of a similar size, the auditor is still heavily involved in the accounts preparation work. It illustrates how accounts preparation work can be used to provide audit evidence.

FILE 1 – COLLINS PARK MANAGEMENT COMPANY LIMITED

Client: Collins Park Management Co Ltd		Prepared by: EAA	Date: 8.12.95
Year/Period End: 31.10.95	File No:	Reviewed by: DGW	Date: 8.12.95

AUDIT FILE INDEX

A ACCOUNTS

1	Final accounts	✓
2	Tax computations	
3	Final journals	
4	Draft accounts, typing instructions	
5	Letter of representation	✓
6	Letter to management	
7	Company accounts disclosure checklists	✓
8	Management accounts/last year's accounts	
9		

B AUDIT COMPLETION
C AUDIT PLANNING
D EXTENSIVE ANALYTICAL REVIEW
E INTANGIBLE ASSETS
F TANGIBLE FIXED ASSETS
G INVESTMENTS IN GROUP AND ASSOCIATED UNDERTAKINGS
H OTHER INVESTMENTS
I STOCK AND WORK IN PROGRESS
J DEBTORS AND PREPAYMENTS
K BANK BALANCES AND CASH
L CREDITORS AND ACCRUALS
M LONG TERM LOANS AND DEFERRED INCOME
N PROVISIONS FOR LIABILITIES AND CHARGES, CONTINGENT LIABILITIES AND FINANCIAL COMMITMENTS
O CAPITAL, RESERVES AND STATUTORY RECORDS
P TAXATION
Q INCOME AND EXPENDITURE – ANALYSIS FOR TAX PURPOSES
R PROFIT AND LOSS
S CASH FLOW STATEMENTS
T POST BALANCE SHEET EVENTS
U VALUE ADDED TAX
V CONSOLIDATION
W ACCOUNTS WORKING PAPERS
X RECORDS RECEIVED
Y COMPUTER REPORTS
Z OBSOLETE WORKING PAPERS

Client: Collins Park Management co Ltd		Prepared by:	Date:	Ref: **A**
Year/Period End: 31.10.95	File No:	Reviewed by:	Date:	

PARTNER COMPLETION

Final

			Initials
1	Have all outstanding items on the initial partner completion been adequately dealt with?	~~Yes~~/N/A*	ADS
2	Has a signed letter of representation been received?	Yes	ADS
3	Where the letter of representation is signed by one director on behalf of the Board, have we seen minutes of a meeting agreeing its contents?	~~Yes~~/N/A*	ADS
4	Are we satisfied that the directors' representations can be relied upon?	Yes	ADS
5	Does the file contain adequate justification of the audit report?	Yes	ADS
6	Has a letter of comment covering all material weaknesses in the system been sent to the client?	~~Yes~~/N/A*	ADS
7	Has the final post balance sheet events programme on **T4** been completed?	~~Yes~~/NCN†*	ADS
8	Does the balance sheet state the name of the director who approves the accounts on behalf of the Board, together with the date of approval?	Yes	ADS
9	Does the copy of the accounts which is being filed with the Registrar contain original signatures on the directors' report, the auditors' report and the balance sheet?	Yes	ADS
10	Does the audit file contain sufficient evidence (where applicable) to support our opinion on the following exemptions taken by the company:		
	(a) filing abbreviated accounts;	~~Yes~~/N/A*	ADS
	(b) disclosure exemptions applicable to small companies under SI 1992 No 2452;	~~Yes~~/N/A*	ADS
	(c) exemption from preparing consolidated accounts within s248 CA 1985.	~~Yes~~/N/A*	ADS
11	Do the working papers and the tax computation reflect final adjustments?	Yes	ADS
12	Have all final journals been recorded and processed to produce a closing trial balance agreeing with the accounts?	Yes	ADS
13	Has the final copy of the accounts been referenced to the file to ensure all lead and **Q** schedules reflect final adjustments?	Yes	ADS

I authorise the signing of the audit report.

Signed AD Smith Partner Date 20.12.95

Second partner (if applicable)

Signed ______________________ Partner Date __________

* Delete as appropriate.

† NCN = not considered necessary.

Collins Park Management Company Limited

FINANCIAL STATEMENTS FOR THE YEAR ENDED

31 OCTOBER 1995

COMPANY NUMBER 9991000

COLLINS PARK MANAGEMENT COMPANY LIMITED

Report of the directors

The directors submit their report and the audited accounts of the company for the year ended 31 October 1995.

Principal activities

The principal activity of the company is the management of amenities at Collins Park, Newtown, Berkshire, for the benefit of the members of the company.

Directors

The following were directors during the year, and their interests in shares of the company were:

	Ord £1 shares	
	31.10.95	*1.11.94*
B A Jones	1	1
J L Smith	1	1

The director retiring by rotation is Mr B A Jones who, being eligible, offers himself for re-election.

Statement of directors' responsibilities

Company law requires the directors to prepare financial statements for each financial year which give a true and fair view of the state of affairs of the company and of the profit or loss of the company for that period. In preparing those financial statements, the directors are required to:

(a) select suitable accounting policies and then apply them consistently;

(b) make judgements and estimates that are reasonable and prudent;

(c) prepare the financial statements on the going concern basis unless it is inappropriate to presume that the company will continue in business.

The directors are responsible for keeping proper accounting records which disclose with reasonable accuracy at any time the financial position of the company and to enable them to ensure that the financial statements comply with the Companies Act 1985. They are also responsible for safe-guarding the assets of the company and hence for taking reasonable steps for the prevention and detection of fraud and other irregularities.

Special exemptions

Advantage has been taken, in the preparation of this report, of special exemptions applicable to small companies.

By Order Of The Board

Secretary

B A Jones

Registered Office:
No 1 Collins Park
Newtown
Berkshire

16 December 1995

(Page 1)

Auditors' Report to the shareholders of Collins Park Management Company Limited

We have audited the financial statements on pages 3 to 5 which have been prepared under the historical cost convention and the accounting policies set out on page 5.

Respective responsibilities of directors and auditors
As described on page 1 the company's directors are responsible for the preparation of financial statements. It is our responsibility to form an independent opinion, based on our audit, on those statements and to report our opinion to you.

Basis of opinion
We conducted our audit in accordance with Auditing Standards issued by the Auditing Practices Board. An audit includes examination, on a test basis, of evidence relevant to the amounts and disclosures in the financial statements. It also includes an assessment of the significant estimates and judgements made by the directors in the preparation of the financial statements, and of whether the accounting policies are appropriate to the company's circumstances, consistently applied and adequately disclosed.

We planned and performed our audit so as to obtain all the information and explanations which we considered necessary in order to provide us with sufficient evidence to give reasonable assurance that the financial statements are free from material misstatement, whether caused by fraud or other irregularity or error. In forming our opinion we also evaluated the overall adequacy of the presentation of information in the financial statements.

Opinion
In our opinion the financial statements give a true and fair view of the state of the company's affairs as at 31 October 1995 and of its profit for the year then ended and have been properly prepared in accordance with the provisions of the Companies Act 1985 applicable to small companies.

Smith, Williams and Taylor

Chartered Accountants
and Registered Auditor

15 The Crescent
Newtown
Berkshire

20 December 1995

(Page 2)

Collins Park Management Company Limited

Profit and Loss account for the year ended 31 October 1995

	NOTE	1995 £	1994 £
Turnover	1	1600	1600
Administrative expenses		(1536)	(1566)
		64	34
Interest receivable		7	9
Profits on ordinary activities before taxation	2	71	43
Tax on profit on ordinary activities		–	–
Profit on ordinary activities after taxation, retained for the financial year		71	43
Retained profit brought forward		65	22
Retained profit carried forward		136	65

There were no recognised gains or losses other than the profit for the current or preceeding financial year.

There were no acquisitions or discontinued operations during the current or preceding financial year.

The notes on page 5 form an integral part of these accounts.

(Page 3)

Collins Park Management Company Limited

Balance Sheet as at 31 October 1995

	NOTE	*1995*		*1994*	
		£	£	£	£
CURRENT ASSETS					
Debtors	4	150		50	
Cash at bank		414		397	
		564		447	
CREDITORS: amounts falling due within one year	3	(396)		(350)	
NET CURRENT ASSETS			168		97
TOTAL ASSETS LESS CURRENT LIABILITIES			168		97
CAPITAL AND RESERVES					
Called up share capital	5		32		32
Profit and loss account			136		65
Shareholders' funds	6		168		97

The notes on page 5 form an integral part of these accounts.

These accounts were approved by the Board of Directors on 16 December 1995.

Advantage has been taken, in the preparation of the accounts, of special exemptions applicable to small companies on the grounds that, in the directors' opinion, the company qualifies as a small company under s246 and s247 of the Companies Act 1985.

____

J L SMITH

(Page 4)

Collins Park Management Company Limited

Notes to the Accounts for the year ended 31 October 1995

1. Accounting policies

Basis of accounting

The accounts have been prepared under the historical cost accounting convention, and in accordance with applicable accounting standards.

Turnover

Turnover is the amount receivable by the company for services rendered.

	1995 £	*1994* £
2. Profit on ordinary activities before taxation		
After charging:		
Auditor's remuneration	100	90
The directors received no remuneration during the year (last year £ nil)		
3. Creditors: amounts falling due within one year		
Trade creditors	329	316
Accruals	67	34
	396	350
4. Debtors		
Trade debtors	150	50
5. Called up share capital		
Authorised ordinary shares of £1	100	100
Allotted, issued and fully paid	32	32
6. Reconciliation of shareholders' funds		
Profit for the financial year	71	43
Opening shareholders' funds	97	54
Closing shareholders' funds	168	97

(Page 5)

Collins Park Management Ltd
No 1 Collins Park
Newtown
Berkshire
Company No. 9991000

Smith, Williams & Taylor
Chartered Accountants
15 The Crescent
Newtown
Berkshire

Dear Sirs

We confirm to the best of our knowledge and belief, and having made appropriate enquiries to other directors and officials of the company, the following representations given to you in connection with your audit of the company's financial statements for the year ended 31 October 1995.

1. We acknowledge as directors our responsibility for the financial statements, which you have prepared for the company. All the accounting records have been made available to you for the purpose of your audit and all the transactions undertaken by the company have been properly reflected and recorded in the accounting records. All other records and related information, including minutes of all management and shareholders' meetings, have been made available to you.

2. The company has no liabilities or contingent liabilities other than those disclosed in the financial statements. In particular, we confirm that the local council have not shown any intention to adopt the private road and as such no provisions or contingencies are necessary.

3. There has been no event since the balance sheet date which requires disclosing or which would materially affect the amounts in the financial statements, other than those already disclosed or included in the financial statements.

4. The company has had at no time during the year any arrangement, transaction or agreement to provide credit facilities (including loans, quasi-loans or credit transactions) for directors nor to guarantee or provide security for such matters.

5. The company has not contracted for, nor authorised any capital expenditure other than as disclosed in the financial statements.

6. There are no laws or regulations which are central to the company's ability to continue operating.

Yours faithfully

B A Jones
Director

J L Smith
Director

Client: Collins Park Management Co Ltd		Prepared by: MJS	Date: 8.12.95	Ref: A7.1
Year/Period End: 31.10.95	File No:	Reviewed by: AJS	Date: 12.12.95	

SIMPLIFIED INTRODUCTORY CHECKLIST

The simplified checklists for small companies have omitted the more unusual disclosure requirements. They are only suitable for small companies which are not part of a group, and assume full advantage has been taken of SI 1992 No 2452. *Complete this introductory checklist to confirm that it is appropriate to use the simplified checklists. For any questions answered 'yes', complete the relevant questions in the full checklists.*

			*Full checklist reference**	*Complete (√)*
1	Does it have more than 250 employees?	Y/N	3.12(a)	—
2	Has it adopted any format other than Balance Sheet Format I and Profit and Loss Account Formats I or II in the Companies Act 1985, or changed formats since last year?	Y/N	2.01 to 2.07, 2.12 to 2.17	—
3	Has it acquired or discontinued any operations, or undergone a reorganisation or reconstruction?	Y/N	11.02 to 11.10, 12.04 to 12.06	—
4	Has it any foreign currency transactions or overseas income?	Y/N	10.01 to 10.02, 13.10, 31.10, **9**(3.03).	—
5	Has it any exceptional or extraordinary items?	Y/N	12.01 to 12.09	—
6	Has it any intangible fixed assets (e.g., goodwill)?	Y/N	6.04, 17.03, 18.01 to 18.04, 31.12, **9**(3.09, 5.04)	—
7	Does it have any investments in shares of other companies?	Y/N	20.02, 23.04, **9**(3.16)	—
8	Does the company have any government grants?	Y/N	27.01, 27.02, 31.05	—
9	Has it any defined benefit or foreign pension schemes, or any other post retirement benefits?	Y/N	8.03, 8.05, 8.06, 29.08, 31.13, Checklist **14**	—
10	Has it any class of shares other than the normal ordinary shares?	Y/N	14.02, 25.20, 28.02 to 28.06, 28.08, 28.12 to 28.14, **9**(3.06 to 3.08)	—
11	Has it purchased any own shares or given financial assistance for the purchase of its shares?	Y/N	3.15, Checklist **12**	—

* *All references are to full Checklist **6** (main checklist), unless specified.*

A7.2

			Full checklist reference*	Complete (√)
12	Has it any debentures, convertible debts or warrants, or any other capital instruments treated as debt (other than normal loans)?	Y/N	25.05 to 25.15	—
13	Has it repurchased or settled any own debt early?	Y/N	9.02	—
14	Does the company have any unusual directors' transactions (other than overdrawn loan accounts and transactions in which the directors have a material interest) or transactions with officers (who are not directors), such as financial arrangements, quasi-loans, guarantees or security or credit transactions?	Y/N	24.01 to 24.12	—
15	Does the company pay unconnected third parties for directors' services?	Y/N	7.03	—
16	Is it a lessor company?	Y/N	Checklist **13**	—
17	Has it any FRS 5 style substance over form transactions (e.g., factoring of debts, consignment stock or sale and leaseback)?	Y/N	1.06 to 1.11	—
18	Is it an investment company?	Y/N	14.09, 28.11, 31.14	—
19	Does it have any interest in a partnership, unlimited company or Scottish firm, where each partner or member is a limited company?	Y/N	**9**(5.05), **10**(4.05 to 4.08)	—

Client: Collins Park Management Co		Prepared by:	Date:	Ref: A7.3
Year/Period End: 31.10.95	File No:	Reviewed by:	Date:	

SIMPLIFIED ANNUAL REVIEW OF CHANGES

This checklist is only suitable for small companies which are not part of a group and assumes full advantage has been taken of SI 1992 No 2452. *The checklist is not intended to be a comprehensive accounts checklist, but highlights the most common areas of change which will require further disclosure. The references are to the Checklist* **2** *(simplified main checklist). This checklist should be marked with a '√' to indicate yes, a '×' for no and a '-' for not applicable.*

		Complete (√)
1	The introductory checklist should be completed every year and any additional disclosures identified should be followed up.	✓
2	The Checklist **2** (simplified main checklist) should normally be used:	
	(a) when statutory accounts are first completed on behalf of a client; or	–
	(b) when the size or nature of the client's business alters significantly.	–
3	Note any significant changes to the accounts and the disclosure requirements. If any are required, either update the existing checklist or complete a new checklist.	–
4	Ensure that a completed copy of the Checklist **2** (simplified main checklist) is held on the Permanent Audit File.	✓
5	If any new FRSs have been published which affect the company, note the disclosure requirements and the dates from which the FRS applies to the company.	–

Conclusion

I have considered the disclosure requirements of this company and the risk of a disclosure error arising from not completing the Checklist **2** (simplified main checklist) this year. In my opinion, it is acceptable to use the simplified 'annual review of changes' checklist.

Prepared by MJS Date 8.12.95

Reviewed by AKS Date 12.12.95

		Changed? Y/N	Checklist 2 reference	Complete (√)
1	Have there been any changes to principal activities?	Y/N	2.01	
2	Have any new directors been appointed or any existing directors retired or resigned?	Y/N	2.02, 2.03	
3	Have the shareholdings of directors changed?	Y/N	2.03(a)	
4	Have any options been granted to or exercised by directors (or immediate family)?	Y/N	2.03(b)	
5	Do political and charitable contributions exceed £200?	Y/N	2.04	
6	Does the aggregate directors' remuneration exceed £60,000?	Y/N	4.07	
7	Has the true and fair override been used?	Y/N	1.01 to 1.04, 4.05	
8	Have any fixed assets been revalued?	Y/N	4.04, 4.18, 4.25, 4.26, 5.03, 6.01 to 6.04, 6.08 to 6.12, 10.02(d), 11.04	
9	Are there any new leasing or hire-purchase contracts:			
	– operating leases?	Y/N	4.10, 12.06, 12.07, 14.08	
	– finance leases and hire-purchase contracts?	Y/N	4.09, 6.05, 6.06, 9.03, 9.04, 12.05, 14.08	
10	Has there been any change in issued or authorised share capital?	Y/N	4.23, 11.01, 11.02	
11	Have any new reserves or provisions been created?	Y/N	10.01, 10.02, 11.03, 11.04	
12	Have there been any transactions between the company and its directors and officers?	Y/N	8.01 to 8.03	
13	Have payments commenced to a new pension scheme?	Y/N	4.08, 12.04, 14.09	
14	Has the company entered into any new financial commitments or contracted for or authorised any capital expenditure?	Y/N	12.03, 12.08	
15	Have there been any prior year adjustments?	Y/N	4.27 to 4.31	
16	Has the company received any new loans?	Y/N	9.01, 9.02	

A7.5

		Changed? Y/N	Checklist 2 reference	Complete (✓)
17	Does the company have any new contingent liabilities or charges on assets?	~~Y~~/N	9.01(c), 12.01, 12.02	—
18	Is a provision required for deferred tax?	~~Y~~/N	4.15 to 4.17, 9.05, 10.02 14.07	—
19	Have there been any gains or losses other than the profit or loss recorded in the profit and loss account?	~~Y~~/N	4.24, 4.25	—
20	Are there any dividends paid or proposed?	~~Y~~/N	3.06, 4.19, 4.21, 9.05	—
21	Are any debtors due after more than one year?	~~Y~~/N	7.05, 7.06	—
22	Are there any long-term contracts?	~~Y~~/N	7.02, 7.04	—
23	Have any accounting policies changed?	~~Y~~/N	14.01 to 14.09	—
24	Have there been any material post-balance sheet events?	~~Y~~/N	13.01	—

B AUDIT COMPLETION

1	Partner review	☐
2	Audit standards questionnaire	☑
3	File completion questionnaire	☑
4	Critical review of accounts questionnaire	☑
5	Audit highlights	☑
6	Justification of audit report	☐
7	Summary of unadjusted errors	☐
8	Queries for partner	☐
9	Final analytical review	☐
10	Points forward to next year	☐
11	Commercial observations on client's business	☐
12	Senior/manager review	☐
13	Cleared audit queries	☐
14		☐
15		☐

Client: Collins Park Management + Co		Prepared by:	Date:	Ref: **B**
Year/Period End: 31.10.95	File No:	Reviewed by:	Date:	

PARTNER COMPLETION

Initial

			Initials
1	Has the audit standards questionnaire been satisfactorily completed?	Yes	ADS
2	Has the file completion questionnaire been satisfactorily completed?	Yes	ADS
3	Has the critical review of accounts questionnaire been satisfactorily completed?	Yes	ADS
4	Has sufficient work been undertaken in view of the level of risk (as revised)* and materiality (as revised)* to enable an audit opinion to be formed?	Yes	ADS
5	Has all original work been reviewed, other than that undertaken by the partner responsible for the audit?	Yes	ADS
6	Have all partner review points been properly cleared?	~~Yes~~/N/A*	ADS

7 List below any other work that needs to be undertaken before the audit report is signed:

____

____

____

____

____

____

I authorise the issue of the accounts for approval.

Signed ADSmith Partner Date 12.12.95

Second partner (if applicable)

Signed ____________________ Partner Date __________

* Delete as appropriate.

Client: Collins Park Management Co		Prepared by: MJS	Date: 8·12·95	Ref: **B2**
Year/Period End: 31.10.95	File No:	Reviewed by: AAS	Date: 12.12.95	

AUDIT STANDARDS QUESTIONNAIRE

SAS No.		Initials
110	Has the audit been planned and performed having considered the risk of material fraud or error?	Yes MJS
120	Has the audit been planned and performed having considered the risk of material misstatement arising from non-compliance with relevant laws and regulations?	Yes MJS
130	Has the appropriateness of the going concern basis been considered?	Yes MJS
140	Do we have an up-to-date letter of engagement?	Yes MJS
150	Has an adequate post balance sheet events review been performed?	Yes MJS
160	Has other information to be issued with the financial statements been reviewed for consistency?	Yes MJS
200	Has the audit plan been reviewed and updated, where necessary?	Yes MJS
210	Do our audit files contain adequate information to provide an understanding of the nature of the client's business?	Yes MJS
220	Has materiality been reviewed and updated, where necessary?	Yes MJS
220	Has the effect on the accounts of any unadjusted errors been considered?	Yes MJS
230	Do the working papers contain an adequate record of the work performed and conclusions drawn?	Yes MJS
240	Has the audit work been properly directed, supervised and reviewed?	Yes MJS
300	Do the files contain sufficient details of the client's accounting systems?	Yes MJS
300	Has the risk assessment been reviewed and updated, where necessary?	Yes MJS
300	Where the risk assessment or materiality has been revised, has sufficient additional testing been undertaken?	Yes MJS
400	Does the file contain sufficient, appropriate audit evidence to enable us to draw reasonable conclusions?	Yes MJS
410	Does the file contain sufficient evidence of analytical review?	Yes MJS
420	Does the file contain sufficient, appropriate evidence assessing the reasonableness of accounting estimates?	Yes MJS
430	Has audit sampling been applied in an appropriate manner?	Yes MJS

Client: Collins Park Management Co		Prepared by: MJS	Date: 8.12.95	Ref: **B2**
Year/Period End: 31.10.95	File No:	Reviewed by: HDS	Date: 12.12.95	

AUDIT STANDARDS QUESTIONNAIRE (*Cont.*)

SAS No.			**Initials**
440	Has a letter of representation been drafted covering all necessary representations?	Yes	MJS
450	Is there sufficient, appropriate evidence that amounts derived from the previous period are free from material misstatement and are appropriately incorporated in the current period's accounts?	Yes	MJS
470	Has an adequate overall review of the accounts been performed?	Yes	MJS
600	Is the audit opinion consistent with the audit evidence and conclusions?	Yes	MJS

Client: Collins Park Management Co		Prepared by: MJS	Date: 8.12.95	Ref: **B3**
Year/Period End: 31.10.95	File No:	Reviewed by: AAS	Date: 12.12.95	

FILE COMPLETION QUESTIONNAIRE

Where work is outstanding prior to review, the outstanding (O/S) column should be ticked in pencil to highlight work required. As and when work is completed, the final column should be initialled, and the tick rubbed out.

Completion (pre-partner review)

	Question		O/S	Initials
1	Do the working papers record all the work done and do all the schedules contain the source of information?	Yes		MJS
2	Has the current file been fully cross-referenced?	Yes		MJS
3	Have all the queries and problems been properly cleared or carried forward to schedule **B8**, queries for partner or **B5** audit highlights?	Yes		MJS
4	Have the budget and actual time summaries been completed, along with explanations of variances?	~~Yes~~/NCN†*		MJS
5	Has the Permanent audit file been updated?	Yes		MJS
6	Have all unadjusted errors been summarised on **B7** and adjusted where necessary?	~~Yes~~/None*		MJS
7	Has the **B2** Audit standards questionnaire been completed?	Yes		MJS
8	Has the **B6** Justification of audit report been completed? (Covered on B5)	~~Yes~~		MJS
9	Have any commercial observations on the client's business been recorded on B11?	~~Yes~~/None*		MJS

Completion (final)

	Question		O/S	Initials
10	Have you confirmed that there have been no changes to the firm's independence during the course of the audit which would prevent reappointment of the firm as auditors for the next financial period?	Yes		MJS
11	Has consultation been undertaken in all circumstances, where it is required by the firm's procedures?	~~Yes~~/NCN†*		MJS
12	Where any fraud, error or breach in laws and regulations have been identified, have the implications on the accounts been fully considered?	~~Yes~~/N/A*		MJS
13	Has the draft letter or the points for comment been prepared?	~~Yes~~/NCN†*		MJS
14	Have all necessary points forward to next year been recorded on **B10**?	~~Yes~~/None*		MJS
15	Has a budget for next year been prepared?	~~Yes~~/NCN†*		MJS

† NCN = not considered necessary.

* Delete as appropriate.

Client: Collins Park Management Co		Prepared by:	Date:	Ref: **B4**
Year/Period End: 31.10.95	File No:	Reviewed by:	Date:	

CRITICAL REVIEW OF ACCOUNTS QUESTIONNAIRE

	Comments	Initials	WP Ref
1 Review accounting policies to determine whether they:			
(a) comply with SSAPs, FRSs or, in their absence, are otherwise acceptable;		MJS	
(b) are consistent with those of the previous period;		MJS	
(c) are consistently applied to all like transactions;		MJS	
(d) are appropriate to the nature of the client's business;		MJS	
(e) are disclosed in accordance with the requirements of SSAP 2.		MJS	
2 Carry out an overall review of the information in the accounts and compare it with other available data, including final analytical review. Note significant variations and obtain explanations thereto.	None	MJS	~~B9~~
3 Consider whether the accounts adequately reflect: (a) the substance of underlying transactions and balances and not merely their form;		MJS	
(b) the information and explanations obtained and conclusions reached on particular aspects of the audit;		MJS	
(c) the proper application of the four fundamental accounting concepts.		MJS	
Schedule points of interest on 'audit highlights'.	None	MJS	B5
4 Consider whether the review reveals any new factors which may affect the presentation of information or disclosures in the accounts.		MJS	
5 Review the accounts for proper preparation in accordance with the Companies Act, SSAPs, FRSs, and other disclosure requirements. State whether or not a disclosure checklist has been completed in respect of the current year. If not completed in current year, state year in which it was last completed.	Yes/~~No*~~ L1994	MJS	
6 Consider whether the information contained in the directors' report and any other document issued with the accounts is consistent with the accounting information in the accounts and has not been unduly influenced by the directors' desire to present matters in a favourable or unfavourable light.		MJS	

Conclusion

1 ~~I have compared the ratios of the final accounts with those of the preliminary*/extensive* analytical review.~~

2 ~~(a) I have obtained, recorded and corroborated explanations for significant fluctuations for principal areas of the accounts*.~~

Or

(b) There were no significant fluctuations requiring explanation*.

3 The directors' report and other published information is consistent with the accounts.

I am satisfied from this critical review that the accounts appear credible and have been properly prepared in accordance with the Companies Act 1985.

Prepared by MJS Date 8.12.95

Reviewed by AAS Date 12.12.95

* Delete as appropriate.

COLLINS PARK MANAGEMENT CO LTD

AUDIT HIGHLIGHTS

Rentals

Control account balanced. Ensures completeness of income, and verifies opening and closing debtors. — Noted

Debtors

Obtained from reconciliation of receipts. All paid after year end. — Noted

Creditors

Determined from review of invoices and accy creditor. Review of payments after year end ensures no other creditors required. — Noted

Payments

Main expenditure is electricity for street lighting and grass cutting, and has been vouched to invoices. All other expenses and income acceptable. — Noted

Post balance sheet events, contingent liabilities & shares

Discussed with directors. They are not aware of any PBSEs, nor of any contingent liabilities. Still no sign of the council seeking to adopt the road. — Noted

Confirmed no change in shareholdings during the year and no going concern problems. There are no laws or regulations that are central to the company's continued operation. — Noted

Conclusion

No problems encountered. Client has adequate books and records and we have obtained all the information and explanations required. Sufficient audit evidence obtained to give a clean audit report. — Agreed

MJS 8·12·95 ADS 12·12·95

C AUDIT PLANNING

1	Audit planning memorandum	✓
2	Professional independence questionnaire	✓
3	Preliminary analytical review	
4	General risk assessment	✓
5	Specific risk assessment	✓
6	Materiality summary	✓
7	Systems overview	✓
8	Points forward from last year	
9	Other planning schedules	
10	Assignment planning – timetable	
11	Budget and performance summary	
12	Time ledger print-out	
13		
14		

Client: Collins Park Management Co		Prepared by:	Date:	Ref: **C1**
Year/Period End: 31.10.95	File No:	Reviewed by:	Date:	

AUDIT PLANNING MEMORANDUM

		Comments	Initials	WP Ref
1	Before commencing any detailed work on the audit, confirm that the Professional independence questionnaire has been satisfactorily completed.		MJS	C2
2	Review terms of engagement letter. Discuss any changes with reporting partner. If appropriate, send revised letter to client, and confirm its return, duly signed.		MJS	PAF
3	Review and update the following on the Permanent audit file: – Background information – Systems notes – Summary of significant laws and regulations – Other (specify):		MJS	PAF
4	Review points forward from last year's schedule. File on current year's working paper file.	None	MJS	~~C8~~
5	Review correspondence file for relevant points arising during the year.	None	MJS	
6	Consider and schedule impact of changes in legislation/SSAPs/FRSs on the accounts.	None	MJS	
7	Where the previous period's audit report was qualified, consider what impact, if any, it will have on the current period's report.	N/A	MJS	
8	Meet/discuss with client current year's accounts and timetable.	NCN	MJS	~~C10~~
9	Consider whether there are any indications that the going concern basis of accounting may not be appropriate.	None	MJS	
10	If appropriate, prepare a brief memo of matters arising from the review of the correspondence file and meeting/discussion with the client.	N/A	MJS	~~C9~~
11	Allocate staff, as appropriate.		MJS	
12	Obtain print-out of the firm's WIP and prepare fee budget. Agree fee estimate with client where necessary. (fixed fee £260)	NCN	MJS	~~C11/C12~~
13	Where the accounts to be audited are available at the planning stage, complete the Analytical review form, based on preliminary figures.	N/A	MJS	~~C3~~
14	Where the accounts to be audited are not available at the planning stage, discuss with management whether there have been any significant changes in the business since the previous period.	No Signif. Changes	MJS	
15	Complete general risk assessment.		MJS	C4
16	Complete specific risk assessment.		MJS	C5
17	Complete materiality summary.		MJS	C6
18	Complete systems overview.		MJS	C7
19	Review/tailor/prepare audit programme as directed by **C5**.		MJS	
20	Brief staff listed below.			

Audit Partner: AL Smith Initials: ALS

Senior/Manager: MJ Stern Initials: MJS

Other: ____________ Initials: ____________

____________ Initials: ____________

Conclusion

I am satisfied that the staff assigned are competent to carry out the planned work and have been adequately briefed.
I am satisfied that the audit has been planned effectively.
The file ~~does~~/does not* require second partner review.

Senior/Manager MJ Stern Date 8.12.95

Partner AL Smith Date 8.12.95

* Delete as appropriate.

Client: Collins Park Management Co		Prepared by: MJS	Date: 8.12.95	Ref: **C2**
Year/Period End:	File No:	Reviewed by:	Date:	

PROFESSIONAL INDEPENDENCE QUESTIONNAIRE

Regulations state that 'a Registered Auditor shall not accept appointment or continue as auditor if the firm has any interest likely to conflict with the proper conduct of the audit'. This questionnaire shall be completed annually for all clients to ensure that the regulations have been complied with.

	YES	NO
1 *Undue dependence on an audit client*		
Do the total fees for this client/group of clients exceed:		
(a) 10%* of gross practice income?		✓
(b) 15%* of the partner's gross income?		✓
Is this client/group of clients highly prestigious?		
* (a) becomes 5% and (b) becomes 10% for listed or public interest audits.		✓
2 *Overdue fees*		
Does the client owe the firm any money which exceeds your normal credit terms?		✓
3 *Litigation*		
Is there any actual or anticipated litigation between yourself and the client in relation to fees, audit work, or other work?		✓
4 *Associated firms*		
Are you or your staff associated with any other practice or organisation which has any dealings with the company?		✓
5 *Family or other personal relationships*		
Do you or any of your staff have any personal or family connections with the company and its officers?		✓
6 *Ex-partners or senior employees*		
(a) Has any officer of the company been a partner or senior employee in the practice?		✓
(b) Is the partner or any senior employee on the audit joining or involved in substantive negotiations with the client?		✓
7 *Financial involvement*		
Do you or any of your staff have any financial involvement in the company in respect of the following:		
(a) any beneficial interest in shares or other investments?		✓
(b) any beneficial interest in trusts?		✓
(c) any trustee investments?		✓
(d) any loans or guarantees?		✓

Client: Collins Park Management Co		Prepared by: MJS	Date: 8.12.95	Ref: **C2**
Year/Period End: 31.10.95	File No:	Reviewed by:	Date:	

PROFESSIONAL INDEPENDENCE QUESTIONNAIRE (*Cont.*)

	YES	NO
8 Goods and services: hospitality		
Have you or any of your staff accepted any material goods or services on favourable terms or received undue hospitality from the company?	☐	✓
9 Provision of other services and specialist valuations		
(a) Are any services in relation to the management of the company performed by the firm?	☐	✓
(b) Where the firm prepares the company's accounting records, is there any reason why the client will not accept responsibility for the records as his own?	☐	✓
(c) Do the accounts include any specialist valuations carried out by the firm or an associated firm?	☐	✓
10 Rotation of audit engagement partner		
Have you been acting as the audit engagement partner for more than seven years?	☐	✓
11 Adequate resources		
Are there any problems over adequately staffing the audit with staff with the necessary expertise?	☐	✓
12 Proper performance		
Are there any aspects of the client, or other factors, that will adversely affect the firm's ability to perform the audit properly?	☐	✓

Conclusion

Where any of the above questions have been answered 'yes', specify what action is proposed to be taken to maintain independence, and to ensure the availability of resources and the ability to perform the audit properly.

Having regard to any safeguards identified above, in my opinion independence is maintained, we have adequate resources and the ability to properly perform the audit.

Partner AD Smith Date 8.12.95

Consultation (to be completed where appropriate)

In my opinion the steps proposed are sufficient to maintain independence and to ensure the availabilty of resources and the ability to perform the audit properly.

Second Partner________________ Date________

Client: Collins Park Management Co		Prepared by:	Date:	Ref: **C4**
Year/Period End:	File No:	Reviewed by:	Date:	

GENERAL RISK ASSESSMENT

The most appropriate category for each point should be ringed. Using this and any further information that is relevant, assess the general risk of the client. Detailed help on what factors may affect our assessment is given on a detailed schedule.

		Low	*Medium*	*High*
1	***External interest in accounts***			
1.1	Share ownership	Director/ Management	Small minority	(External interest)
1.2	Accounts requested by third party? Specify:	(No)	Possibly	Yes
1.3	Is there a potential going concern problem?	(No)	Possibly	Yes
2	***Management of business***			
2.1	Management experience/competence	(Good)	Satisfactory	Poor
2.2	Management changes (past/future)	(None)	Some	Many
2.3	Management influence	(Low risk)	Medium risk	High risk
2.4	Existence of fraud or error	(Low risk)	Medium risk	High risk
2.5	Breaches of significant laws or regulations	(Low risk)	Medium risk	High risk
3	***Accounting***			
3.1	Accounting systems	(Good)	Satisfactory	Poor
3.2	Type of business	(Mainly credit)	Mixed	Mainly cash
3.3	Contentious accounting issues	(None)	Some	Many
3.4	Audit history	(Good)	Satisfactory	Poor
4	***Business environment***			
4.1	Nature of business/industry Specify:	(Low risk)	Medium risk	High risk
4.2	Track record	(Established)	–	New

Conclusion: (Identify major risk areas and give an overall assessment of the job.)

No major general risk areas

Overall general risk assessment is:	***(Low)***	***Medium***	***High***

Detailed general risk assessment attached ~~YES~~/NO*

MJS Preparer 8.12.95 Date
ADS Reviewer 8.12.95 Date

* Delete as appropriate.

Client: Collins Park Management Co		Prepared by: MJS	Date: 8·12·95	Ref: **C5**
Year/Period End: 31.10.95	File No:	Reviewed by: A&S	Date: 8.12.95	

SPECIFIC RISK ASSESSMENT

Objective: *To ensure that all material risk areas are identified and appropriate audit work is planned and performed.*

	High, Medium or Low risk?	Nature of risks	Standard audit prog required? Y/N	Comments/details of alternative procedures
D Extensive analytical review			N	
E Intangible assets		N/A		
F Tangible fixed assets		N/A		
G Investments in group and associated undertakings		N/A		
H Other investments		N/A		
I Stock and WIP		N/A		
J Debtors and prepayments	L		N	Determine debtors from control account & ensure subsequently paid.
K Bank and cash	L		N	Reconcile bank. Obtain & check bank letter
L Creditors and accruals	L		N	Determine creditors from review of invoices and after date payments.
M Long-term loans and deferred income		N/A		
N Provisions and contingencies	L		N	Discuss with directors. Confirm no laws and regulations central to company
O Capital and reserves	L		N	Confirm no movements in shares.

Client: Collins Park Management Co		Prepared by:	Date:	Ref: **C5**
Year/Period End: 31.10.95	File No:	Reviewed by:	Date:	

SPECIFIC RISK ASSESSMENT (*cont.*)

	High, Medium or Low risk?	Nature of risks	Standard audit prog required? Y/N	Comments/details of alternative procedures
P Taxation		N/A		Mutual Trading
R Profit and loss – income	L		N	Covered by rental control account
– expenditure	L		N	Vouch all payments
– wages		N/A		
– other	L		N	Covered by accountancy work
T Post balance sheet events	L		N	Discuss with directors confirm in letter of representation
U VAT		N/A		
V Consolidation		N/A		
Other		N/A		

Conclusion

I am satisfied that the planned audit programmes are suitable to produce sufficient appropriate audit evidence.

Prepared by MJS

Date 8.12.95

Reviewed by ASS

Date 8.12.95

TABLE OF INHERENT RISK ASSESSMENT FACTORS

Tests of detail only

Specific risk

General risk	L	M	H
L	1.2	1.5	1.8
M	1.5	1.8	2.1
H	1.8	2.1	2.5

Client: Collins Park Management Co		Prepared by:	Date:	Ref: **C6**
Year/Period End: 31.10.95	File No:	Reviewed by:	Date:	

MATERIALITY SUMMARY

MATERIALITY RANGES

Range of turnover and gross assets	Percentage of turnover and gross assets	Materiality ranges
£0 – £500,000	3.0%	£1 – £15,000
£500,001 – £1,000,000	2.5%	£15,001 – £25,000
£1,000,001 – £2,000,000	2.0%	£25,001 – £40,000
£2,000,001 – £5,000,000	1.5%	£40,001 – £75,000
over £5,000,000	1.0%	over £75,000

APPLICATION OF MATERIALITY RANGES TO BUSINESS

	Initial assessment			Final assessment		
	Percentage %	Anticipated results £	Materiality level £	Percentage %	Final results £	Materiality level £
Turnover	3%	1,600	48	3%	1600	48
Gross assets	3%	500	15	3%	564	17
Profit/(loss) before tax		50			71	
Adjustment for unusual items		-			-	
Adjusted profit/(loss)	10%	50	5	10%	71	7

	This year	Last year (final)
OVERALL INITIAL AUDIT MATERIALITY SET AT	£ 35	£ 30

Comments

Level of acceptable accounting differences : £ Nil

Conclusion

Based on the anticipated results, I am satisfied that the above figure represents an appropriate initial audit materiality.

MJS	Preparer	8·12·95	Date
ADS	Reviewer	8.12.95	Date

	This year
REVISED AUDIT MATERIALITY	£ 35

Comments

Conclusion

Based on the final results, I am satisfied that the above figure represents an appropriate final audit materiality.

MJS	Preparer	8·12·95	Date
ADS	Reviewer	12.12.95	Date

Client: Collins Park Management Co		Prepared by: MJS	Date: 8.12.95	Ref: C7
Year/Period End: 31.10.95	File No:	Reviewed by: ABS	Date: 8.12.95	

SYSTEMS OVERVIEW

***Objective**: To ascertain the company's system of recording and processing transactions and to assess its adequacy as a basis for the preparation of the accounts.*

1 Accounting records

Estimated transactions for whole year unless specified

Tick as appropriate	Manual	Computerised	Prepared by us	Volume		Value £
(a) Sales Day Book					Number of invoices	
(b) Cash Receipts Book	✓			32	Number of entries	1600
(c) Sales Ledger					Number of accounts	
(d) Purchase Day Book					Number of invoices	
(e) Cash Payments Book	✓			12	Number of entries	1550
(f) Purchase Ledger					Number of accounts	
(g) Petty Cash Book					Number of entries	
(h) Fixed Asset Register					Number of assets	
(i) Stock Ledger					Number of lines	
(j) Payroll					Number of employees	
(k) Nominal Ledger						
(l) Management Accounts				Frequency		
(m) Financial Statements			✓			
(n) Other (specify):						

2 *Sales system*
(Detail below the categories of income received and how a sale is first recorded.)

"Rental" income only – flat contribution to costs by each member.

Client: Collins Park Management Co		Prepared by: MJS	Date: 8·12·95	Ref: C7
Year/Period End:	File No:	Reviewed by: ADS	Date: 8.12.95	

SYSTEMS OVERVIEW (*cont.*)

3 Purchases system

(**Detail below the way a liability is first recognised.**)

Receipt of invoice or 'Petty Cash' claim

4 Details of computer system

N/A

Conclusion

	Initials	Date
1 The above notes are an adequate record of the client's systems*. ~~The above systems require further documentation which is filed on ______ *~~	MJS	8·12·95
2 These systems do/~~do not*~~ provide a reliable basis for the preparation of statutory accounts ~~(only when supplemented by our own accounts preparation work)*~~.	MJS	8·12·95

* Delete where not appropriate.

Client	File No.	Ref.
Collins Park Management Co Ltd		K3

Subject	Prepared by	Date
Bank Reconciliation	MJS	8/12/95
	Reviewed by	Date
	ADS	12/12/95
	Accounting Dates	31·10·95

		£	£	
Opening balance			397.21	
Bankings per schedule	W2	1,500.00		
Interest rec'd		6.72		
			1,506.72	
			1,903.93	
Cheques per schedule	W4		1,490.43	
Balance as at 31·10·95			£413.50	
Balance per bank statement dated 31·10·95			£413.50	Agreed to bank letter

Client	File No.	Ref.
Collins Park Management Co Ltd		L1

Subject	Prepared by	Date
Creditors and accruals	MJS	8/12/95
	Reviewed by ADS	Date 12/12/95
	Accounting Dates	31·10·95

	1995 £	1994 £
Accountancy and audit	260.00	240.00
Grass cuttings	68.54	41.22
Street lighting accrual	67.12	68.42
2/3 × £100.68 (Nov bill)		
	£395.66	£349.64

Conclusion

Grass cutting and street lighting agreed to invoices. Review of after date payments confirms no other creditors or accruals required.

Client	Collins Park Management Co Ltd	File No.	Ref. Q3
Subject	Rental Control A/C	Prepared by MJS	Date 8/12/95
		Reviewed by ADS	Date 12/12/95
		Accounting Dates	31·10·95

	£	£
Opening balance o/s at 31·10·94	50.00	
Rents due 32 flats @ £50	1,600.00	
Paid per W2		1,500.00
Closing balance o/s at 31·10·95		150.00
	1,650.00	1,650.00

Rents o/s	No. 4	50.00	Paid	5·11·95
	No. 5	50.00		1·12·95
	No. 29	50.00		5·12·95
		£150.00		

Reconciliation of receipts

Flat										
	√ 1	√ 2	√ √ 3	Dr 4	Dr 5	√ 6	√ 7	√ 8	√ 9	√ 10
	√ 11	√ 12	√ 13	√ 14	√ 15	√ 16	√ 17	√ 18	√ 19	√ 20
	√ 21	√ 22	√ 23	√ 24	√ 25	√ 26	√ 27	√ 28	Dr 29	√ 30
	√ 31	√ 32								

√ = Paid
Dr = Debtor

Conclusion

Control a/c balances. Opening debtor paid. Closing debtors obtained from reconciliation and subsequently paid.

Client: Collins Park Management Co Ltd	File No.	Ref. W2	
Subject: Summary of bankings	Prepared by MJS		Date 8/12/95
	Reviewed by ADS		Date 12/12/95
	Accounting Dates	31·10·95	

	Rents £									
Nov 94	400.00	No's	√ 1,	√ 3,	√ 7,	√ 9,	√ 12,	√ 15,	√ 17,	√ 18
Dec 94	250.00	No's	√ 6,	√ 10,	√ 13,	√ 22,	√ 31			
Jan 95	350.00	No's	√ 2,	√ 8,	√ 11,	√ 19,	√ 20,	√ 23,	√ 24	
Feb 95	50.00	No's	√ 27							
May 95	150.00	No's	√ 3,	√ 25,	√ 32					
June 95	100.00	No's	√ 28,	√ 30						
Sept 95	200.00	No's	√ 14,	√ 16,	√ 21,	√ 26				
K3	£1,500.00									

√ = to reconciliation of receipts

Q3

Client	Collins Park Management Co Ltd	File No.	Ref. W4
Subject	Summary of cheque payments	Prepared by	Date 8/12/95
		Reviewed by	Date 12/12/95
		Accounting Dates	31·10·95

Grass cuts	Audit/ accy	Electricity	Sundries	
£	£	£	£	
41.22√	240.00	102.63√	18.00	Registrar of Co's
77.29√		204.21√		
76.34√		224.43√	10.25	Stationery
78.92√		187.12√		
67.12√			10.50	Refreshments for AGM
77.00√				
75.40√				
493.29	240.00	718.39	38.75	
			Total	£1,490.43

√ Invoice seen

K3

File No.		Ref	Y1
Prepared by:	MJS	Date	8/12/95
Reviewed by:	ADS	Date	12/12/95
Accounting Dates			31/10/95

Client **Collins Park Management Co Ltd**

TRIAL BALANCE

	Ref	Balance B/fwd		Bank Account		Access Account		Ref	Adjustments				Profit & Loss Account		Balance Sheet	
		Debit	Credit	Debit	Credit	Debit	Credit		Debit	Credit	Accruals	Prepayments	Debit	Credit	Debit	Credit
Bank		397.21		1,506.72	1,490.43										413.50	
Share capital			32.00													32.00
Profit & loss a/c			65.57													65.57
'Ground rents'		50.00			1,500.00							150.00		1,600.00		
Electricity			34.21	718.39							67.12		751.30			
Grass cuttings			75.43	493.29							68.54		486.40			
Audit & accountancy			240.00	240.00							260.00		260.00			
Sundry expenses				38.75									38.75			
Interest received					6.72									6.72		
Debtors											150.00				150.00	
Creditors												395.66				395.66
													1,536.45	1,606.72	563.50	493.23
Profit													70.27			70.27
		447.21	447.21	2,997.15	2,997.15						545.66	545.66	1,606.72	1,606.72	563.50	563.50

FILE 2 – ROBERTS DESIGN LIMITED

ROBERTS DESIGN LIMITED

DIRECTORS:	Mr E Roberts Mrs K Roberts
SECRETARY:	Mrs K Roberts
REPORTING ACCOUNTANTS:	Jones Watson & Co Chartered Accountants 24 Barracks Square Oldtown Yorkshire
BANKERS:	Capital Bank plc
REGISTERED OFFICE:	100 Plumstone Court Newtown Berkshire
COMPANY NUMBER:	9992000

ROBERTS DESIGN LIMITED

DIRECTORS' REPORT

The Directors present the annual report and financial statements for the period ended 30 June 1995.

Principal activities

The principal activity of the company is that of subcontract design and drawing services.

Incorporation and share capital

The company was incorporated as Roberts Design Limited on 22 June 1994 and commenced trading on 1 July 1994. The authorised share capital of the company on incorporation was £100 divided into 100 ordinary shares of £1 each.

On 30 June 1994, one share of £1 each in the original share capital of the company was transferred by each of the company's formation agents to Mr E Roberts and Mrs K Roberts. All money due on shares allotted has been received in cash.

Directors

The following were directors for the period and their interest in the share capital of the company at the date of incorporation, or date of appointment if later, and at the end of the period were:

	£1 ordinary shares	
	30/6/95	*On incorporation or appointment*
Company Formation Ltd (resigned 30/6/94)	–	1
Company Formation Services Ltd (resigned 30/6/94)	–	1
Mr E Roberts (appointed 30/6/94)	1	1
Mrs K Roberts (appointed 30/6/94)	1	1

Advantage has been taken, in the preparation of this report, of special exemptions applicable to small companies.

By Order of the Board.

100 Plumstone Court
Newtown
Berkshire

K Roberts
Company Secretary

2 September 1995

[Page 1]

ACCOUNTANTS' REPORT TO THE SHAREHOLDERS OF

ROBERTS DESIGN LIMITED

We report on the accounts for the year ended 30 June 1995 set out on pages 3 to 7.

Respective responsibilities of directors and reporting accountant

As described on page 4 the company's directors are responsible for the preparation of the accounts, and they consider that the company is exempt from an audit. It is our responsibility to carry out procedures designed to enable us to report our opinion.

Basis of opinion

Our work was conducted in accordance with the Statement of Standards for Reporting Accountants, and so our procedures consisted of comparing the accounts with the accounting records kept by the company, and making such limited enquiries of the officers of the company as we considered necessary for the purposes of this report. These procedures provide only the assurance expressed in our opinion.

Opinion

In our opinion:

(a) the company accounts are in agreement with the accounting records kept by the company under s221 of the Companies Act 1985;

(b) having regard only to, and on the basis of, the information contained in those accounting records:
   - (i) the accounts have been drawn up in a manner consistent with the accounting requirements specified in s249C(6) of the Act; and
   - (ii) the company satisfied the conditions for exemption from an audit of the accounts for the year specified in s249A(4) of the Act and did not, at any time within that year, fall within any of the categories of companies not entitled to the exemption specified in s249B(1).

The financial statements were approved by the Board of Directors on 2 September 1995.

For the year in question, the company was entitled to exemption from an audit under 249A(2) of the Companies Act 1985. No notice has been deposited under 249B(2) of the Act in relation to the accounts for the financial year. The directors acknowledge their responsibilities for:

(a) ensuring that the company keeps accounting records which comply with s221 of the Companies Act 1985; and

(b) preparing accounts which give a true and fair view of the state of affairs of the company, as at the end of the financial year, and of its profit or loss for the financial year in accordance with the requirements of s226 of the Companies Act 1985, and which otherwise comply with the requirements of that Act relating to accounts, so far as applicable to the company.

Advantage has been taken of the exemptions conferred by section A of Part III of Schedule 8 to the Companies Act 1985, on the grounds that, in the directors' opinion, the company qualifies as a small company under s246 and s247 of the Companies Act 1985.

Advantage has been taken, in the preparation of the accounts, of special exemptions applicable to small companies on the grounds that, in the directors' opinion, the company qualifies as a small company under s246 and s247 of the Companies Act 1985.

Jones Watson & Co
Chartered Accountants
4 September 1995

24 Barracks Square
Oldtown
Yorkshire

[Page 2]

ROBERTS DESIGN LIMITED

PROFIT AND LOSS ACCOUNT
FOR THE PERIOD ENDED 30 JUNE 1995

	Notes	£
Turnover	1	97,553
Administrative expenses		(77,341)
		20,212
Other interest receivable and similar income		427
		20,639
Interest payable and similar charges		(466)
Profit on ordinary activities before taxation	2	20,173
Tax on profit on ordinary activities		(4,998)
Profit on ordinary activities after taxation		15,175
Dividends paid	3	(6,000)
Retained profit for the year and carried forward		£9,175

There were no acquisitions or discontinued operations during the year.
There were no gains or losses other than the profit for the year.

[Page 3]

ROBERTS DESIGN LIMITED

BALANCE SHEET
AS AT 30 JUNE 1995

	Notes	£	£
Fixed assets			
Tangible assets	4		3,825
Current assets			
Debtors	5	2,170	
Cash at bank and in hand		18,399	
		20,569	
Creditors: amounts falling due within one year	6	15,217	
Net current assets			5,352
Total assets less current liabilities			£9,177
Capital and reserves			
Called up share capital	7		2
Profit and loss account			9,175
Shareholders' funds	8		£9,177

The notes on pages 5 to 7 form an integral part of these accounts.

The financial statements were approved by the directors on 2 September 1995.

For the year in question, the company was entitled to exemption from an audit under s249A(2) of the Companies Act 1985. No notice has been deposited under s249B(2) of the Act in relation to the accounts for the financial year. The directors acknowledge their responsibilities for:

(a) ensuring that the company keeps accounting records which comply with s221 of the Companies Act 1985; and
(b) preparing accounts which give a true and fair view of the state of affairs of the company, as at the end of the financial year, and of its profit or loss for the financial year in accordance with the requirements of s226 of the Companies Act 1985, and which otherwise comply with the requirements of that Act relating to accounts, so far as applicable to the company.

Advantage has been taken, in the preparation of the accounts, of special exemptions applicable to small companies on the grounds that, in the directors' opinion, the company qualifies as a small company under s246 and s247 of the Companies Act 1985.

Mr E Roberts
DIRECTOR

[Page 4]

ROBERTS DESIGN LIMITED

NOTES TO THE FINANCIAL STATEMENTS
FOR THE PERIOD ENDED 30 JUNE 1995

(1) Accounting policies

The financial statements have been prepared under the historical cost convention in accordance with normal fundamental accounting concepts, and comply with all applicable accounting standards.

Turnover
Turnover is the amount receivable for drawing services provided in the UK during the period excluding VAT.

Depreciation
The company's tangible assets are depreciated over their expected useful lives using the following rates:

Motor vehicles 25% on reducing balance

Taxation
The charge for taxation is based on the profit for the year as adjusted for disallowable items. Tax deferred or accelerated is accounted for in respect of all material timing differences to the extent that it is probable that a liability or asset will crystallise. Timing differences arise from the inclusion of items of income and expenditure in tax computations in periods different from those in which they are included in the accounts. Provision is made at the rate which is expected to be applied when the liability or asset is expected to crystallise.

Pensions
The company makes payments into defined contribution pension schemes in respect of the directors. Payments are accounted for on the accruals basis.

(2) Profit on ordinary activities before taxation

Is stated after charging:

Depreciation	1,275
Directors' emoluments	62,749
Pension contributions	9,200

(3) Dividends

Interim dividend (£1,000 per share)	2,000
Final dividend (£2,000 per share)	4,000
	£6,000

[Page 5]

ROBERTS DESIGN LIMITED

NOTES TO THE FINANCIAL STATEMENTS
FOR THE PERIOD ENDED 30 JUNE 1995

(4) Tangible assets

	Motor vehicle £
Cost	
Additions	5,100
As at 30 June 1995	5,100
Depreciation	
Charge for period	1,275
As at 30 June 1995	1,275
Net book value	
As at 30 June 1995	£3,825

(5) Debtors

Trade debtors	1,990
Others	180
	£2,170

(6) Creditors: amounts falling due within one year

Bank loans and overdrafts	183
Trade creditors	416
Taxation and social security	8,898
Directors' loan	3,688
Accruals	1,032
ACT payable	1,000
	£15,217

[Page 6]

ROBERTS DESIGN LIMITED

NOTES TO THE FINANCIAL STATEMENTS FOR THE PERIOD ENDED 30 JUNE 1995

(7) Called up share capital

Authorised Ordinary shares of £1 each	100
Allotted, called up and fully paid Ordinary shares of £1 each	2

During the period, 2 ordinary shares of £1 each were issued on the incorporation of the company. These were issued at par value for cash.

(8) Reconciliation of shareholders' funds

	Share capital £	*Profit & loss* £	*Total* £
As at 1 July 1994	2	—	2
Profit for the year	—	9,175	9,175
As at 30 June 1995	2	9,175	9,177

(9) Capital commitments

Contracted for, not provided	Nil
Authorised, not contracted for	Nil

(10) Contingent liabilities

There were no contingent liabilities at 30 June 1995.

[Page 7]

ROBERTS DESIGN LIMITED

DETAILED PROFIT AND LOSS ACCOUNT FOR THE PERIOD ENDED 30 JUNE 1995

	£	£
INCOME		97,553
Add: Interest receivable		427
		97,980
EXPENSES		
Directors' remuneration	66,388	
Motor expenses	5,695	
Health insurance	119	
Stationery and postage	1,408	
Accountancy and professional advice	1,650	
Bank charges	232	
Bank interest	39	
Loan interest	195	
Sundry	415	
Depreciation	1,275	
Use of home as office	390	
		77,807
Net profit before tax		20,173
Corporation tax		4,998
		15,175
Dividends paid		6,000
RETAINED PROFIT FOR PERIOD		£9,175

[Page 8]

ACCOUNTANTS' REPORT TO THE SHAREHOLDERS OF

ROBERTS DESIGN LTD

We report on the accounts for the year ended 30 June 1995 set out on pages 3 to 7.

Respective responsibilities of directors and reporting accountant

As described on page 4 the company's directors are responsible for the preparation of the accounts, and they consider that the company is exempt from an audit. It is our responsibility to carry out procedures designed to enable us to report our opinion.

Basis of opinion

Our work was conducted in accordance with the Statement of Standards for Reporting Accountants, and so our procedures consisted of comparing the accounts with the accounting records kept by the company, and making such limited enquiries of the officers of the company as we considered necessary for the purposes of this report. These procedures provide only the assurance expressed in our opinion.

Opinion

In our opinion:

(a) the accounts are in agreement with the accounting records kept by the company under s221 of the Companies Act 1985;

(b) having regard only to, and on the basis of, the information contained in those accounting records:

  (i) the accounts have been drawn up in a manner consistent with the accounting requirements specified in s249C(6) of the Act; and

  (ii) the company satisfied the conditions for exemption from an audit of the accounts for the year specified in s249A(4) of the Act and did not, at any time within that year, fall within any of the categories of companies not entitled to the exemption specified in s249B(1).

Jones Watson & Co
Chartered Accountants
4 September 1995

24 Barracks Square
Oldtown
Yorkshire

[Page 2]

ROBERTS DESIGN LIMITED

ABBREVIATED BALANCE SHEET
AS AT 30 JUNE 1995

	Notes	£	£
Fixed assets			
Tangible assets	2		3,825
Currents assets			
Debtors		2,170	
Cash at bank and in hand		18,399	
		20,569	
Creditors: amounts falling due within one year		15,217	
Net current assets			5,352
Total assets less current liabilities			£9,177
Capital and reserves			
Called up share capital	3		2
Profit and loss account			9,175
			£9,177

The notes on page 3 form an integral part of these accounts.

The financial statements were approved by the Board of Directors on 2 September 1995.

For the year in question, the company was entitled to exemption from an audit under s249A(2) of the Companies Act 1985. No notice has been deposited under s249B(2) of the Act in relation to the accounts for the financial year. The directors acknowledge their responsibilities for:

(a) ensuring that the company keeps accounting records which comply with s221 of the Companies Act 1985; and
(b) preparing accounts which give a true and fair view of the state of affairs of the company, as at the end of the financial year, and of its profit or loss for the financial year in accordance with the requirements of s226 of the Companies Act 1985, and which otherwise comply with the requirements of that Act relating to accounts, so far as applicable to the company.

Advantage has been taken of the exemptions conferred by section A of Part III of Schedule 8 to the Companies Act 1985, on the grounds that, in the directors' opinion, the company qualifies as a small company under s246 and s247 of the Companies Act 1985.

Advantage has been taken, in the preparation of the accounts, of special exemptions applicable to small companies on the grounds that, in the directors' opinion, the company qualifies as a small company under s246 and s247 of the Companies Act 1985.

Mr E Roberts
DIRECTOR

ROBERTS DESIGN LIMITED

NOTES TO THE ABBREVIATED FINANCIAL STATEMENTS
FOR THE PERIOD ENDED 30 JUNE 1995

(1) Accounting policies

The financial statements have been prepared under the historical cost convention in accordance with normal fundamental accounting concepts, and comply with all applicable accounting standards.

Turnover
Turnover is the amount receivable for drawing services provided in the UK during the period excluding VAT.

Depreciation
The company's tangible assets are depreciated over their expected useful lives using the following rates:

Motor vehicles — 25% on reducing balance

Taxation
The charge for taxation is based on the profit for the year as adjusted for disallowable items. Tax deferred or accelerated is accounted for in respect of all material timing differences to the extent that it is probable that a liability or asset will crystallise. Timing differences arise from the inclusion of items of income and expenditure in tax computations in periods different from those in which they are included in the accounts. Provision is made at the rate which is expected to be applied when the liability or asset is expected to crystallise.

Pensions
The company makes payments into defined contribution pension schemes in respect of the directors. Payments are accounted for on the accruals basis.

(2) Tangible assets

	Total £
Cost	
Additions	5,100
As at 30 June 1995	5,100
Depreciation	
Charge for period	1,275
As at 30 June 1995	1,275
Net book value	
As at 30 June 1995	£3,825

(3) Called up share capital

Authorised	
Ordinary shares of £1 each	100
Allotted, called up and fully paid	
Ordinary shares of £1 each	2

During the year, 2 ordinary shares of £1 each were issued on the incorporation of the company. These were issued at par value for cash.

Client	File No.	Ref.
Roberts Design Limited		A2
Subject	**Prepared by**	**Date**
Tax computation	KM	11/8/95
	Reviewed by	**Date**
	EAA	17/8/95
	Accounting Dates	30·6·95

Corporation tax

			£
Profit before tax			20,173
add: depreciation			1,275
less: interest receivable			(427)
capital allowances			(1,275)
Schedule D Case I			19,746
Schedule D Case III		K1	247
Profits chargeable to corporation tax			19,993
Corporation tax @ 25%			4,998.25
less: ACT recoverable		Y1	(1,500.00)
Due at 30/6/95		L1	(3,498.25)

Capital allowances

	Motor vehicle £		*Capital allowances*
Addition	5,100	F1	
WDA @ 25%	(1,275)		£1,275
WDV c.f.	3,825		

Deferred tax

The only timing difference for deferred tax purposes is £30 interest receivable at the year end. This has not been provided for as it is not material.

ROBERTS DESIGN LIMITED

2 September, 1995

Jones Watson & Co
24 Barracks Square
Oldtown
Yorkshire

Dear Sirs

We confirm to the best of our knowledge and belief the following representations given to you in connection with your review of the company's accounts for the year ended 30 June 1995.

1. We acknowledge as directors our responsibility for the accounts, which you have prepared for the company. All the accounting records have been made available to you for the purpose of your review and all the transactions undertaken by the company have been properly reflected and recorded in the accounting records.
2. In our opinion, the accounting policies are appropriate to the company and conform with generally accepted accounting principles. We confirm that all transactions and balances have been accounted for in accordance with these accounting policies.
3. We confirm that all assets included in the balance sheet exist and are recoverable at the value recorded.
4. We confirm that all liabilities have been fully recorded and correctly classified.
5. We confirm that all turnover has been fully recorded and correctly classified.
6. The company has had at no time during the year any arrangement, transaction or agreement to provide credit facilities (including loans, quasi-loans or credit transactions) for directors, nor to guarantee or provide security for such matters.
7. The company has no contingent liabilities other than those disclosed in the accounts.
8. There has been no event since the balance sheet date which requires disclosing or which would materially affect the amounts in the accounts, other than those already disclosed or included in the accounts.
9. The company has not contracted for, nor authorised any capital expenditure other than as disclosed in the accounts.

Yours faithfully

E Roberts K Roberts

100 Plumstone Court, Newtown, Berkshire
Directors: E Roberts, Mrs K Roberts
Telephone (01989) 517238 Fax (01989) 517240

Registered No 9992000 England

ROBERTS DESIGN LTD

COMPANIES' ACCOUNTS DISCLOSURE CHECKLIST

Checklists used:

1 Simplified introductory checklist
2 Simplified main checklist
4 Simplified formats
5 Simplified abbreviated accounts

Checklists 2 and 4 have not been included in this particular case study. Checklists 1 and 5 are included.

NB Checklists 2 and 4 are included in the case study 'Bright-a-Light Ltd'.

Client: Roberts Design Ltd		Prepared by: EAA	Date: 18.8.95	Ref: A7.1
Year/Period End: 30.6.95	File No:	Reviewed by: ADS	Date: 21.8.95	

SIMPLIFIED INTRODUCTORY CHECKLIST

The simplified checklists for small companies have omitted the more unusual disclosure requirements. They are only suitable for small companies which are not part of a group, and assume full advantage has been taken of SI 1992 No 2452. *Complete this introductory checklist to confirm that it is appropriate to use the simplified checklists. For any questions answered 'yes', complete the relevant questions in the full checklists.*

			*Full checklist reference**	*Complete (✓)*
1	Does it have more than 250 employees?	Y/N	3.12(a)	—
2	Has it adopted any format other than Balance Sheet Format I and Profit and Loss Account Formats I or II in the Companies Act 1985, or changed formats since last year?	Y/N	2.01 to 2.07, 2.12 to 2.17	—
3	Has it acquired or discontinued any operations, or undergone a reorganisation or reconstruction?	Y/N	11.02 to 11.10, 12.04 to 12.06	—
4	Has it any foreign currency transactions or overseas income?	Y/N	10.01 to 10.02, 13.10, 31.10, **9**(3.03).	—
5	Has it any exceptional or extraordinary items?	Y/N	12.01 to 12.09	—
6	Has it any intangible fixed assets (e.g., goodwill)?	Y/N	6.04, 17.03, 18.01 to 18.04, 31.12, **9**(3.09, 5.04)	—
7	Does it have any investments in shares of other companies?	Y/N	20.02, 23.04, **9**(3.16)	—
8	Does the company have any government grants?	Y/N	27.01, 27.02, 31.05	—
9	Has it any defined benefit or foreign pension schemes, or any other post retirement benefits?	Y/N	8.03, 8.05, 8.06, 29.08, 31.13, Checklist **14**	—
10	Has it any class of shares other than the normal ordinary shares?	Y/N	14.02, 25.20, 28.02 to 28.06, 28.08, 28.12 to 28.14, **9**(3.06 to 3.08)	—
11	Has it purchased any own shares or given financial assistance for the purchase of its shares?	Y/N	3.15, Checklist **12**	—

* *All references are to full Checklist **6** (main checklist), unless specified.*

			Full checklist reference*	Complete (✓)
12	Has it any debentures, convertible debts or warrants, or any other capital instruments treated as debt (other than normal loans)?	Y/N	25.05 to 25.15	—
13	Has it repurchased or settled any own debt early?	Y/N	9.02	—
14	Does the company have any unusual directors' transactions (other than overdrawn loan accounts and transactions in which the directors have a material interest) or transactions with officers (who are not directors), such as financial arrangements, quasi-loans, guarantees or security or credit transactions?	Y/N	24.01 to 24.12	—
15	Does the company pay unconnected third parties for directors' services?	Y/N	7.03	—
16	Is it a lessor company?	Y/N	Checklist **13**	—
17	Has it any FRS 5 style substance over form transactions (e.g., factoring of debts, consignment stock or sale and leaseback)?	Y/N	1.06 to 1.11	—
18	Is it an investment company?	Y/N	14.09, 28.11, 31.14	—
19	Does it have any interest in a partnership, unlimited company or Scottish firm, where each partner or member is a limited company?	Y/N	**9**(5.05), **10**(4.05 to 4.08)	—

Checklist 5

Client: Roberts Design Ltd		Prepared by: EAA	Date: 18.8.95	Ref: A7.2
Year/Period End: 30.6.95	File No:	Reviewed by: ADS	Date: 21.8.95	

SIMPLIFIED ABBREVIATED ACCOUNTS

This checklist is only suitable for small companies which are not part of a group and assumes full advantage has been taken of SI 1992 No 2452. *The checklist should be marked with a '√' to indicate yes, a '×' for no and a '-' for not applicable. This checklist merely summarises the relevant legislation; detailed requirements should be obtained from the Act itself. If you intend to use the Checklist* ***4*** *(simplified annual review of changes) in subsequent years, file this checklist on the Permanent Audit File.*

		Complete (√)
1.01	The balance sheet must contain a statement immediately above the director's signature* stating that advantage is taken of the exemptions conferred by Section A of Part III of Sch 8 to the CA 1985, together with a statement of the grounds on which, in the directors' opinion, the company is entitled to those exemptions (Sch 8.23).	√
1.02	Where an audit is required, attach a special report of the auditors to the abbreviated accounts, to include:	
	(a) a statement that, in the auditors' opinion, the company is entitled to the exemptions claimed in the directors' statement, and the accounts are properly prepared in accordance with Sch 8;	–
	(b) the full text of the auditors' report on the shareholders' accounts and, if qualified, any further material necessary to understand the qualification; and	–
	(c) the name of the auditors (Sch 8.24, PN8).	–
1.03	Where an independent accountants' report is required, attach the reporting accountants' report on the full statutory accounts to the abbreviated accounts (s249E(2), Sch 8.25A).	√
1.04	Paragraphs **1.01** and **1.02** above do not apply to a dormant company which has elected not to appoint auditors, but the accounts must include a statement by the directors, immediately above the director's signature, that the company was dormant throughout the year (s250(4)(c), Sch 8.25).	–
1.05	A directors' report and profit and loss account are not required (Sch 8.18,20).	√
1.06	An abbreviated balance sheet may be filed, showing only those items to which a letter or roman number is assigned in the balance sheet format adopted under Part I of Sch 4 (Sch 8.17(1)).	√
1.07	Disclose the accounting policies (Sch 8.19(1)).	√
1.08	Show the corresponding amounts for the preceding year, except where indicated (Sch 8.19(1)).	√
1.09	State the authorised share capital (Sch 8.19(1)).	√
1.10	State the number and aggregate nominal value of shares allotted (Sch 8.19(1)).	√
1.11	For each class of fixed assets (tangible and investments), disclose the cost or valuation and accumulated depreciation at the beginning and end of the year, additions and disposals, transfers, depreciation and revaluations. Comparative figures are not required (Sch 8.19(1)).	√

* *or immediately above any statement required by s246(1A) (see Checklist* ***2*** *(simplified main checklist), para 5.01).*

Complete (✓)

1.12 For each item included under creditors, show:

(a) the total amount falling due after five years and not repayable by instalments; and —

(b) the total amount payable by instalments, any part of which is payable after five years, together with the total amount of instalments falling due after five years (Sch 8.19(1)). —

1.13 State the total amount of creditors secured (Sch 8.19(1)). —

1.14 State the aggregate amount of any debtors falling due after more than one year (Sch 8.17(2)(a)). —

1.15 State the aggregate amount of any creditors falling due after more than one year, if not shown on the face of the balance sheet (Sch 8.17(2)(b)). —

1.16 If any loans or other transactions in favour of directors or officers exist, disclose the details required by the Checklist **2** (simplified main checklist), paragraphs **8.01** to **8.03** (Sch 8.19(3)). —

Additional disclosures

1.17 If the full accounts disclose additional information (see the Checklist **2** (simplified main checklist), para **1.01**), then that additional information should be disclosed in the abbreviated accounts to the extent that it relates to any disclosure arising from **1.01** to **1.16** above (s226(4)). —

1.18 If, in special circumstances, the full accounts depart from the provisions of the Act (see the Checklist **2** (simplified main checklist), paragraphs **1.02** to **1.04**), then that departure should be disclosed in the abbreviated accounts to the extent that it relates to any disclosure arising from **1.01** to **1.16** above (s226(5)). —

1.19 The registered number of the company must be shown in a prominent position (s706(2)(a)). ✓

Client Roberts Design Ltd	Year end 30.6.95

C1 · Clearance and Conclusions

The reporting accountant should perform such procedures as are necessary to provide a reasonable basis on which to express the opinions which are to be provided in the report:

- accounts in agreement with the accounting records;
- accounts prepared in a manner consistent with the specified accounting requirements;
- entitlement to exemption from an audit.

In the performance of these procedures the reporting accountant should plan, control and record his work.

Checklist

		Yes/No	*Initials*
1	Has D1 · *Planning memorandum* been satisfactorily completed?	Yes	EAA
2	Have E1 and E2 · *Work programmes* been fully completed?	Yes	EAA
3	Have all final journals been recorded and processed to produce a closing trial balance agreeing with the accounts?	Yes	EAA
4	Have all queries and problems been properly cleared or carried forward to C2 · *Points for partner/highlights*?	Yes	EAA
5	Does the file contain evidence of 'partner' review?	Yes	EAA
6	Have all the partner review points been cleared?	Yes	EAA
7	Have all matters of concern been discussed with the directors, and explanations noted and resolved?	Yes	EAA
	If not: has an appropriate explanatory paragraph or qualification been included in the report and the underlying reasons recorded on file?	N/A	
8	Does the balance sheet contain a statement from the directors acknowledging their responsibilities?	Yes	EAA

Conclusion

I am satisfied that procedures necessary to support the opinions in our report have been properly performed and recorded.

Senior/Manager EA Arbuthnott Date 18.8.95

Partner AJ Smith Date 21.8.95

CRM Release 1 3/2

Client Roberts Design Ltd	Year end 30.6.95

D1 · Planning Memorandum

	Comments	Initials	WP Ref
1 *Entitlement* Confirm that the client appears to be entitled to exemption from an audit by completing the planning column of *Work Programme E1*.		EAA	E1
2 *Independence* Confirm that we can act as reporting accountants. (Consider, e.g., independence, outstanding fees, ability to service client, client's integrity.)	No independence problems	EAA	
3 *Engagement letter* (a) Ensure terms of our engagement are still valid. (b) If appropriate, send revised letter to client and confirm its return, duly signed.	Letter sent 4.7.94	EAA	
4 *Knowledge of client* (a) Review and update Permanent File. (b) Review correspondence file for relevant points arising during the year and/or discuss with client.	No relevant points	EAA EAA	
5 *Procedures* By reference to *Work Programmes E1 and E2* consider the work to be carried out and note if any additional procedures are considered appropriate.		EAA	E2
6 *Timetable and budget* Prepare a note of the time schedule, staff allocation and fee budget.	Not necessary fee agreed £1650		D2

Conclusion

I am satisfied that the work has been planned effectively and the client appears to be entitled to exemption from audit.

Senior/Manager EAA Date 10.8.95

Partner AJS Date 10.8.95

CRM Release 0	*3/3*

Jones Watson & Co

24 Barracks Square, Oldtown, Yorkshire

Tel: 01978 623897 Fax: 01978 623938

1 June 1995

E Roberts Esq
Roberts Design Limited
100 Plumstone Court
Newtown
Berkshire

Dear Mr Roberts

As we approach the next year end, I am writing to ask you to confirm that you are still eligible for the audit exemption. I would, therefore, like you to complete the attached questionnaire and return it to our offices as soon as possible (at least two weeks before your year end). This will ensure appropriate action can be taken should you be found to be ineligible for the exemption.

If you have any queries, then please call me on the number above.

Yours sincerely

A D Smith

. . . .

1. I/we confirm that the company is not, nor has it been during the period:

    1.1 a public company;

    1.2 a banking or insurance company;

    1.3 enrolled in the list maintained by the Insurance Brokers' Registration Council under s4 of the Insurance Brokers' (Registration) Act 1977;

    1.4 an authorised person or an appointed representative under the Financial Services Act 1986;

    1.5 a special registered body as defined in s117(1) of the Trade Union and Labour Relations (Consolidation) Act 1992, or an employers' association as defined in s122 of that Act; or

    1.6 A parent company or a subsidiary undertaking.

2. I/we confirm that no shareholders have lodged a statement with us requesting an audit.

3. I/we confirm that I am/we are unaware of any other reason why the company may need to have an audit.

Signed on behalf of the board Date

Client Roberts Design Ltd	Year end 30.6.95

E1 · Entitlement to Exemption from Audit

Objective: To obtain and record sufficient evidence to enable us to form an opinion as to whether the company is entitled to exemption from audit.

	Planning – Initials & Date	*Final – Initials & Date*	*Ref/ Comments*
According to the information contained in the accounting records and discussions with client:			
1 Confirm that: • turnover is over £90,000 and not more than £350,000 (and income not more than £250,000 for a charity); • gross assets are not more than £1,400,000.	EAA 10.8.95	EAA 18.8.95	
2 Confirm that the company qualifies as a small company under s246 Companies Act 1985.	EAA 10.8.95	EAA 18.8.95	
3 Confirm that at no time during the year was the company: • a plc ✓ • a banking or insurance company ✓ • an authorised person or an appointed representative under the Financial Services Act 1986 ✓ • an insurance broker enrolled on the list maintained by the IBRC ✓ • a 'special register' body or employers' association as defined in the Trade Union and Labour Relations (Consolidation) Act 1992 ✓ • a parent company ✓ • a subsidiary undertaking ✓	EAA 10.8.95	EAA 18.8.95	The company was not set up as a subsidiary of the formation agency. The company's Articles of Association do not require an audit.
4 Optional additional procedure: Obtain the directors' confirmation that members holding 10 per cent or more of the nominal value of the company's share capital or of any class thereof had not deposited a notice requiring an audit more than one month before the year end.	✓ covered in pre-year end letter EAA	EAA 18.8.95	

Conclusion *(to be signed off at the final stage)*

The company appears to be entitled to exemption from audit and a report can be prepared.

~~The company is not entitled to exemption from audit and a report must not be prepared. (In this case advise the client partner immediately.)*~~

	Name	Signature	Date
Senior	EA Arbuthnott	EAA	18.8.95
Manager/Partner	AJ Smith	AJS	21.8.95

* Delete whichever conclusion is not applicable.

There are no commercial pressures (e.g. loans, banks) that may require an audit EAA 10.8.95

Client Roberts Design Ltd	Year end 30.6.95

E2 · Accounts (a) In Agreement with Accounting Records and (b) Consistent with Specified Accounting Requirements

Objective: To obtain and record sufficient evidence to form an opinion as to whether the company's accounts are in accordance with the accounting records and with the accounting requirements of the Companies Act 1985.

	Covered by Accountancy Yes	*Results Satisfactory Yes/No*	*Ref/ Comments*	*Initials & Date*
1 (a) Check all current year items appearing in the accounts on the face of the profit and loss account, balance sheet and notes to the trial balance; (b) include on file a copy of the cross-referenced accounts and trial balance.	Yes Yes	Yes Yes		EAA 18.8.95
2 Check all items from the trial balance to the nominal ledger.	Yes	Yes		EAA 18.8.95
3 On a test basis check the figures in the nominal ledger to the prime books and vice versa, including: (a) the stock figure in the nominal ledger to the stock records; (b) trade debtors and creditors in the nominal ledger to supporting list of balances.	Yes	Yes		EAA 18.8.95
4 Where the make-up of items in the nominal ledger is unclear, or where the accounts are prepared directly from the basic records, check items to the underlying records.	Yes	Yes		EAA 18.8.95
5 Agree the comparative figures to the previous year's accounts and note any changes in amounts or wordings.	N/A	—		
6 (a) Read the accounts to consider whether the amounts appear reasonable and the descriptions appropriate; (b) discuss any matters of concern with directors; (c) obtain and note explanations.	Yes N/A N/A	Yes — —	None	EAA 18.8.95
7 (a) Consider the accounts in relation to the accounting requirements of the Companies Act; (b) complete a disclosure checklist tailored to the company's circumstances.	Yes Yes	Yes Yes	A7.1 & A 7.2	EAA 18.8.95
8 Other tests (if required):				

Client Roberts Design Ltd	Year end 30.6.95

E2 contd.

Conclusion

Subject to the matters highlighted on C2 · *Points for partner/highlights*, in my opinion, sufficient evidence has been obtained from the checks recorded overleaf to conclude that the accounts are in agreement with the accounting records and with the applicable accounting requirements of the Companies Act 1985.

	Name	**Signature**	**Date**
Senior	EA Arbuthnott	EAA	18.8.95
Manager/Partner	AD Smith	ADS	21.8.95

Alternative conclusion (*any alternative conclusion must be referred to on C2*)

	Name	**Signature**	**Date**
Senior			
Manager/Partner			

Client	File No.	Ref.	
Roberts Design Limited		F1	
Subject	Prepared by		Date
Fixed Assets	KM		11/8/95
	Reviewed by		Date
	EAA		17/8/95
	Accounting Dates	30·6·95	

Motor vehicle

	£
Cost	
Addition – Escort J921 XYO	5,100.00
As at 30.6.95	5,100.00
Dep'n	
Charge for period @ 25%	1,275.00
As at 30.6.95	1,275.00
NBV at 30.6.95	3,825.00
	Agreed to TB

	£
Amount paid (per W5)	5,300.00
less warranty & RFL	200.00
Capital	5,100.00

Client		File No.	Ref.
Roberts Design Limited			J1
Subject: Debtors		Prepared by: KM	Date: 11/8/95
		Reviewed by: EAA	Date: 17/8/95
		Accounting Dates: 30·6·95	

		1992
		£
Trade debtors		
29.6.95 Invoice 49 – Paid 3.7.95	W2	1,989.74
Accrued income:bank interest – estimated		180.00
	Agreed to TB	£2,169.74

Client		File No.	Ref.
Roberts Design Limited			K1
Subject		Prepared by	Date
Bank & cash		KM	11/8/95
		Reviewed by	Date
		EAA	17/8/95
		Accounting Dates	30·6·95

	Dr	Cr			£
Current account 1968510			W1	√ β	2,652.71
Premier Interest account 71878883					
	£	£			
Receipts	17,500.00		W5		
Payments		2,000.00	W1		
Interest received – gross	246.69		A2		
Balance c.fwd.		15,746.69		√ β	15,746.69
	£17,746.69	£17,746.69			
					£18,399.40

Small business loan No. 6331319	Dr	Cr			
	£	£			
Advance		2,045.40	W1		
Repayments	2,057.99		W5		
Interest paid		195.09			
Balance c.f.	182.50		L1	√ β	£182.50
	£2,240.49	£2,240.49			

Key

√ Agreed to trial balance Y1
β Agreed to Year end bank statement.

Client		File No.	Ref.
Roberts Design Ltd			L1
Subject		**Prepared by**	**Date**
Creditors		KM	11/8/95
		Reviewed by	**Date**
		EAA	17/8/95
		Accounting Dates	30·6·95

				£		£	
Bank loan				K1		182.50	TB
Trade creditors – access				W6		416.50	TB
Taxation & social security	TB	TB					
Corporation tax	(4,998.25 – 1,500.00 ACT)			3,498.25	A2		
PAYE & NI			W11	2,179.62	TB		
VAT			U1	3,220.72	TB	8,898.59	
Directors' loan – see below						3,688.00	TB
Accruals							
Bank charges			TB	11.60			
Accountancy			TB	1,020.00			
						1,031.60	
ACT – dividend 30·6·95						1,000.00	TB
						15,217.19	

Directors' loan account	*Dr*	*Cr*	
Paid into bank account 1 July 1994		3,300.00	W1
Share capital	2.00		
Use of home as office		390.00	
Balance at 30 June 1995	3,688.00		
	£3,690.00	£3,690.00	

TB = Trial balance Y1

Client		File No.	Ref.
Roberts Design Ltd			Q7
Subject		Prepared by	Date
Directors' emoluments		KM	11/8/95
		Reviewed by	Date
		EAA	17/8/95
		Accounting Dates	30·6·95

		Gross	*E'ers NI*	*Total*
		£	£	£
Mr E Roberts		48,000	4,896	52,896
Mrs K Roberts		12,000	1,224	13,224
	W11	60,000	6,120	66,120
Benefits in kind – E Roberts		2,749	268	3,017
		£62,749	£6,388	£69,137

Benefits – per P11D

1300 Ford Escort <18,000 business miles <4 yrs old		
List price £8,500 @ 35% × $\frac{2}{3}$		1,983.33
Fuel benefit: [640 × $\frac{9}{12}$] + [670 × $\frac{3}{12}$]		647.50
Access card – payments for petrol etc. – s198 claim agreed as all business expenses		—
Health insurance	W5	118.51
		£2,749.34

Client	File No.	Ref.
Roberts Design Ltd		U1

Subject	Prepared by	Date
VAT Control	KM	10/8/95
	Reviewed by EAA	Date 17/8/95
	Accounting Dates 30·6·95	

			Dr £		Cr £
Output VAT				W2	16,723.50
Input VAT		W4	424.02		
Payments		W4	12,318.08		
Access payments		W6	857.04		
Scale charge	3 @£23.83 + 1 @ £24.87				96.36
Balance at 30·6·95		L1	3,220.72		
			£16,819.86		£16,819.86

VAT turnover reconciliations

Turnover per accounts	£97,553
@ 17½%	17,072
Year end debtor – on cash basis	(348)
Outputs per control account	£16,724
Outputs per VAT returns	96,113
Year end debtor	1,990
Scale charge	(550)
Turnover per accounts	£97,553

Client		File No.	Ref.
Roberts Design Ltd			W1
Subject Bank Control account		Prepared by	Date
		Reviewed by	Date
		Accounting Dates	

			Dr £			*Cr* £
Account opened on 1·7·94						
Receipts	Sales		112,286.49	W2		
	1·7·94	Directors' current a/c	3,300.00	L1		
	6·7·94	Bank loan	2,045.40	K2		
	13·5·95	Transfer from premier interest a/c	2,000.00	K1		
Payments	Recorded payments				W4	91,241.45
	Unrecorded payments				W5	25,737.73
	Balance c/fwd 30·6·95					2,652.71
			£119,631.89			£119,631.89

Client	File No.	Ref.
Roberts Design Ltd		W2

Subject	Prepared by	Date
Sales invoices summary	KM	10/8/95
	Reviewed by	**Date**
	EAA	17/8/95
	Accounting Dates	30·6·95

			Net £	*VAT* £	*Gross* £
July – Sept	1–13		25,788.16	4,512.90	30,301.06
Oct – Dec	14–25		23,812.43	4,167.18	27,979.61
Jan – Mar	26–38		26,032.14	4,555.62	30,587.76
Apr – June	39–48		19,930.26	3,487.80	23,418.06
			95,562.99	16,723.50	112,286.49
			TB	TB U1	W1
Invoice	49	J1	1,989.74	348.20	2,337.94
			£97,552.73	£17,071.70	£114,624.43

Client		File No.	Ref.
Roberts Design Limited			W4
Subject		**Prepared by**	**Date**
Summary of Cash Book Payments		KM	10/8/95
		Reviewed by	**Date**
		EAA	17/8/95
		Accounting Dates	30·6·95

Recorded in cash book

	Total	*VAT*	*Salary*	*Stationery & postage*	*Sundry*	*ACT*	*Access*
	£	£	£	£	£	£	£
July	3,699.98	94.84	3,064.04	31.10	510.00		
August	6,577.81	22.05	6,039.55	85.70	40.01		390.50
September	6,189.88	35.56	5,507.12	163.20	40.00		444.00
October	10,137.33	26.03	5,432.88	142.00	4,047.85		488.57
November	8,280.30	23.54	5,510.00	121.50	2,040.00		585.26
December	6,452.48	46.48	5,674.00	225.60	40.00		466.40
January	11,129.89	20.82	5,746.00	123.40	4,193.95	500.00	545.72
February	6,151.17	18.57	5,510.00	66.10	40.00		516.50
March	6,380.61	59.25	5,510.00	138.50	200.00		472.86
April	10,139.77	26.92	5,436.07	90.00	4,156.28		430.50
May	9,941.75	26.36	5,268.72	86.14	4,025.00		535.53
June	6,160.48	23.60	5,510.00	134.86			492.02
Total	£91,241.45	£424.02	£64,208.38	£1,408.10	£19,333.09	£500.00	£5,367,86
	W1	U1	↓		↓		W6

Salary	32,296.97	Accy	630.00	
Deductions	28,911.41	VAT	12,318.08	U1
W11		Dividend	6,000.00	
		Other	385.01	
	£64,208.38			
			£19,333.09	

Client		File No.	Ref.
Roberts Design Limited			W5
Subject		Prepared by	Date
Unrecorded payments on bank account		KM	10/8/95
		Reviewed by	Date
		EAA	17/8/95
		Accounting Dates	30·6·95

Bank charges	*Bank interest*	*Overdraft insurance*	*RAC*	*Loan*	*Transfers to premium*	*Health insurance*
£	*£*	*£*	*£*	*£*	*£*	*£*
57.00	23.90	2.00	81.00	187.09	3,000.00	16.93
63.70	1.73	1.00	95.00	187.09	1,500.00	16.93
48.10		1.00		187.09	2,000.00	16.93
51.90		1.00		187.09	1,000.00	16.93
		1.00		187.09	3,000.00	16.93
		1.00		187.09	3,000.00	16.93
		1.00		187.09	4,000.00	16.93
		1.00		187.09		
		1.00		187.09		
		1.00		187.09		
		1.00		187.09		
		1.00				
220.70	25.63	13.00	176.00	2,057.99	17,500.00	118.51
				K2	K1	Q7

Car insurance	*Other*	
£	*£*	
45.40	5,300.00	— Payment for Escort
25.50	F1	
25.50		
25.50		
25.50		
25.50		
25.50		
25.50		
25.50		
25.50		
25.50		
25.50		
325.90	5,300.00	

Total £25,737.73

W1

Client		File No.	Ref.
Roberts Design Ltd			W6
Subject		**Prepared by**	**Date**
Access Control Account		KM	10/8/95
		Reviewed by	**Date**
		EAA	17/8/95
		Accounting Dates	30·6·95

		Dr £	*Cr* £
Payments	W4	5,367.86	
Purchases – see below			5,784.36
Creditor – per statement 30·6·95	L1	416.50	
		£5,784.36	£5,784.36

Analysis of Access purchases

	Total £	*VAT* £	*Motor* £	*Sundry* £
July	390.50	53.69	306.81	30.00
August	444.00	66.13	377.87	–
September	488.57	72.77	415.80	–
October	585.26	87.16	498.10	–
November	466.40	69.46	396.94	–
December	545.72	81.28	464.44	–
January	516.50	76.93	439.57	–
February	472.86	70.43	402.43	–
March	430.50	64.12	366.38	–
April	535.53	79.76	455.77	–
May	492.02	73.28	418.74	–
June	416.50	62.03	354.47	–
Total	£5,784.36	£857.04	£4,897.32	£30.00

U1

Client	Roberts Design Ltd	File No.	Ref. W11
Subject	Wages control account	Prepared by KM	Date 10/8/95
		Reviewed by EAA	Date 17/8/95
		Accounting Dates	30·6·95

		Dr £		*Cr* £
Wages control				
Gross wages			Q7	60,000.00
				268.00
E'ers NIC			Q7	6,120.00
Pension deductions		9,200.00		
PAYE		11,822.55		
NIC		9,800.48		
		268.00		
Net wages	W4	35,296.97		
		66,120.00 + 268.00		66,120.00 + 268.00
Deductions control				
Pensions				9,200.00
PAYE				11,822.55
NIC				9,800.48
				268.00
Payments	W4	28,911.41		
PAYE Creditor	£2,179.62 LI TB	981.62		
NIC Creditor		930.00		
		268.00		
		30,823.03 + 268.00		30,823.03 + 268.00

Wages Summary

	Gross	*Pension*	*Tax*	*E'ees NI*	*Net*	*E'ers NI*
Edward	48,000.00	7,200.00	10,149.03	2,957.60	27,693.37	4,896.00
Katy	12,000.00	2,000.00	1,673.52	722.88	7,603.60	1,224.00
	60,000.00	9,200.00	11,822.55	3,680.48	35,296.97	6,120.00 + 268.00

File No.	Ref Y1.1
Prepared by: KM	Date 11/08/95
Reviewed by: EAA	Date 17/08/95
Accounting Dates	30.06.95

Client **Roberts Design Ltd**

Key = μ casts checked
√ agreed to accounts

TRIAL BALANCE

	Ref	Balance B/fwd		Bank Account		Access Account		Ref	Adjustments				Profit & Loss Account		Balance Sheet	
		Debit	Credit	Debit	Credit	Debit	Credit		Debit	Credit	Accruals	Prepayments	Debit	Credit	Debit	Credit
Turnover					95,562.99							1,989.74		97,552.73		
								6	6,120.00							
Wages								5	60,000.00				66,388.00			
								12	268.00							
								12		268.00					W11	
Deduction control account				28,911.41				7		30,823.03					L1	2,179.62
								6	9,200.00	6,120.00						
Wages control account				35,296.97				5, 7	11,822.55	60,000.00						
									9,800.48							
				176.00												
Motor expenses				325.90		4,897.32		8	96.36				5,695.58			
								1	200.00							
Bank charges				220.70							11.60	L1	232.30			
				13.00												
Bank interest				25.63									38.63			
Loan interest								3	195.09				195.09			
Postage and stationery				1,408.10									1,408.10			
Health insurance				118.51									118.51			
Accountancy				630.00							1,020.00	L1	1,650.00			
Sundry expenses				385.01		30.00							415.01			
Use of home as office								10	390.00				390.00			
Interest received								4		246.69		180.00		426.69		
Dividends				6,000.00									6,000.00			
Taxation – P & L								11	4,998.25				4,998.25			
ACT				500.00						L1	1,000.00			L1	1,500.00	
Depreciation								2	1,275.00				1,275.00			
				74,011.23	95,562.99	4,927.32			104,365.73	97,457.72	2,031.60	2,169.74	88,804.47	97,979.42	1,500.00	2,179.62

File No.		Ref	Y1.2
Prepared by:	KM	Date	11/8/95
Reviewed by:	EAA	Date	17/8/95
Accounting Dates		30.6.95	

Client **Roberts Design Ltd**

TRIAL BALANCE

	Ref	Balance B/fwd		Bank Account		Access Account		Ref	Adjustments				Profit & Loss Account		Balance Sheet	
		Debit	Credit	Debit	Credit	Debit	Credit		Debit	Credit	Accruals	Prepayments	Debit	Credit	Debit	Credit
Motor vehicle				5,300.00				1		200.00				(F1)	5,100.00	
Accumulated depreciation								2		1,275.00					(F1)	1,275.00
Current account				119,631.89	116,979.18									(K1)	2,652.71	
Premier account				17,500.00	2,000.00			4	246.69					(K1)	15,746.69	
Access account				5,367.86			5,784.36				416.50	(L1)			–	–
				12,318.08												
VAT account				424.02	16,723.50	857.04		8		96.36					(L1)	3,220.72
Loan account				2,057.99	2,045.40			3		195.09					(K1)	182.50
Director's current account					3,300.00			9,10	2.00	390.00					(L1)	3,688.00
Share capital								9		2.00						2.00
Debtors & prepayments											2,169.74			(J1)	2,169.74	
Creditors & accruals												2,448.10				2,448.10
Tax creditor								11		4,998.25					(L1)	4,998.25
Page 2				162,599.84	141,048.08	857.04	5784.36		248.69	7,156.70	2,586.24	2,448.10			25,669.14	15,814.57
Page 1				74,011.23	95,562.99	4,927.32			104,365.73	97,457.72	2,031.60	2,169.74	88,804.47	97,979.42	1,500.00	2,179.62
Profit for the year													9,174.95			9,174.95
				236,611.07	236,611.07	5,784.36	5,784.36		104,614.42	104,614.42	4,617.84	4,617.84	97,979.42	97,979.42	27,169.14	27,169.14

Client		File No.	Ref.
Roberts Design Limited			Y2.1
Subject		**Prepared by**	**Date**
Journals		KM	11/8/95
		Reviewed by	**Date**
		EAA	17/8/95
		Accounting Dates	30·6·95

		Dr £	*Cr* £
(1)	Dr Motor expenses	200.00	
	Cr Motor vehicle		200.00
	Being: warranty. RFL purchased with car		
(2)	Dr Depreciation	1,275.00	
	Cr Acc. depn motor vehicle		1,275.00
	Being: depreciation charge for period		
(3)	Dr Loan interest	195.09	
	Cr Loan account		195.09
	Being: loan interest		
(4)	Dr Deposit a/c	246.69	
	Cr Interest rec'd		246.69
	Being: deposit a/c interest		
(5)	Dr Wages	60,000.00	
	Cr Wages control		60,000.00
	Being gross wages for period.		
(6)	Dr Wages	6,120.00	
	Cr Wages control		6,120.00
	Being Er's NIC for period		

Client: Roberts Design Limited	File No.	Ref. Y2.2
Subject: Journals	Prepared by: KM	Date: 11/8/95
	Reviewed by: EAA	Date: 17/8/95
	Accounting Dates: 30·6·95	

		Dr £	*Cr* £
(7)	Dr Wages control – PAYE	11,822.55	
	– NI	9,800.48	
	– pensions	9,200.00	
	Cr Deductions control		30,823.03
	Being: deductions for period		
(8)	Dr Motor expenses	96.36	
	Cr VAT control		96.36
	Being: scale change		
(9)	Dr Directors' current a/c	2.00	
	Cr Share capital		2.00
	Being: unpaid share capital		
(10)	Dr P & L use of home as office	390.00	
	Cr Directors' current account		390.00
	Being: Use of home as office		
(11)	Dr P & L tax charge	4,998.25	
	Cr Corporation tax creditors		4,498.25
	Being: corporation tax provision for the year		
(12)	Dr Wages control	268.00	
	Cr Deductions control		268.00
	Being: class 1A NIC		

FILE 3 – BRIGHT-A-LIGHT LTD

Client: Bright-a-Light Ltd		Prepared by: KM	Date: 23.6.95
Year/Period End: 31.3.95	File No:	Reviewed by: EAA	Date: 27.6.95

AUDIT FILE INDEX

A ACCOUNTS

1	Final accounts	✓
2	Tax computations	✓
3	Final journals	
4	Draft accounts, typing instructions	
5	Letter of representation	✓
6	Letter to management	
7	Company accounts disclosure checklists	✓
8	Management accounts/last year's accounts	
9		

B AUDIT COMPLETION
C AUDIT PLANNING
D EXTENSIVE ANALYTICAL REVIEW
E INTANGIBLE ASSETS
F TANGIBLE FIXED ASSETS
G INVESTMENTS IN GROUP AND ASSOCIATED UNDERTAKINGS
H OTHER INVESTMENTS
I STOCK AND WORK IN PROGRESS
J DEBTORS AND PREPAYMENTS
K BANK BALANCES AND CASH
L CREDITORS AND ACCRUALS
M LONG TERM LOANS AND DEFERRED INCOME
N PROVISIONS FOR LIABILITIES AND CHARGES, CONTINGENT LIABILITIES AND FINANCIAL COMMITMENTS
O CAPITAL, RESERVES AND STATUTORY RECORDS
P TAXATION
Q INCOME AND EXPENDITURE – ANALYSIS FOR TAX PURPOSES
R PROFIT AND LOSS
S CASH FLOW STATEMENTS
T POST BALANCE SHEET EVENTS
U VALUE ADDED TAX
V CONSOLIDATION
W ACCOUNTS WORKING PAPERS
X RECORDS RECEIVED
Y COMPUTER REPORTS
Z OBSOLETE WORKING PAPERS

Client: Bright-a-Light Ltd		Prepared by: DGW	Date: 18.7.95	Ref: **A**
Year/Period End: 31.3.95	File No:	Reviewed by: MJ	Date: 18.7.95	

PARTNER COMPLETION

Final		**Initials**
1 Have all outstanding items on the initial partner completion been adequately dealt with?	Yes/~~N/A*~~	DGW
2 Has a signed letter of representation been received?	Yes	DGW
3 Where the letter of representation is signed by one director on behalf of the Board, have we seen minutes of a meeting agreeing its contents?	~~Yes~~/N/A*	DGW
4 Are we satisfied that the directors' representations can be relied upon?	Yes	DGW
5 Does the file contain adequate justification of the audit report?	Yes	DGW
6 Has a letter of comment covering all material weaknesses in the system been sent to the client?	~~Yes~~/N/A*	DGW
7 Has the final post balance sheet events programme on **T4** been completed?	Yes/~~NCN†*~~	DGW
8 Does the balance sheet state the name of the director who approves the accounts on behalf of the Board, together with the date of approval?	Yes	DGW
9 Does the copy of the accounts which is being filed with the Registrar contain original signatures on the directors' report, the auditors' report and the balance sheet?	Yes	DGW
10 Does the audit file contain sufficient evidence (where applicable) to support our opinion on the following exemptions taken by the company:		
(a) filing abbreviated accounts;	~~Yes~~/N/A*	DGW
(b) disclosure exemptions applicable to small companies under SI 1992 No 2452;	~~Yes~~/N/A*	DGW
(c) exemption from preparing consolidated accounts within s248 CA 1985.	~~Yes/~~N/A*	DGW
11 Do the working papers and the tax computation reflect final adjustments?	Yes	DGW
12 Have all final journals been recorded and processed to produce a closing trial balance agreeing with the accounts?	Yes	DGW
13 Has the final copy of the accounts been referenced to the file to ensure all lead and **Q** schedules reflect final adjustments?	Yes	DGW

I authorise the signing of the audit report.

Signed DG Watson Partner Date 19.7.95

Second partner (if applicable)

Signed M Jones Partner Date 19.7.95

* Delete as appropriate.
† NCN = not considered necessary.

BRIGHT-A-LIGHT LIMITED

COMPANY NUMBER: 9993000

FINANCIAL STATEMENTS FOR THE YEAR ENDED 31 MARCH 1995

AUDITORS:	JONES WATSON & CO Registered Auditors and Chartered Accountants 24 Barracks Square Oldtown Yorkshire
REGISTERED OFFICE:	12 Westend Industrial Estate Oldtown Yorkshire

BRIGHT-A-LIGHT LIMITED

DIRECTORS' REPORT
The directors submit their report, together with the accounts of the company for the year ended 31 March 1995.

PRINCIPAL ACTIVITIES
The principal activity of the company is the supply of packaged fuels.

DIRECTORS
The following persons were directors during the year and their shareholdings in the company at the beginning and end of the year were:

	Ordinary £1 Shares
K Strike	9,900
B Strike	100

STATEMENT OF DIRECTORS' RESPONSIBILITIES
Company law requires the directors to prepare financial statements for each financial year which give a true and fair view of the state of affairs of the company and of the profit or loss of the company for that period. In preparing those financial statements, the directors are required to:

- select suitable accounting policies and then apply them consistently;
- make judgements and estimates that are reasonable and prudent;
- prepare the financial statements on the going concern basis, unless it is inappropriate to presume that the company will continue in business.

The directors are responsible for keeping proper accounting records which disclose with reasonable accuracy at any time the financial position of the company and to enable them to ensure that the financial statements comply with the Companies Act 1985. They are also responsible for safeguarding the assets of the company and hence for taking reasonable steps for the prevention and detection of fraud and other irregularities.

AUDITORS
Jones Watson & Co., in accordance with the Companies Act 1985, retire and offer themselves for reappointment.

SMALL COMPANY EXEMPTIONS
Advantage has been taken, in the preparation of this report, of special exemptions applicable to small companies.

BY ORDER OF THE BOARD

B STRIKE
Secretary

Date: 17 July 1995

Page 1

AUDITORS' REPORT TO THE MEMBERS OF BRIGHT-A-LIGHT LIMITED

FOR THE YEAR ENDED 31 MARCH 1995

We have audited the financial statements on pages 3 to 8, which have been prepared under the historical cost convention and the accounting policies set out on page 5.

Respective responsibilites of directors and auditors

As described on page 1 the company's directors are responsible for the preparation of financial statements. It is our responsibility to form an independent opinion, based on our audit, on those statements and to report our opinion to you.

Basis of opinion

We conducted our audit in accordance with Auditing Standards issued by the Auditing Practices Board. An audit includes examination, on a test basis, of evidence relevant to the amounts and disclosures in the financial statements. It also includes an assessment of the significant estimates and judgements by the directors in the preparation of the financial statements, and of whether the accounting policies are appropriate to the company's circumstances, consistently applied and adequately disclosed.

We planned and performed our audit so as to obtain all the information and explanations which we considered necessary in order to provide us with sufficient evidence to give reasonable assurance that the financial statements are free from material misstatement, whether caused by fraud, or other irregularity or error. In forming our opinion, we also evaluated the overall adequacy of the presentation of information in the financial statements.

Opinion

In our opinion the financial statements give a true and fair view of the state of the company's affairs as at 31 March 1995 and of its profit for the year then ended and have been properly prepared in accordance with the provisions of the Companies Act 1985 applicable to small companies

Jones Watson & Co

Registered Auditors and
Chartered Accountants
24 Barracks Square
Oldtown
Yorkshire

Date: 19 July 1995

Bright-a-Light Limited

Profit and Loss account
for the year ended 31 March 1995

	Note	*1995*		*1994*	
		£	*£*	*£*	*£*
Turnover	1		858,901		675,324
Cost of sales			691,119		538,830
Gross profit			167,782		136,494
Distribution costs		36,560		29,585	
Administrative expenses		105,658		80,282	
			142,218		109,867
			25,564		26,627
Other operating income			10,530		3,134
Interest payable and similar charges			(18,774)		(19,418)
Profit on ordinary activities before taxation	2		17,320		10,343
Tax on profit on ordinary activities	4		5,630		2,732
Profit for financial year			11,690		7,611
Retained profit brought forward			15,981		8,370
Retained profit carried forward			£27,671		£15,981

There are no recognised gains or losses other than as disclosed above.

There have been no discontinued activities or acquisitions in the current or preceding accounting period.

Bright-a-Light Limited
Balance sheet at 31 March 1995

	Note	*1995*		*1994*	
		£	£	£	£
Fixed assets					
Tangible assets	5		£159,007		157,862
Current assets					
Stocks		26,003		22,860	
Debtors	6	127,542		75,172	
Cash in hand		461		123	
		154,006		98,155	
Creditors: amounts falling due within one year	7	(161,295)		(106,512)	
Net current liabilities			(7,289)		(8,357)
Total assets less current liabilities			151,718		149,505
Creditors: amounts falling due after more than one year	8		114,047		123,524
			£37,671		£25,981
Funds employed					
Called up share capital	10		10,000		10,000
Profit and loss account			27,671		15,981
Shareholders' funds	11		£37,671		£25,981

The notes on pages 5 to 8 form an integral part of these accounts.

Advantage has been taken, in the preparation of the accounts, of special exemptions applicable to small companies on the grounds that, in the directors' opinion, the company qualifies as a small company under s246 and s247 of the Companies Act 1985. The accounts were approved by the Board of Directors on 17 July 1995, and are signed on its behalf by:

K Strike

K Strike

Page 4

Bright-a-Light Limited

Notes to the Accounts
for the year ended 31 March 1995

1 Accounting policies

Accounting convention
The financial statements have been prepared under the historical cost convention of accounting, and comply with all applicable accounting standards.

Turnover
Turnover represents the amounts receivable, excluding VAT, by the company for goods and services provided in the UK.

Depreciation
Depreciation is calculated to write off the cost of the assets over their expected useful lives using the following rates;

Freehold buildings	11.1% on 1994 net book value (1994:2% on the cost)
Plant and equipment	20% on the net book value
Motor vehicles	25% on the net book value
Fixtures and fittings	15% on the net book value

The useful economic life of the freehold buildings has been revised to 10 years to reflect the poor condition of the buildings.

Stock
Stock is valued at the lower cost and net realisable value. Cost is calculated using the first in, first out (FIFO) method of valuation.

Deferred taxation
The charge for taxation is based on the profit for the year as adjusted for disallowable items. Tax deferred or accelerated is accounted for in respect of all material timing differences to the extent that it is probable that a liability or asset will crystallise. Timing differences arise from the inclusion of items of income and expenditure in tax computations in periods different from those in which they are included in the accounts. Provision is made at the rate which is expected to be applied when the liability or asset is expected to crystallise.

Pensions
The company operates a defined contribution pension scheme. The assets of the scheme are held separately from those of the company in an independently administered fund. Contributions are charged to the profit and loss account as they become payable in accordance with the rules of the scheme.

Leased assets
Where assets are financed by finance leases, the assets are included in the balance sheet at cost less depreciation in accordance with the company's normal accounting policies. The future rental payments are shown as a liability. Interest is charged to the profit and loss account over the period of the lease in proportion to the balance of the capital outstanding. Rentals payable under operating leases are charged to the profit and loss account as incurred.

Bright-a-Light Limited

Notes to the Accounts
for the year ended 31 March 1995

2 Profit on ordinary activities before taxation	*1995*	*1994*
	£	£
After charging or including:		
Depreciation for year	12,914	5,436
Auditor's remuneration	1,800	1,600
Directors' emoluments (note 3)	19,488	18,388
Finance charges on finance leases	1,055	–

3 Directors and employees	*1995*	*1994*
	£	£
Directors:		
Emoluments: for service as directors	17,450	17,042
Pension costs (defined contribution scheme)	2,038	1,346
Benefits in kind	5,543	5,614
	£25,031	£24,002

4 Taxation

	1995	*1994*
	£	£
Taxation based on the adjusted profit for the year:		
Corporation tax @ 25%	5,630	2,742
Overprovision in the previous year	–	(10)
	£5,630	£2,732

The directors do not consider that any provision is required for deferred taxation under the accounting policy set out in Note 1.

Unprovided deferred tax – accelerated capital allowances	£127	£121

Bright-a-Light Limited

Notes to the Accounts for the year ended 31 March 1995

5 Tangible assets

	Land	*Freehold buildings*	*Plant & equipment*	*Motor vehicles*	*Fixtures & fittings*	*Total*
	£	£	£	£	£	£
Cost						
At 1 April 1994	95,935	47,967	4,500	16,975	1,753	167,130
Additions	–	–	–	16,345	326	16,671
Disposals	–	–	–	(5,000)	–	(5,000)
At 31 March 1995	95,935	47,967	4,500	28,320	2,079	178,801
Depreciation						
At 1 April 1994	–	960	1,650	6,207	451	9,268
Charge for year	–	5,223	570	6,875	246	12,914
Disposals	–	–	–	(2,388)	–	(2,388)
At 31 March 1995	–	6,183	2,220	10,694	697	19,794
Net book amounts						
As at 31 March 1995	£95,935	£41,784	£2,280	£17,626	£1,382	£159,007
As at 1 April 1994	£95,935	£47,007	£2,850	£10,768	£1,302	£157,862

The net book amount of motor vehicles includes £5,997 (1994 £–) in respect of assets held under finance leases. The depreciation charged in the year on these assets amounts to £2,998 (1994 £–).

(6) Debtors

	1995	*1994*
	£	£
Trade debtors	121,192	73,196
Other debtors	4,773	940
Prepayments and accrued income	1,577	1,036
	£127,542	£75,172

(7) Creditors: amounts due within one year

Bank loans and overdrafts	56,129	41,661
Trade creditors	82,808	51,109
Taxation and social security	9,786	3,823
Other creditors	8,197	7,895
Accruals and deferred income	2,285	2,024
Obligations under finance leases	2,090	—
	£161,295	£106,512

(8) Creditors: amounts due after more than one year

Amounts repayable by instalments

	Bank loans		*Finance leases*		*Total*	
	1995	*1994*	*1995*	*1994*	*1995*	*1994*
	£	£	£	£	£	£
Due 1–2 years	13,767	14,524	2,572	—	16,339	14,524
Due 3–5 years	38,196	39,793	2,475	—	40,671	39,793
Due after 5 years	57,037	69,207	—	—	57,037	69,207
	£109,000	£123,524	£5,047	—	£114,047	£123,524

(9) Secured liabilities

The business development loans and overdraft facility are secured by a mortgage debenture incorporating a fixed and floating charge over the assets of the company and a mortgage over the freehold property.

The obligations under finance leases are secured on the finance lease assets included under tangible assets.

(10) Share capital

		1995	*1994*
		£	£
Ordinary shares of £1 each	Authorised	10,000	10,000
	Allotted, issued and fully paid	10,000	10,000

(11) Reconciliation of movement in shareholders' funds

	1995	*1994*
	£	£
Profit for the financial year	11,690	7,611
Opening shareholders' funds	25,981	18,370
Closing shareholders' funds	37,671	25,981

(12) Capital commitments and contingencies

There are no capital commitments and contingencies at the year end (last year £Nil).

BRIGHT-A-LIGHT LIMITED

TRADING AND PROFIT AND LOSS ACCOUNT
FOR THE YEAR ENDED 31 MARCH 1995

	Note	*1995*		*1994*	
		£	£	£	£
SALES			858,901		675,324
COST OF GOODS SOLD:					
Opening stock		22,860		31,797	
Purchases		694,262		529,893	
Closing stock		(26,003)		(22,860)	
			691,119		538,830
			167,782		136,494
Rents and rates received			10,530		3,134
			178,312		139,628
EXPENSES:					
Delivery costs	1	36,560		29,585	
Yard and establishment	2	25,127		18,958	
Management expenses	3	42,957		38,103	
Office expenses	4	10,802		11,023	
Finance and administration	5	13,646		6,762	
Loan interest		13,912		17,069	
Bank charges and interest		3,807		2,349	
Finance charges on finance leases		1,055		—	
Depreciation		12,914		5,436	
Loss on the sale of fixed assets		212		—	
			160,992		129,285
Net profit for the year before tax			£17,320		£10,343

BRIGHT-A-LIGHT LIMITED

SUMMARY OF EXPENSES
FOR THE YEAR ENDED 31 MARCH 1995

	1995 £	*1994* £
(1) Delivery costs		
Wages and National Insurance	15,624	14,661
Pensions	424	—
Petrol and oil	6,365	5,794
Repairs and renewals	8,696	5,771
Licences and insurances	2,637	2,502
Miscellaneous	2,814	857
	£36,560	£29,585
(2) Yard and establishment		
Wages and National Insurance	6,760	5,526
Repairs and maintenance	8,380	3,227
Light and heat	1,219	1,076
Rates	5,804	5,921
Insurance	2,860	3,020
Miscellaneous	104	188
	£25,127	£18,958
(3) Management expenses		
Salaries and National Insurance	30,790	29,905
Pensions	2,038	1,346
Travelling	1,652	1,666
Motor expenses	5,371	3,014
Miscellaneous	1,232	2,172
Agents' commission	1,874	—
	£42,957	£38,103
(4) Office expenses		
Telephone	2,624	2,161
Computer leasing/expenses	1,336	2,271
Printing and stationery	1,343	1,861
Postage	1,536	1,188
Advertising	2,790	2,007
Repairs and maintenance	124	44
Miscellaneous	1,049	1,491
	£10,802	£11,023
(5) Finance and administration		
Miscellaneous	25	—
Credit card charges	408	247
Accountancy	4,400	6,150
Bad debts written off	8,425	120
Legal and professional fees	388	245
	£13,646	£6,762

BRIGHT-A-LIGHT LIMITED

CORPORATION TAX COMPUTATIONS
YEAR ENDED 31 MARCH 1995

		£
Net profit per accounts		17,320
Add:	Depreciation	12,914
	Loss on the sale of fixed assets	212
		30,446
Less:	Rent received	10,530
	Capital allowances	4,927
	Depreciation on leased car	2,998
Schedule 'D(1)' profits		11,991
Schedule 'A' income		10,530
Profits chargeable to corporation tax		£22,521
Tax at 25%		£5,630

CAPITAL ALLOWANCES

	B/fwd	*Added*	*Disposals*	*W.D.A.*	*C/fwd*
	£	£	£	£	£
Fixtures & fittings/plant & machinery	3,696	326	—	1,006	3,016
Motor vehicles pool	10,738	**7,350	(2,402)	3,921	11,765
				£4,927	

** Excludes Peugeot 405, purchased on finance lease

BRIGHT-A-LIGHT LTD
12 Westend Industrial Estate, Oldtown, Yorkshire
Tel: (0772) 124578 Fax: (0772) 124580

Jones Watson & Co
24 Barracks Square
OLDTOWN
Yorkshire

17 July 1995

Dear Sirs

We confirm to the best of our knowledge and belief the following representations given to you in connection with your audit of the company's financial statements for the period ending 31 March 1995.

1. We acknowledge as directors our responsibility for the financial statements, which you have prepared for the company. All the accounting records have been made available to you for the purpose of your audit and all the transactions undertaken by the company have been properly reflected and recorded in the accounting records. All other records and related information, including minutes of all management and shareholder's meetings, have been made available to you.
2. The company has no liabilities or contingent liabilities other than those disclosed in the financial statements.
3. There has been no event since the balance sheet date which requires disclosing or which would materially affect the amounts in the financial statements, other than those already disclosed or included in the financial statements.
4. The company has had at no time during the year any arrangement, transaction or agreement to provide credit facilities (including loans, quasi-loans or credit transactions) for directors, nor to guarantee or provide security for such matters.
5. The company has not contracted for, nor authorised any capital expenditure other than as disclosed in the financial statements.
6. We confirm that we are not aware of any breaches in laws or regulations that are central to our business.
7. We confirm that in our opinion, the amount relating to freehold land and buildings should be split to give two thirds of the value to the land and one third to the buildings. The economic useful life of the buildings is ten years.

Yours faithfully

K Strike B Strike

Client: Bright-a-Light Ltd		Prepared by: EAA	Date: 22·6·95	Ref: A7.1
Year/Period End: 31.3.95	File No:	Reviewed by: DGW	Date: 3.7.95	

SIMPLIFIED INTRODUCTORY CHECKLIST

The simplified checklists for small companies have omitted the more unusual disclosure requirements. They are only suitable for small companies which are not part of a group, and assume full advantage has been taken of SI 1992 No 2452. *Complete this introductory checklist to confirm that it is appropriate to use the simplified checklists. For any questions answered 'yes', complete the relevant questions in the full checklists.*

			*Full checklist reference**	*Complete (✓)*
1	Does it have more than 250 employees?	~~Y~~/N	3.12(a)	—
2	Has it adopted any format other than Balance Sheet Format I and Profit and Loss Account Formats I or II in the Companies Act 1985, or changed formats since last year?	~~Y~~/N	2.01 to 2.07, 2.12 to 2.17	—
3	Has it acquired or discontinued any operations, or undergone a reorganisation or reconstruction?	~~Y~~/N	11.02 to 11.10, 12.04 to 12.06	—
4	Has it any foreign currency transactions or overseas income?	~~Y~~/N	10.01 to 10.02, 13.10, 31.10, **9**(3.03).	—
5	Has it any exceptional or extraordinary items?	~~Y~~/N	12.01 to 12.09	—
6	Has it any intangible fixed assets (e.g., goodwill)?	~~Y~~/N	6.04, 17.03, 18.01 to 18.04, 31.12, **9**(3.09, 5.04)	—
7	Does it have any investments in shares of other companies?	~~Y~~/N	20.02, 23.04, **9**(3.16)	—
8	Does the company have any government grants?	~~Y~~/N	27.01, 27.02, 31.05	—
9	Has it any defined benefit or foreign pension schemes, or any other post retirement benefits?	~~Y~~/N	8.03, 8.05, 8.06, 29.08, 31.13, Checklist **14**	—
10	Has it any class of shares other than the normal ordinary shares?	~~Y~~/N	14.02, 25.20, 28.02 to 28.06, 28.08, 28.12 to 28.14, **9**(3.06 to 3.08)	—
11	Has it purchased any own shares or given financial assistance for the purchase of its shares?	~~Y~~/N	3.15, Checklist **12**	—

* *All references are to full Checklist* **6** *(main checklist), unless specified.*

			*Full checklist reference**	*Complete* (✓)
12	Has it any debentures, convertible debts or warrants, or any other capital instruments treated as debt (other than normal loans)?	Y/N	25.05 to 25.15	—
13	Has it repurchased or settled any own debt early?	Y/N	9.02	—
14	Does the company have any unusual directors' transactions (other than overdrawn loan accounts and transactions in which the directors have a material interest) or transactions with officers (who are not directors), such as financial arrangements, quasi-loans, guarantees or security or credit transactions?	Y/N	24.01 to 24.12	—
15	Does the company pay unconnected third parties for directors' services?	Y/N	7.03	—
16	Is it a lessor company?	Y/N	Checklist **13**	—
17	Has it any FRS 5 style substance over form transactions (e.g., factoring of debts, consignment stock or sale and leaseback)?	Y/N	1.06 to 1.11	—
18	Is it an investment company?	Y/N	14.09, 28.11, 31.14	—
19	Does it have any interest in a partnership, unlimited company or Scottish firm, where each partner or member is a limited company?	Y/N	**9**(5.05), **10**(4.05 to 4.08)	—

Client: Bright-a-Light Ltd		Prepared by: EAA	Date: 22.6.95	Ref: A7.2
Year/Period End: 31.3.95	File No:	Reviewed by: JGW	Date: 3.7.95	

SIMPLIFIED MAIN CHECKLIST

This checklist is only suitable for small companies which are not part of a group and assumes full advantage has been taken of SI 1992 No 2452. *The checklist should be marked with a '√' to indicate yes, a '×' for no and a '-' for not applicable. The checklist merely summarises the relevant legislation and standards; detailed requirements should be obtained from the Act or SSAPs/FRSs themselves. If you intend to use Checklist* ***4*** *(simplified annual review of changes) in subsequent years, file this checklist on the Permanent Audit File.*

1 General

Complete (√)

True and fair view

1.01 The accounts must show a true and fair view. Disclose any additional information necessary to achieve this (s226(4)). [✓]

1.02 If, in special circumstances, compliance with any provision of the Act is inconsistent with the requirement to give a true and fair view, then depart from that provision to the extent necessary, but disclose the departure, the reasons for it and the effect in a note to the accounts (s226(5)). [–]

1.03 Where a departure continues in subsequent accounts, the disclosures required by **1.02** above should include corresponding amounts for the previous year (UITF 7.5). [–]

1.04 Where a departure affects only the corresponding amounts, the disclosures required by **1.02** above should be given for those corresponding amounts (UITF 7.6). [–]

Other general requirements

1.05 Immaterial items need not be disclosed, but only if the disclosure is required by Sch. 4 (Sch 4.86). [✓]

1.06 The registered number of the company must be shown in a prominent position (s706(2)(a)). [✓]

1.07 In the case of an undertaking not trading for profit, all references to profit and loss account may be construed as references to income and expenditure account (s262(2)). [–]

2 Directors' report

2.01 State the principal activities during the year of the company and any significant changes (s234(2)). [✓]

2.02 State the names of the directors, who served at any time during the year (s234(2)). [✓]

2.03 For each person who was a director at the end of the year, give details (even if nil), as shown by the register of directors' interests, of:

(a) the interest (direct or indirect) in the shares or debentures of the company, including any held by the director's immediate family, at the beginning of the period (or date of appointment, if later) and at the end of the period (Sch 7.2A); and [✓]

Complete (√)

(b) any right to subscribe for shares or debentures of the company which was granted to or exercised by the director or a member of the director's immediate family (excluding family members who are directors). If any such right was granted or exercised, state the number of shares or the amount of debenture (Sch 7.2B). [—]

NB Immediate family includes spouse, and infant child or step-child (s328, Sch 7.2B(3)). The above disclosures may be dealt with in the notes to the accounts (Sch 7.2(1)).

2.04 Give totals for each of UK political and charitable donations, if together they are more than £200. For each political contribution exceeding £200, name the recipient or party and the amount (Sch 7.3). [—]

2.05 Immediately above the signature on the directors' report, the report should include a statement that advantage has been taken, in the preparation of the report, of special exemptions applicable to small companies (s246(1B)). [✓]

2.06 If the audit firm acts as trustees, and the trust holds in aggregate one per cent or more of the issued capital of the company, details of the trust investment must be disclosed in the directors' report or the auditors' report (ICAEW Handbook 1.201 para 9.4(c), ACCA Handbook 2.1 para 50(c)). [—]

3 Auditors' and reporting accountants' reports

Auditors' report requirements

3.01 The content of the audit report should be consistent with SAS 600 (SAS 600.2 to 600.9). [✓]

3.02 The audit report should contain a clear expression of opinion on the accounts and on any further matters required by statute or other requirements applicable to the particular engagement, and in particular whether they:

(a) have been properly prepared in accordance with the Companies Act 1985 applicable to small companies; and [✓]

(b) give a true and fair view (s235(2), Sch 8.14(3), SAS 600.5). [✓]

3.03 If, in the opinion of the auditors, the information given in the directors' report is inconsistent with the annual accounts, they must state that fact (s235(3)). [—]

3.04 The auditors must state in their report if in their opinion:

(a) proper accounting records have not been kept by the company; [—]

(b) proper returns adequate for their audit have not been received from branches not visited by them; [—]

(c) the company's accounts are not in agreement with the accounting records and returns (s237(2)); and [—]

(d) all the information and explanations necessary for the purposes of their audit have not been obtained (s237(3)). [—]

3.05 If the requirements of Sch 6 (see Section 4, 'Directors' emoluments' and Section 8, 'Directors' and officers' loans and transactions') are not complied with in the annual accounts, the auditors must give the required particulars in their report, so far as they are reasonably able to do so (s237(4)). [—]

Complete (✓)

3.06 If the audit report is qualified and the company proposes to make a distribution, the auditors must state whether, in their opinion, the matter in respect of which their report is qualified is material for determining whether the distribution would contravene the Companies Act provisions. This may form part of the normal audit report, or be submitted subsequently in writing (s271(4), PN8). [—]

3.07 The audit report must refer to any significant departure from SSAPs/FRSs:

(a) which is not adequately disclosed in the notes to the accounts; or [—]

(b) with which the auditors do not concur (Fwd Acctg Stds, para 10(b)). [—]

Reporting accountants' report

3.08 The reporting accountants' report should be addressed to the shareholders of the company (s249A(2)). [—]

3.09 The reporting accountants' report must state whether, in the opinion of the reporting accountant:

(a) the accounts are in agreement with the accounting records kept by the company under s221 CA1985; [—]

(b) having regard only to, and on the basis of, the information contained in those accounting records, those accounts have been drawn up in a manner consistent with the accounting requirements specified in s249C(6) of the Act; and [—]

(c) having regard only to, and on the basis of, the information contained in those accounting records, the company satisfied the conditions for exemption from an audit of the accounts for the year specified in s249A(4) of the Act, (as amended by s249A(5) for charities) and did not, at any time within that year, fall within any of the categories of companies not entitled to the exemption specified in s249B(1)(a) to (f) (s249C(2),(3)). [—]

4 Profit and loss account

Income

4.01 Where, in the directors' opinion, the company supplies substantially different markets, state the percentage of its turnover that, in the opinion of the directors, is attributable to those markets (Sch 4.55(2), 8.9(2)). [—]

Depreciation

4.02 State the total charge for depreciation or provision in respect of diminution in value, and if appropriate the amount of any provision for diminution written back (Sch 4.19, Format note 17). [✓]

4.03 State the nature and amount of any adjustment to accumulated depreciation resulting from a revision of an asset's useful economic life (SSAP 12.18). Not material [—]

4.04 State the effect on the charge for the year of:

(a) any change in the depreciation method, if material, and the reasons for the change (SSAP 12.26); and [—]

(b) any revaluation in the year, if material (SSAP 12.27). [—]

4.05 If no depreciation is provided on investment properties as a result of SSAP 19, this represents a departure from the requirements of the Act. Follow the disclosure requirements in **1.02** to **1.04** above (SSAP 19.17). [—]

		Complete (√)

Directors' emoluments

4.06 Disclose the aggregate amount, including amounts received from the company and others, of:

(a) emoluments (including 'golden hellos', taxable expenses allowances, money value of benefits and amounts paid to connected parties for directors' services) (Sch 6.1); and ✓

(b) compensation for loss of office (including any non-cash benefits). State the nature of any non-cash benefits. Distinguish between amounts from the company and others (Sch 6.8,10(3)). —

NB Pension contributions paid or payable should always be included in the total for directors' emoluments.

4.07 Disclose the number of directors waiving emoluments and the aggregate amount waived, unless the aggregate emoluments of all directors is under £60,000 (Sch 6.2, 6). —

Other expenses

4.08 If the company has a defined contribution pension scheme, disclose the nature of the scheme (i.e., defined contribution), the pension cost charge for the period and any outstanding or prepaid contributions at the balance sheet date (SSAP 24.87). ✓

4.09 Disclose the finance charges on finance leases/hire-purchase (SSAP 21.53). ✓

4.10 Disclose amounts relating to operating lease rentals (other than hire of plant and machinery) (Sch 4.53(6), 8.6, SSAP 21.55). —

4.11 Disclose the auditors' remuneration, including expenses and non-cash benefits. State the nature of any non-cash benefits (s390A(3)). ✓

Taxation

4.12 Disclose any special circumstances that affect the tax charge or credit for the period, or that may affect future periods, and quantify the effects (FRS 3.23). —

4.13 Disclose separately on the face of the profit and loss account, as part of the tax charge or credit, the effects of a fundamental change in the basis of taxation (FRS 3.23). —

4.14 Disclose the tax attributable to franked investment income and any irrecoverable ACT (SSAP 8.22(a)). —

4.15 Include deferred tax as part of the tax on profit on ordinary activities specifying UK deferred tax separately (SSAPs 8.22(a), 15.33). —

4.16 Show the amount of any unprovided deferred tax in respect of the period, analysed into its major components (SSAP 15.35). ✓

4.17 Adjustments to deferred tax resulting from changes in tax rates and allowances should be disclosed separately as part of the tax charge for the year (SSAP 15.36). —

4.18 State the tax treatment of any amounts transferred to or from the revaluation reserve (Sch 4.34(4)). —

Complete (✓)

Reserves and dividends

4.19 State the aggregate of dividends paid and proposed (excluding ACT) (Sch 4.3(7)(b), SSAP 8.24). [—]

4.20 Disclose any amount set aside or proposed to be set aside to or withdrawn from reserves (Sch 4.3(7)(a)). [—]

4.21 If a material illegal dividend was paid during the year or is proposed, disclose the fact that it is illegal, and the consequences (i.e., that it may be repayable by the shareholders) (s226(4), SAS 120, para 23). [—]

FRS 3 primary statements and additional notes

4.22 Where there are no acquisitions or discontinued operations during the current or preceding year, state this fact immediately below the profit and loss account (FRS 3.14). [✓]

4.23 Provide a note reconciling the opening and closing totals of shareholders' funds of the period (FRS 3.28). [✓]

4.24 If there are no gains or losses other than the profit or loss for the period, a statement of this fact immediately below the profit and loss account, will satisfy the requirements of **4.25** below (FRS 3.57). [✓]

4.25 Provide a primary statement, with the same prominence as the other primary statements, showing the total of the recognised gains and losses and its components (FRS 3.27). [—]

4.26 Where there is a material difference between the result as disclosed in the profit and loss account and the result on an unmodified historical cost basis, provide a note, immediately following the profit and loss account or the statement of total recognised gains and losses, showing:

(a) a reconciliation of the reported profit or loss on ordinary activities before tax to the equivalent historical cost amount; and [—]

(b) the retained profit for the year on the historical cost basis (FRS 3.26). [—]

Prior year adjustments

4.27 If the comparative amount is not comparable with the current year, it must be adjusted, and particulars of the adjustment and the reasons for it given (Sch 4.4(2), 58(2)). [—]

4.28 State the reason for each prior year adjustment (Sch 4.4(2), 58(2)). [—]

4.29 Restate the comparative figures for the preceding period in the primary statements and notes and adjust the opening balance of reserves for the cumulative effect (Sch 4.4(2), FRS 3.29). [—]

4.30 Show the cumulative effect at the foot of the statement of total recognised gains and losses for the current period (FRS 3.29). [—]

4.31 Show the effect on the results for the preceding period where practical (FRS 3.29). [—]

Complete (✓)

Balance sheet

5 General

5.01 The balance sheet must contain, immediately above the signature of the directors:

(a) a statement that advantage has been taken, in the preparation of the accounts, of special exemptions applicable to small companies; and ✓

(b) a statement of the grounds on which, in the directors' opinion, the company is entitled to those exemptions (s246(1A)). ✓

5.02 Give particulars where the original purchase price or production cost of an asset is unknown, and the earliest known cost is used in its place (Sch 4.51(1)). —

5.03 Where the value of an asset is shown in a note because it differs materially from its book amount, the note should also show the tax effects, if any, that would arise if the asset were sold at that value (SSAP 15.42). —

5.04 Disclose the amount of any interest capitalised and included in the production cost of any asset (Sch 4.26(3)(b)). —

6 Fixed assets

6.01 State at purchase price or production cost unless revalued (Sch 4.17, UITF 5.6). ✓

6.02 For each class of fixed asset (i.e., tangible and investments), disclose the aggregate:

(a) cost or valuation at the beginning and end of the year; ✓

(b) additions, disposals and transfers during the year; ✓

(c) revaluations during the year; —

(d) accumulated depreciation at the beginning and end of the year; and ✓

(e) charge for depreciation, the amount released on disposals and other adjustments to depreciation during the year (Sch 4.42, SSAP 12.25). ✓

Comparative figures are not required (Sch 4.58(3)(d)).

6.03 If any fixed asset is included at a valuation, state which items and the basis of valuation, and give details of the historical cost and accumulated depreciation (Sch 4.33). —

6.04 For revalued fixed assets (not listed investments) show:

(a) the year in which the assets were revalued; —

(b) the amount of each valuation; and —

(c) if valued during the year, the names or qualifications of the valuers and the basis of the valuation (Sch 4.43). —

6.05 Disclose the gross amount of fixed assets held under finance leases/hire-purchase separately from owned assets (by class of asset), together with the accumulated depreciation and depreciation for the period (SSAP 21.49). —

6.06 As an alternative to **6.05** above, combine finance lease/hire-purchase assets with owned assets, but disclose the net amount included in the overall total, and the amount of depreciation allocated for the year relating to finance lease/hire-purchase assets (SSAP 21.50). ✓

Complete (✓)

6.07 Show the gross amount of any non-depreciable assets (such as land) when mixed with a depreciable asset (as in freehold land and buildings) (SSAP 12.25). ✓

6.08 Include investment properties at open market value (SSAP 19.11, 15). —

6.09 State the names of persons valuing investment property, or particulars of their qualifications, plus the basis of valuation. If any property has been valued by an employee or officer of the company, state this fact (SSAP 19.12). —

6.10 Disclose temporary changes in the value of investment properties as a movement on an investment revaluation reserve and in the statement of total recognised gains and losses, even if this results in a deficit on the investment revaluation reserve (SSAP 19.13). —

NB A permanent deficit, or its reversal, should be charged to the profit and loss account for the period.

6.11 Where property assets are valued on a basis which has regard to the trading potential attached to those properties, the assets should be disclosed separately and a note should state that:

(a) this practice has been followed; and —

(b) the amount at which the assets are stated does not exceed their open market value (SSAP 22.15). —

6.12 Where fixed asset investments are included at a valuation which is not market value, state the method used and the reason for adopting it (Sch 4.31(3)). —

7 Current assets

7.01 Current assets should be stated at the lower of cost (purchase price or production cost) and net realisable value (Sch 4.22, 23). ✓

7.02 For long-term contracts:

(a) show within debtors as 'amounts recoverable on contracts', the amount by which the recorded turnover is in excess of payments on account (SSAP 9.30(a)); —

(b) show within creditors the balance of payments on account in excess of amounts matched with turnover, or offset against long-term contract balances (SSAP 9.30(b)); —

(c) disclose 'long-term contract balances' separately within stocks (at cost net of transfers to cost of sales, less losses, less payments on account not matched with turnover) showing:

(i) net cost less foreseeable losses; and —

(ii) applicable payments on account (SSAP 9.30(c)); and —

(d) show the amount by which the provision or accrual for foreseeable losses exceeds the costs incurred (after transfers to cost of sales) within either provisions for liabilities and charges or creditors (SSAP 9.30(d)). —

7.03 If stocks are shown at current cost, identify the items in question and state the basis of valuation adopted (Sch 4.33(2)). ✓

7.04 Where different bases have been adopted for different types of stocks and long-term contracts, the amounts included in the accounts for each type will need to be stated (SSAP 9.14). —

7.05 Disclose the aggregate amount of debtors falling due after one year (Format note 5, Sch 8.5(a)). —

Complete (√)

7.06 Where the amount of debtors due after more than one year is so material in the context of the total net current assets, they should be disclosed on the face of the balance sheet (UITF 4.3). —

7.07 Where the amount repayable on any debt owed by the company exceeds the value of the consideration originally received, and the surplus is treated as an asset, it should be subject to annual amortisation, and fully written off before repayment of the debt. If the current amount is not shown separately in the balance sheet, disclose the asset in a note (Sch 4.24). —

NB This treatment is not consistent with the requirements of FRS 4 (FRS 4 App 1.5).

8 Directors' and officers' loans and transactions

8.01 Paragraphs **8.02** and **8.03** below do not apply to:

(a) a transaction, arrangement or agreement between one company and another in which a director in the former is interested only by virtue of his directorship in both companies (Sch 6.18(a));

(b) a contract of service between a company and one of its directors (Sch 6.18(b));

(c) a transaction, arrangement or agreement which was not entered into during the financial year, and which did not subsist at any time during that year (Sch 6.18(c)); or

(d) any transaction or arrangement where the transaction is entered into in the normal course of business and on an 'arm's-length' basis (Sch 6.20).

8.02 In respect of any directors' loans, state:

(a) that the transaction was made or subsisted (as the case may be) during the year (Sch 6.22(2)(a)); —

(b) the principal terms (Sch 6.22(1)); —

(c) the name of the person for whom it was made and, where that person is or was connected with the director, state the name of that director (Sch 6.22(2)(b)); —

(d) the amount of liability, in respect of principal and interest, at the beginning and the end of the year (Sch 6.22(d)); —

(e) the maximum amount of the liability during that year (Sch 6.22(d)); —

(f) the amount of unpaid interest due (Sch 6.22(d)); and —

(g) the amount of any provision made for any anticipated failure to repay the liability (Sch 6.22(2)(d)). —

NB Comparative figures are not required (Sch 4.58(3)(a)).

8.03 Subject to the exclusions below, in respect of any transactions in which a director has a material interest, state:

(a) that the transaction was made or subsisted (as the case may be) during the year (Sch 6.22(2)(a)); —

(b) the principal terms (Sch 6.22(1)); —

(c) the name of the person for whom it was made (Sch 6.22(2)(b)); —

(d) the name of the director with the material interest (Sch 6.22(2)(b)); and —

(e) the value of the transaction (Sch 6.22(2)(f). —

NB Comparative figures are not required (Sch 4.58(3)(c)).

Complete (✓)

A transaction is not material if it is not so in the opinion of the majority of the board excluding the interested director(s) (Sch 6.17).

Does not apply where the total amount did not exceed £1,000 during the year, or if more, did not exceed the lower of £5,000 or 1 per cent of the company's net assets at the year end (Sch 6.25).

9 Creditors

9.01 For creditors, show:

(a) the total amount falling due after five years and not repayable by instalments; [—]

(b) the total amount payable by instalments, any part of which is payable after five years, together with the total amount of instalments falling due after five years (Sch 4.48(1) 8.68); and [✓]

(c) in respect of each item under 'creditors' in the balance sheet the total amount secured (Sch 4.48(4), 8.6). [✓]

9.02 Analyse capital instruments treated as liabilities (debt) between debts maturing:

(a) in one year or less, or on demand; [✓]

(b) between one and two years; [✓]

(c) between two and five years; and [✓]

(d) in five years or more (FRS 4.33). [✓]

NB Maturity should be determined by the earliest date on which repayment can be required (FRS 4.34).

9.03 Show finance lease/hire-purchase liabilities separately from other obligations and liabilities, either by way of note or on the balance sheet (SSAP 21.51). [✓]

9.04 Analyse finance lease/hire-purchase liabilities between amounts payable within one year, two to five years, and after five years (SSAP 21.52). [✓]

9.05 ACT on proposed dividends should be included as a current tax liability and, if recoverable, set against any deferred tax account, or if none, shown as a deferred asset (SSAP 8.26, 27). [—]

10 Provisions for liabilities and charges

10.01 For each class of provision for liabilities and charges, unless the only movement relates only to the transfer out for the purpose of which the provision was established, show:

(a) the amount at the beginning and end of the year; [—]

(b) the amount transferred to or from the provision during the year; and [—]

(c) the source and application of any such movement (Sch 4.46(2)). [—]

NB Comparative figures are not required (Sch 4.58(3)(d)).

Complete (√)

10.02 In respect of deferred taxation, disclose separately:

(a) the amount provided and the amount unprovided, analysed into their major components (SSAP 15.37, 15.40); ✓

(b) transfers to and from the provision arising from any movement on reserves (SSAP 15.39); —

(c) other transfers to and from the provision (SSAP 15.38); and —

(d) the amount of potential deferred taxation arising from the revaluation of an asset which does not constitute a timing difference (SSAP 15.41). —

11 Capital and reserves

11.01 Disclose the aggregate of:

(a) authorised share capital; ✓

(b) allotted share capital; ✓

(c) called up share capital; and ✓

(d) the amount of called up share capital that has been paid (Sch 4.38(1)(a), Format note 12). ✓

11.02 If the company has allotted any shares during the year, state the reason for making the allotment, the number allotted, their aggregate nominal value and the consideration received (Sch 4.39). —

11.03 For each class of reserves show:

(a) the amount at the beginning and end of the year; ✓

(b) the amount transferred to or from the provision during the year; and ✓

(c) the source and application of any such movement (Sch 4.46(2)). ✓

NB Comparative figures are not required (Sch 4.58(3)(d)).

11.04 Show separately the net investment revaluation reserve relating to investment properties (SSAP 19.15). —

Other disclosures

12 Contingencies and commitments

12.01 State the particulars (and amount if practicable) of any charge on the assets of the company to secure the liability of any other person (Sch 4.50(1)). —

Complete
(✓)

12.02 For any other contingent liability not provided for, and any material contingent gain if it is probable that the gain will be realised, disclose:

(a) the amount or a prudent estimate of the financial effect before tax (or a statement that it is not practicable to make such an estimate); —

(b) the legal nature of the contingency; —

(c) the uncertainties that are expected to affect the ultimate outcome; —

(d) an explanation of the tax implications, where necessary for the proper understanding of the financial position; and —

(e) whether any valuable security has been given for the liability, and if so, details of the security (Sch 4.50(2), SSAP 18.16,17,18,20). —

12.03 State the estimated amount, if practicable, of future capital expenditure (including irrecoverable VAT, if appropriate), relating to:

(a) amounts contracted for but not provided for in the accounts; and —

(b) amounts authorised by the directors, but not contracted for (Sch 4.50(3), SSAP 5.6). —

12.04 Give particulars of any pension commitments:

(a) provided for in the accounts; —

(b) not provided for in the accounts; and —

(c) included in (a) and (b) above which relate to pensions payable to past directors (Sch 4.50(4)). —

12.05 Disclose commitments under finance leases/hire-purchase agreements entered into before the year end, which start after the year end (SSAP 21.54). —

12.06 If the standard straight line treatment for reverse premiums and other incentives received or receivable in respect of operating leases is not used, disclose the following:

(a) an explanation of the specific circumstances that render the standard treatment misleading; —

(b) a description of the basis used and the amounts involved; and —

(c) the effect of the departure on the results for the current and prior period (UITF 12.8). —

12.07 State the amount of any commitments under operating leases for the next 12 months, split between land and buildings and other operating leases, and analysing each between leases which expire in the next year, in the second to fifth years inclusive, and over five years from the balance sheet date (SSAP 21.56). —

12.08 Give particulars of any other financial commitments not provided for, but relevant to assessing the company's state of affairs (Sch 4.50(5)). —

Complete
(√)

13 Post-balance sheet events

13.01 Disclose for any non-adjusting events, or the reversal of any transactions entered into primarily for window dressing purposes:

(a) the nature of the event; —

(b) an estimate of the financial effect, before taxation, or a statement that it is not practicable to make such an estimate; and —

(c) an explanation of the tax implications, where necessary for a proper understanding of the financial position (SSAP 17.24, 25). —

14 Accounting policies

14.01 State the accounting policies used for dealing with items which are judged material or critical to the accounts (Sch 4.36, SSAP 2.18). ✓

14.02 If accounts are prepared on the basis of assumptions which differ from any of the generally accepted fundamental concepts (going concern, accruals, consistency and prudence), or accounting policies are not consistently applied (either within the same accounts, or from year to year) then particulars of the departure, the reasons for it and the effects must be disclosed (Sch 4.15, SSAP 2.17). ✓

14.03 Turnover should be the amount derived from ordinary activities, and stated after trade discounts, VAT and any other sales taxes. If it is desirable to show the gross turnover as well, then show the VAT as a deduction in arriving at turnover exclusive of VAT (s262(1), SSAP 5.8). ✓

14.04 State the accounting policy applied to stocks. For long-term contracts, disclose the methods of ascertaining turnover and attributable profit (SSAP 9.32). ✓

14.05 For each major class of depreciable asset, disclose the depreciation methods used, and the estimated useful economic life or rate of depreciation (Sch 4.36, SSAP 12.25). ✓

14.06 Explain the accounting policy on research and development expenditure (SSAP 13.30). —

14.07 State the accounting policy for deferred tax (SSAP 15.24–28, 32A). ✓

14.08 Disclose the lessee's policies for the treatment of operating leases and finance leases (including hire-purchase contracts) (SSAP 21.57). ✓

14.09 State the accounting policy used for defined contribution pension schemes (SSAP 24.87(b)). ✓

15 Abbreviated accounts

15.01 If abbreviated accounts are being filed, complete simplified Checklist **5** (abbreviated accounts). ✓

Not included in this model file. See Roberts Design Ltd for an example of checklist 5.

Client: Bright-a-Light Ltd		Prepared by: EAA	Date: 22.6.95	Ref: A7.3
Year/Period End: 31.3.95	File No:	Reviewed by: DGW	Date: 3.7.95	

SIMPLIFIED FORMATS

This checklist is only suitable for small companies which are not part of a group and assumes full advantage has been taken of SI 1992 No 2452. *The checklist should be marked with a '√' to indicate yes, a '×' for no and a '-' for not applicable. Select and complete the format used by the client. If you intend to use Checklist **4** (simplified annual review of changes) in subsequent years, file this checklist on the Permanent Audit File.*

1 Profit and Loss Account Format 1

		Complete (√)
1	Turnover	√
2	Cost of sales	√
3	Gross profit or loss	√
4	Distribution costs	√
5	Administrative expenses	√
6	Other operating income	√
	Operating profit or loss (FRS 3.14)	—
7	Income from other fixed asset investments	—
8	Other interest receivable and similar income	—
9	Amounts written off investments	—
10	Interest payable and similar charges	√
	Profit or loss on ordinary activities before taxation (Sch 4.3(6))	√
11	Tax on profit or loss on ordinary activities	√
12	Profit or loss on ordinary activities after taxation	—
13	Other taxes not shown under the above items	—
14	Profit or loss for the financial year	√
	Transfers to and from reserves (Sch 4.3(7)(a))	—
	Dividends paid and proposed (Sch 4.3(7)(b))	—

3 BALANCE SHEET FORMAT 1

	Complete (√)
A ***Called up share capital not paid***	—
B ***Fixed assets***	✓
I Tangible assets	✓
1 Land and buildings	✓
2 Plant and machinery, etc.	✓
II Investments	—
1 Other investments other than loans	—
2 Others	—
C ***Current assets***	✓
I Stocks	✓
1 Stocks	✓
2 Payments on account	—
II Debtors	✓
1 Trade debtors	✓
2 Others	✓
III Investments	—
1 Other investments	—
IV Cash at bank and in hand	✓
D ***Prepayments and accrued income***	—
E ***Creditors: amounts falling due within one year***	✓
1 Bank loans and overdrafts	✓
2 Trade creditors	✓
3 Taxation and social security (Format note 9)	✓
4 Other creditors	✓
F ***Net current assets (liabilities)***	✓
G ***Total assets less current liabilities***	✓
H ***Creditors: amounts falling due after more than one year***	✓
1 Bank loans and overdrafts	✓
2 Trade creditors	—
3 Taxation and social security (Format note 9)	—
4 Other creditors	✓
I ***Provisions for liabilities and charges***	—
J ***Accruals and deferred income***	—
K ***Capital and reserves***	✓
I Called up share capital	✓
II Share premium account	—
III Revaluation reserve	—
IV Other reserves	—
V Profit and loss account	✓
Shareholders' funds (FRS 4.38)	✓

B AUDIT COMPLETION

1	Partner review	✓
2	Audit standards questionnaire	✓
3	File completion questionnaire	✓
4	Critical review of accounts questionnaire	✓
5	Audit highlights	✓
6	Justification of audit report	✓
7	Summary of unadjusted errors	✓
8	Queries for partner	
9	Final analytical review	✓
10	Points forward to next year	
11	Commercial observations on client's business	
12	Senior/manager review	
13	Cleared audit queries	✓
14		
15		

Client: Bright-a-Light Ltd		Prepared by: DGW	Date: 3.7.95	Ref: **B**
Year/Period End: 31.3.95	File No:	Reviewed by: MJ	Date: 5.7.95	

PARTNER COMPLETION

Initial

			Initials
1	Has the audit standards questionnaire been satisfactorily completed?	Yes	DGW
2	Has the file completion questionnaire been satisfactorily completed?	Yes	DGW
3	Has the critical review of accounts questionnaire been satisfactorily completed?	Yes	DGW
4	Has sufficient work been undertaken in view of the level of risk ~~(as revised)~~* and materiality ~~(as revised)~~* to enable an audit opinion to be formed?	Yes	DGW
5	Has all original work been reviewed, other than that undertaken by the partner responsible for the audit?	Yes	DGW
6	Have all partner review points been properly cleared?	Yes/~~N/A*~~	DGW

7 List below any other work that needs to be undertaken before the audit report is signed:

____

____

____

____

____

____

I authorise the issue of the accounts for approval.

Signed DG Watson Partner Date 3.7.95

Second partner (if applicable)

Signed M Jones Partner Date 5.7.95

* Delete as appropriate.

Client: Bright-a-Light Ltd		Prepared by: DGW	Date: 3/7/95	Ref: **B1**
Subject: Partners review	File No:	Reviewed by:	Date:	
		Accounting dates:		

(1)	Provide for bad debt on J4.2 £5,953	Now done	Y2
(2)	Agree no deferred tax provision, but still need a note of unprovided deferred tax in accts.	Amended	
(3)	Surely finance lease creditor is secured on the finance lease asset. Note required in accounts.	Amended	
(4)	Put through adjustment above and finalise the tax position.	Done	Y2
(5)	Pass to MJ.	Done	

EAA 4.7.95

Client: Bright-a-Light Ltd		Prepared by: EAA	Date: 3·7·95	Ref: **B2**
Year/Period End: 31·3·95	File No:	Reviewed by: DGW	Date: 3·7·95	

AUDIT STANDARDS QUESTIONNAIRE

SAS No.		Initials
110	Has the audit been planned and performed having considered the risk of material fraud or error?	Yes EAA
120	Has the audit been planned and performed having considered the risk of material misstatement arising from non-compliance with relevant laws and regulations?	Yes EAA
130	Has the appropriateness of the going concern basis been considered?	Yes EAA
140	Do we have an up-to-date letter of engagement?	Yes EAA
150	Has an adequate post balance sheet events review been performed?	Yes EAA
160	Has other information to be issued with the financial statements been reviewed for consistency?	Yes EAA
200	Has the audit plan been reviewed and updated, where necessary?	Yes EAA
210	Do our audit files contain adequate information to provide an understanding of the nature of the client's business?	Yes EAA
220	Has materiality been reviewed and updated, where necessary?	Yes EAA
220	Has the effect on the accounts of any unadjusted errors been considered?	Yes EAA
230	Do the working papers contain an adequate record of the work performed and conclusions drawn?	Yes EAA
240	Has the audit work been properly directed, supervised and reviewed?	Yes EAA
300	Do the files contain sufficient details of the client's accounting systems?	Yes EAA
300	Has the risk assessment been reviewed and updated, where necessary?	Yes EAA
300	Where the risk assessment or materiality has been revised, has sufficient additional testing been undertaken?	Yes EAA
400	Does the file contain sufficient, appropriate audit evidence to enable us to draw reasonable conclusions?	Yes EAA
410	Does the file contain sufficient evidence of analytical review?	Yes EAA
420	Does the file contain sufficient, appropriate evidence assessing the reasonableness of accounting estimates?	Yes EAA
430	Has audit sampling been applied in an appropriate manner?	Yes EAA

Client: Bright-a-Light Ltd		Prepared by: EAA	Date: 3.7.95	Ref: **B2**
Year/Period End: 31.3.95	File No:	Reviewed by: DGW	Date: 3.7.95	

AUDIT STANDARDS QUESTIONNAIRE (*Cont.*)

SAS No.			Initials
440	Has a letter of representation been drafted covering all necessary representations?	Yes	EAA
450	Is there sufficient, appropriate evidence that amounts derived from the previous period are free from material misstatement and are appropriately incorporated in the current period's accounts?	Yes	EAA
470	Has an adequate overall review of the accounts been performed?	Yes	EAA
600	Is the audit opinion consistent with the audit evidence and conclusions?	Yes	EAA

Client: Bright-a-Light		Prepared by: EAA	Date: 22.6.95	Ref: **B3**
Year/Period End: 31.3.95	File No:	Reviewed by: DAW	Date: 3.7.95	

FILE COMPLETION QUESTIONNAIRE

Where work is outstanding prior to review, the outstanding (O/S) column should be ticked in pencil to highlight work required. As and when work is completed, the final column should be initialled, and the tick rubbed out.

Completion (pre-partner review)

	Question		O/S	Initials
1	Do the working papers record all the work done and do all the schedules contain the source of information?	Yes		EAA
2	Has the current file been fully cross-referenced?	Yes		EAA
3	Have all the queries and problems been properly cleared or carried forward to schedule **B8**, queries for partner or **B5** audit highlights?	Yes		EAA
4	Have the budget and actual time summaries been completed, along with explanations of variances?	~~Yes~~/NCN†*		EAA
5	Has the Permanent audit file been updated?	Yes		EAA
6	Have all unadjusted errors been summarised on **B7** and adjusted where necessary?	Yes/~~None*~~		EAA
7	Has the **B2** Audit standards questionnaire been completed?	Yes		EAA
8	Has the **B6** Justification of audit report been completed?	Yes		EAA
9	Have any commercial observations on the client's business been recorded on B11?	~~Yes~~/None*		EAA

Completion (final)

	Question		O/S	Initials
10	Have you confirmed that there have been no changes to the firm's independence during the course of the audit which would prevent reappointment of the firm as auditors for the next financial period?	Yes		EAA
11	Has consultation been undertaken in all circumstances, where it is required by the firm's procedures?	Yes/~~NCN†~~*		EAA
12	Where any fraud, error or breach in laws and regulations have been identified, have the implications on the accounts been fully considered?	~~Yes~~/N/A*		EAA
13	Has the draft letter or the points for comment been prepared?	~~Yes~~/NCN†*		EAA
14	Have all necessary points forward to next year been recorded on **B10**?	~~Yes~~/None*		EAA
15	Has a budget for next year been prepared?	Yes/~~NCN†*~~		EAA

† NCN = not considered necessary.

* Delete as appropriate.

Client: Bright-a-Light Ltd		Prepared by: EAA	Date: 22.6.95	Ref: **B4**
Year/Period End: 31.3.95	File No:	Reviewed by: DGW	Date: 3.7.95	

CRITICAL REVIEW OF ACCOUNTS QUESTIONNAIRE

	Comments	Initials	WP Ref
1 Review accounting policies to determine whether they:			
(a) comply with SSAPs, FRSs or, in their absence, are otherwise acceptable;		EAA	
(b) are consistent with those of the previous period;		EAA	
(c) are consistently applied to all like transactions;		EAA	
(d) are appropriate to the nature of the client's business;		EAA	
(e) are disclosed in accordance with the requirements of SSAP 2.		EAA	
2 Carry out an overall review of the information in the accounts and compare it with other available data, including final analytical review. Note significant variations and obtain explanations thereto.		EAA	B9
3 Consider whether the accounts adequately reflect: (a) the substance of underlying transactions and balances and not merely their form;		EAA	
(b) the information and explanations obtained and conclusions reached on particular aspects of the audit;		EAA	
(c) the proper application of the four fundamental accounting concepts.		EAA	
Schedule points of interest on 'audit highlights'.		EAA	B5
4 Consider whether the review reveals any new factors which may affect the presentation of information or disclosures in the accounts.		EAA	
5 Review the accounts for proper preparation in accordance with the Companies Act, SSAPs, FRSs, and other disclosure requirements. State whether or not a disclosure checklist has been completed in respect of the current year. If not completed in current year, state year in which it was last completed.	Yes/~~No~~*	EAA	A7
6 Consider whether the information contained in the directors' report and any other document issued with the accounts is consistent with the accounting information in the accounts and has not been unduly influenced by the directors' desire to present matters in a favourable or unfavourable light.		EAA	

Conclusion

1 I have compared the ratios of the final accounts with those of ~~the preliminary*/extensive* analytical review~~ last year.

2 (a) I have obtained, recorded and corroborated explanations for significant fluctuations for principal areas of the accounts*.

Or

~~(b) There were no significant fluctuations requiring explanation*.~~

3 The directors' report and other published information is consistent with the accounts.

I am satisfied from this critical review that the accounts appear credible and have been properly prepared in accordance with the Companies Act 1985.

Prepared by EA Arbuthnott Date 22.6.95

Reviewed by DG Watson Date 3.7.95

* Delete as appropriate.

Bright-a-Light Limited

Audit highlights report for the year ended 31 March 1995

Fixed assets

The main change to fixed assets in the year was the purchase of two lorries and a new Peugeot 405, the latter being financed by a finance lease. Two vehicles from the pool purchased during the management buyout were sold.

The value of freehold land and buildings has been split $\frac{1}{3}$ buildings and $\frac{2}{3}$ land. Due to the poor quality of the buildings, the useful economic life of the freehold buildings has been reduced to 10 years to reflect the state of the buildings and the depreciation charge has jumped significantly as a result. We need to get written representation from the client for the split of the cost of the freehold property. No problems were found during the audit.

Stock

The client is holding roughly the same level of stock as last year, but with more solid fuel and fewer leisure products. No problems were found during the course of the audit work.

Debtors

The level of trade debtors has jumped significantly during the year, due to the increased turnover. However, the client appears to be having some collection problems and bad debts have been reviewed carefully. I have agreed a provision of £2,501.16 with Mr Srike, but I feel that an additional provision is still necessary in relation to J Austins, Distributors. This business is run by Mr Strike's brother-in-law who is in severe financial difficulties, and I think it unlikely that the company will ultimately collect the debt (see **J4.2** for further details). No other problems were encountered.

Bank and cash

All bank accounts and loans were reconciled satisfactorily to the bank confirmation letter and bank statements. A new loan account was opened in the year.

Creditors

Creditors due within one year have increased significantly due mainly to bank loans (see above), trade creditors and corporation tax. Trade creditors have risen significantly due to the increased volume of trade. The major balances were reconciled to suppliers' statements (**L3.1** and **L3.2**) and no problems were encountered. The corporation tax payable for 1995 was calculated by us. The client has not yet paid the corporation tax due for last year nor made any accrual for interest payable. The client has also not made any provision for deferred tax. However, the amounts involved are immaterial (see **P5**) and creditors are fairly stated.

Capital and reserves

The shareholdings have not changed during the year and all relevant documents have been filed with the Registrar of Companies.

Profit and loss account
The planned work was completed and no problems were encountered during the course of the audit.

VAT turnover reconciliation
VAT outputs were satisfactorily reconciled to the turnover in the accounts.

Contingent liabilities and post-balance sheet events
I have reviewed the cash book, invoices, bank statements and minute books after the year end, and no items requiring disclosure were found. In addition, the solicitor's have confirmed that they are not aware of any such matters. The going concern programme has been completed and the going concern basis is appropriate.

Conclusion
I am satisfied that adequate audit evidence has been obtained and that the accounts show a true and fair view.

Agreed D G Watson
3.7.95

Client: Bright-a-Light Ltd		Prepared by: EAA	Date: 3.7.95	Ref: **B6**
Year/Period End: 31.3.95	File No:	Reviewed by: DGW	Date: 3.7.95	

JUSTIFICATION OF AUDIT REPORT

This form should be used to schedule any problems encountered during the audit which could have an impact on the audit report

1 Was the audit report qualified in the previous period? If yes, give details:	~~Yes~~/No*
2 Have there been any problems with books and records? If yes, specify:	~~Yes~~/No*
3 Have you encountered problems obtaining from the directors all information and explanations necessary for the audit? If yes, specify:	~~Yes~~/No*
4 Have you had problems obtaining adequate returns from branches not visited? If yes, specify:	~~Yes~~/~~No~~/N/A*
5 Are there any problems with going concern? (Ref **T3**)	~~Yes~~/No*
6 Have any other problems occurred which could have an impact on the audit report? If yes, specify:	~~Yes~~/No*

Conclusion

Where there are any 'yes' answers, detail below what effect they will have on the audit report.

I am satisfied that an unqualified report is appropriate*

or

In my opinion, the attached fundamental uncertainty and/or qualification is appropriate*

EAA	Preparer	3.7.95	Date
DGW	Reviewer	3.7.95	Date

* Delete as appropriate.

Client: Bright-a-Light Ltd		Prepared by: EAA	Date: 19.6.95	Ref: **B7**
Year/Period End: 31.3.95	File No:	Reviewed by: DGW	Date: 3.7.95	

SUMMARY OF UNADJUSTED ERRORS

FINAL MATERIALITY £15,000

Narrative	*Extrapolated errors*		*Actual errors*		*Profit and loss*	*Balance sheet*
	DR	CR	DR	CR		
J4.2 Additional bad						
debt provision not						
agreed by client						
P&L			5923		(5923)	
Bad debt provision				5923		(5923)
P5 Deferred tax provision						
P&L			127		(127)	
Deferred tax provision				127		(127)
P7 Interest of CT						
liability						
P&L			56		(56)	
Creditors				56		(56)
Total of potential adjustments					(6106)	(6106)

Conclusion

Unadjusted errors are below materiality. No need to adjust
EAA 23.6.95

Adjust for bad debt only. Why pay extra tax?
DGW

Client: Bright-a-Light Ltd		Prepared by: EAA	Date: 22.6.95	Ref: **B9**
Year/Period End: 31.3.95	File No:	Reviewed by: DGW	Date: 3.7.95	

FINAL ANALYTICAL REVIEW

Identify any significant movements in the figures below and record explanations.

Updated for final adjustments

		This year £	1994 £	19 £	19 £	WP Ref
A1	Turnover (credit)	745,584	526,074			B9.1
A2	Turnover (cash)	113,317	149,250			
A	Total turnover (A1 + A2)	858,901	675,324			
B	Trade purchases	694,262	529,893			
C	Gross profit	167,782	136,494			
D	Net profit ~~(adjusted*)~~	17,320	10,343			
E	Tangible assets	159,007	157,862			
F	Stock	26,003	22,860			
G	Trade debtors	121,192	73,196			
H	Cash at bank/in hand	461	123			
I	Total current assets	154,006	98,155			
J	Total assets	313,013	256,017			
K	Trade creditors	82,808	51,109			
L	Bank O/D and short-term borrowings	56,129	41,662			
M	Total current liabilities	161,295	106,512			
N	Total borrowings (incl O/D)	165,129	165,186			
O	Net assets/shareholders' funds	37,671	25,981			
Gross profit (%)	(C/A × 100)	19.5%	20.2%			
Net profit (%)	(D/A × 100)	2.0%	1.5%			
Debtors' credit	(G/A1 × 365)	59 days	51 days			B9.1
Creditors' settlement	(K/B × 365)	44 days	35 days			B9.1
Stock turnover	(B/F)	26.7	23.2			
Liquidity current ratio	(I/M)	0.95	0.92			B9.1
Liquidity quick ratio	((I–F)/M)	0.79	0.71			B9.1
Gearing 1	(N/J)	0.53	0.65			B9.1
Gearing 2	(N/O)	4.38	6.36			
Other key indicators for the business (specify):						

* Delete if not adjusted for directors' bonuses and pensions.

Client Bright-a-Light Ltd		File No.	Ref. B9.1	
Subject Final Analytical Review Commentary		Prepared by EAA		Date 22/6/95
		Reviewed by DGW		Date 3/7/95
		Accounting Dates	31·3·95	

Turnover and Gross Profit Rates

The company's turnover is much higher this year than last year, reflecting continued growth in the client's business. The gross profit ratio has fallen slightly from 20.2% to 19.5%. This is due to a deliberate policy of maintaining lower prices to boost turnover.

Debtor days

Debtor days has risen from 51 to 59 days, which reflects the difficulties that the client has collecting debts in the current recession. Bad debts have been reviewed in some detail during the audit, and provisions made where necessary.

Creditor days

The period for creditors' settlement has also risen from 35 to 44 days. The client is experiencing some cashflow problems, mainly due to the recession and debt collection.

Current and quick ratios

These have risen slightly in the year mainly as a result of the increased stock turnover.

Gearing

The ratio of borrowing to total assets and net assets has fallen in the year. This reflects the slight improvement in the company's asset base. The borrowings in real terms remain almost identical.

Client Bright-a-Light Ltd	File No.	Ref. B13
Subject Points for Manager	Prepared by KM	Date 15/6/95
	Reviewed by EAA	Date 16/6/95
	Accounting Dates	31·3·95

1. Fixed Assets

The Co has entered into a lease with Chartered Leases plc for a Peugeot 405. This has not been capitalised and I am unsure whether this is correct. In addition no disclosure of it as an operating lease has been made in the accounts.	Reviewed the terms of the lease and it is clearly a finance lease. The client is responsible for maintaining, repairing and insuring the car. When the lease is finished the client will get a rebate of 97.5% of the sale proceeds. I have calculated the appropriate adjustments.

2. Debtors

(a) Total bad debts that need providing are £2,501-16	To be adjusted – agreed with client.
(b) No provision has been made for J Austin, the director's brother-in-law. The debt is £5,923. No cash has been received but directors consider it to be good. I do not see how they can justify this.	Has not yet been adjusted and client is unwilling to do so. Therefore have treated it as an error – see schedule of unadjusted errors, B7

3. Sales R4.1 to R4.3

Not able to trace payment for one of items selected as customer now bust. Owes a total of £295.89.	Included in adjustment of £2,501 agreed with client.

C AUDIT PLANNING

1	Audit planning memorandum	✓
2	Professional independence questionnaire	✓
3	Preliminary analytical review	✓
4	General risk assessment	✓
5	Specific risk assessment	✓
6	Materiality summary	✓
7	Systems overview	✓
8	Points forward from last year	
9	Other planning schedules	
10	Assignment planning – timetable	✓
11	Budget and performance summary	
12	Time ledger print-out	
13		
14		

Client: Bright-a-Light Ltd		Prepared by: EAA	Date: 8·6·95	Ref: **C1**
Year/Period End: 31.3.95	File No:	Reviewed by: DGW	Date: 8.6.95	

AUDIT PLANNING MEMORANDUM

		Comments	Initials	WP Ref
1	Before commencing any detailed work on the audit, confirm that the Professional independence questionnaire has been satisfactorily completed.		EAA	C2
2	Review terms of engagement letter. Discuss any changes with reporting partner. If appropriate, send revised letter to client, and confirm its return, duly signed.	updated 23·3·95 Returned Signed	EAA	PAF
3	Review and update the following on the Permanent audit file: – Background information – Systems notes – Summary of significant laws and regulations – Other (specify):	PAF updated	EAA	PAF
4	Review points forward from last year's schedule. File on current year's working paper file.	None	EAA	C8
5	Review correspondence file for relevant points arising during the year.	None	EAA	
6	Consider and schedule impact of changes in legislation/SSAPs/FRSs on the accounts.	FRS4 now applies	EAA	
7	Where the previous period's audit report was qualified, consider what impact, if any, it will have on the current period's report.	N/A	EAA	
8	Meet/discuss with client current year's accounts and timetable.		EAA	~~C10~~
9	Consider whether there are any indications that the going concern basis of accounting may not be appropriate.	None	EAA	
10	If appropriate, prepare a brief memo of matters arising from the review of the correspondence file and meeting/discussion with the client.	None	EAA	C9
11	Allocate staff, as appropriate.	KM	EAA	
12	Obtain print-out of the firm's WIP and prepare fee budget. Agree fee estimate with client where necessary.	Not included in Model file	EAA	~~C11/C12~~
13	Where the accounts to be audited are available at the planning stage, complete the Analytical review form, based on preliminary figures.	Accounts prep assignment	EAA	C3
14	Where the accounts to be audited are not available at the planning stage, discuss with management whether there have been any significant changes in the business since the previous period.	None	EAA	
15	Complete general risk assessment.		EAA	C4
16	Complete specific risk assessment.		EAA	C5
17	Complete materiality summary.		EAA	C6
18	Complete systems overview.		EAA	C7
19	Review/tailor/prepare audit programme as directed by **C5**.		EAA	
20	Brief staff listed below.			

Audit Partner: DG Watson Initials: DGW
Senior/Manager: EA Arbuthnott Initials: EAA
Other: KPF Martin Initials: KM
__________ Initials: __________

Conclusion

I am satisfied that the staff assigned are competent to carry out the planned work and have been adequately briefed.
I am satisfied that the audit has been planned effectively.
The file does/~~does not~~* require second partner review.

Senior/Manager EA Arbuthnott Date 8·6·95
Partner DG Watson Date 8.6.95

* Delete as appropriate.

Client: Bright-a-Light Ltd		Prepared by: DGW	Date: 8.6.95	Ref: C2
Year/Period End: 31.3.95	File No:	Reviewed by: MJ	Date: 8.6.95	

PROFESSIONAL INDEPENDENCE QUESTIONNAIRE

Regulations state that 'a Registered Auditor shall not accept appointment or continue as auditor if the firm has any interest likely to conflict with the proper conduct of the audit'. This questionnaire shall be completed annually for all clients to ensure that the regulations have been complied with.

	YES	NO
1 *Undue dependence on an audit client*		
Do the total fees for this client/group of clients exceed:		
(a) 10%* of gross practice income?		✓
(b) 15%* of the partner's gross income?		✓
Is this client/group of clients highly prestigious?		
* (a) becomes 5% and (b) becomes 10% for listed or public interest audits.		✓
2 *Overdue fees*		
Does the client owe the firm any money which exceeds your normal credit terms?		✓
3 *Litigation*		
Is there any actual or anticipated litigation between yourself and the client in relation to fees, audit work, or other work?		✓
4 *Associated firms*		
Are you or your staff associated with any other practice or organisation which has any dealings with the company?		✓
5 *Family or other personal relationships*		
Do you or any of your staff have any personal or family connections with the company and its officers?	✓	
6 *Ex-partners or senior employees*		
(a) Has any officer of the company been a partner or senior employee in the practice?		✓
(b) Is the partner or any senior employee on the audit joining or involved in substantive negotiations with the client?		✓
7 *Financial involvement*		
Do you or any of your staff have any financial involvement in the company in respect of the following:		
(a) any beneficial interest in shares or other investments?		✓
(b) any beneficial interest in trusts?		✓
(c) any trustee investments?		✓
(d) any loans or guarantees?		✓

Client: Bright-a-Light Ltd		Prepared by:	Date:	Ref: **C2**
Year/Period End: 31.3.95	File No:	Reviewed by:	Date:	

PROFESSIONAL INDEPENDENCE QUESTIONNAIRE (*Cont.*)

	YES	NO
8 *Goods and services: hospitality*		
Have you or any of your staff accepted any material goods or services on favourable terms or received undue hospitality from the company?		✓
9 *Provision of other services and specialist valuations*		
(a) Are any services in relation to the management of the company performed by the firm?		✓
(b) Where the firm prepares the company's accounting records, is there any reason why the client will not accept responsibility for the records as his own?		✓
(c) Do the accounts include any specialist valuations carried out by the firm or an associated firm?		✓
10 *Rotation of audit engagement partner*		
Have you been acting as the audit engagement partner for more than seven years?	✓	
11 *Adequate resources*		
Are there any problems over adequately staffing the audit with staff with the necessary expertise?		✓
12 *Proper performance*		
Are there any aspects of the client, or other factors, that will adversely affect the firm's ability to perform the audit properly?		✓

Conclusion

Where any of the above questions have been answered 'yes', specify what action is proposed to be taken to maintain independence, and to ensure the availability of resources and the ability to perform the audit properly.

K Strike + B Strike are both close personal friends of mine, and have been clients for eight years. In order to safeguard independence, the file will be subjected to a second partner review.

Having regard to any safeguards identified above, in my opinion independence is maintained, we have adequate resources and the ability to properly perform the audit.

Partner DA Watson Date 8.6.95

Consultation (to be completed where appropriate)

In my opinion the steps proposed are sufficient to maintain independence and to ensure the availabilty of resources and the ability to perform the audit properly.

Second Partner M Jones Date 8.6.95

Client Bright-a-Light Ltd	File No.	Ref. C3	
Subject Preliminary analytical review	Prepared by EAA		Date 8/6/95
	Reviewed by DGW		Date 8/6/95
	Accounting Dates		

A preliminary review of the accounting records, and discussion with the directors has indicated the following expected changes over last year.

1 Turnover has increased, but the directors feel that this has been achieved mainly by competitive pricing, and thus GP% is likely to have fallen slightly.

2 Trade debtors seem considerably higher than previous years. We need to watch out for potential bad debts.

3 The directors have been extremely busy, particularly around the year end. This has resulted in some controls slipping – such as debtors not being chased. This in turn has put pressure on their cashflow. The overdraft and trade creditors have both increased.

Client: Bright-a-Light Ltd		Prepared by: EAA	Date: 8.6.95	Ref: **C4**
Year/Period End:	File No:	Reviewed by: DGW	Date: 8.6.95	

GENERAL RISK ASSESSMENT

The most appropriate category for each point should be ringed. Using this and any further information that is relevant, assess the general risk of the client. Detailed help on what factors may affect our assessment is given on a detailed schedule.

		Low	*Medium*	*High*
1	***External interest in accounts***			
1.1	Share ownership	(Director/ Management)	Small minority	External interest
1.2	Accounts requested by third party?	No	(Possibly)	Yes
	Specify: Capital Bank			
1.3	Is there a potential going concern problem?	(No)	Possibly	Yes
2	***Management of business***			
2.1	Management experience/competence	(Good)	Satisfactory	Poor
2.2	Management changes (past/future)	(None)	Some	Many
2.3	Management influence	(Low risk)	Medium risk	High risk
2.4	Existence of fraud or error	(Low risk)	Medium risk	High risk
2.5	Breaches of significant laws or regulations	(Low risk)	Medium risk	High risk
3	***Accounting***			
3.1	Accounting systems	(Good)	Satisfactory	Poor
3.2	Type of business	(Mainly credit)	Mixed	Mainly cash
3.3	Contentious accounting issues	(None)	Some	Many
3.4	Audit history	(Good)	Satisfactory	Poor
4	***Business environment***			
4.1	Nature of business/industry	(Low risk)	Medium risk	High risk
	Specify:			
4.2	Track record	Established	(–)	New

Conclusion: (Identify major risk areas and give an overall assessment of the job.)

No major general risk areas

Overall general risk assessment is: ***(Low)*** ***Medium*** ***High***

Detailed general risk assessment attached ~~YES~~/NO*

EAA	Preparer	8.6.95	Date
DGW	Reviewer	8.6.95	Date

* Delete as appropriate.

Client: Bright-a-Light Ltd		Prepared by: EAA	Date: 8·6·95	Ref: **C5**
Year/Period End: 31. 3. 95	File No:	Reviewed by: DGW	Date: 8.6.95	

SPECIFIC RISK ASSESSMENT

Objective: *To ensure that all material risk areas are identified and appropriate audit work is planned and performed.*

	High, Medium or Low risk?	Nature of risks	Standard audit prog required? Y/N	Comments/details of alternative procedures
D Extensive analytical review			N	
E Intangible assets		N/A		
F Tangible fixed assets	L		Y	
G Investments in group and associated undertakings		N/A		
H Other investments		N/A		
I Stock and WIP	L		Y	
J Debtors and prepayments	H L	Recoverability of trade debtors other debtors	Y	
K Bank and cash	L		Y	
L Creditors and accruals	L		Y	
M Long-term loans and deferred income	L		Y	
N Provisions and contingencies	L		Y	
O Capital and reserves	L		Y	

Client: Bright-a-Light Ltd		Prepared by: EAA	Date: 8·6·95	Ref: C5
Year/Period End: 31.3.95	File No:	Reviewed by: DGW	Date: 8.6.95	

SPECIFIC RISK ASSESSMENT (*cont.*)

	High, Medium or Low risk?	Nature of risks	Standard audit prog required? Y/N	Comments/details of alternative procedures
P Taxation	L		Y	
R Profit and loss – income	L		Y	
– expenditure	L		Y	
– wages	L		Y	
– other	L		Y	
T Post balance sheet events	L		Y	
U VAT	L		Y	
V Consolidation		N/A		
Other				

Conclusion

I am satisfied that the planned audit programmes are suitable to produce sufficient appropriate audit evidence.

Prepared by EA Arbuthnott

Date 8·6·95

Reviewed by DG Watson

Date 8.6.95

TABLE OF INHERENT RISK ASSESSMENT FACTORS

Tests of detail only

General risk \ Specific risk	L	M	H
L	1.2	1.5	1.8
M	1.5	1.8	2.1
H	1.8	2.1	2.5

Client: Bright-a-Light Ltd		Prepared by: EAA	Date: 8.6.95	Ref: **C6**
Year/Period End: 31.3.95	File No:	Reviewed by: DGW	Date: 8.6.95	

MATERIALITY SUMMARY

Materiality ranges

Range of turnover and gross assets	Percentage of turnover and gross assets	Materiality ranges
£0 – £500,000	3.0%	£1 – £15,000
£500,001 – £1,000,000	2.5%	£15,001 – £25,000
£1,000,001 – £2,000,000	2.0%	£25,001 – £40,000
£2,000,001 – £5,000,000	1.5%	£40,001 – £75,000
over £5,000,000	1.0%	over £75,000

Application of materiality ranges to business

	Initial assessment			Final assessment		
	Percentage %	Anticipated results £	Materiality level £	Percentage %	Final results £	Materiality level £
Turnover	2.5%	855,000	21,375	2.5%	858,900	21,472
Gross assets	3.0%	330,000	9,900	3.0%	324,500	9,735

Profit/(loss) before tax		30,000			18,000	
Adjustment for unusual items		–			–	
Adjusted profit/(loss)	10%	30,000	3,000	10%	18,000	1,800

	This year	Last year (final)
Overall initial audit materiality set at	£ 15,000	£ 12,000

Comments

Materiality set mid-way between turnover and gross assets figures.

Conclusion

Based on the anticipated results, I am satisfied that the above figure represents an appropriate initial audit materiality.

EA Arbuthnott	Preparer	8.6.95	Date
DG Watson	Reviewer	8.6.95	Date

	This year
Revised audit materiality	£ 15,000

Comments

No revision necessary

Conclusion

Based on the final results, I am satisfied that the above figure represents an appropriate final audit materiality.

EA Arbuthnott	Preparer	30.6.95	Date
DG Watson	Reviewer	3.7.95	Date

Client: Bright-a-Light Ltd		Prepared by: EAA	Date: 8.6.95	Ref: **C6**
Year/Period End: 31.3.95	File No:	Reviewed by: DGW	Date: 8.6.95	

ACCOUNTANCY WORK PLANNING

1 Level of acceptable accounting differences

If the accounts are to be prepared by us, specify below the level of accounting differences which do not require further investigation.

	This year	Last year
OVERALL LEVEL OF ACCEPTABLE DIFFERENCES	£ 1,000	£ 1,000

If different levels are to be set for the different areas of the accounts preparation, specify these below:

Area	*Level of acceptable differences* This year	Last year
Bank	£ Nil	£
	£	£
	£	£
	£	£
	£	£

2 Analysis work required

Analysis will be required at the following levels:

Income:

1	Turnover	NCN†/~~By category~~*
2	Dividends and interest received/receivable	NCN†/~~all items~~*
3	Rents received/receivable	NCN†/~~all items~~*
4	Management charges	NCN†/~~all items~~*
5		
6		

Expenditure:

7	Directors' emoluments	~~NCN†~~/in full*
8	Interest payable	NCN†/~~all items over~~ £ *
9	Subscriptions and donations	NCN†/~~all items over~~ £ *
10	Insurance (cover and premiums)	NCN†/~~in full, ensuring all areas covered~~*
11	Repairs and renewals	~~NCN†~~/all items over £ 500 *
12	Legal, professional and audit	~~NCN~~†/all items over £ 500 *
13	Entertaining	NCN†/~~all items over £~~ *
14	Sundry expenses	~~NCN~~†/all items over £ 1,000 *
15		
16		

* Delete as appropriate.

† NCN = not considered necessary.

Client: Bright-a-Light Ltd		Prepared by: EAA	Date: 8.6.95	Ref: C7
Year/Period End: 31.3.95	File No:	Reviewed by: DAW	Date: 8.6.95	

SYSTEMS OVERVIEW

Objective: *To ascertain the company's system of recording and processing transactions and to assess its adequacy as a basis for the preparation of the accounts.*

1 Accounting records

Estimated transactions for whole year unless specified

Tick as appropriate	Manual	Computerised	Prepared by us	Volume		Value £'000
(a) Sales Day Book	✓			1,175	Number of invoices	900
(b) Cash Receipts Book	✓			350	Number of entries	850
(c) Sales Ledger		✓		120	Number of accounts	128
(d) Purchase Day Book	✓			500	Number of invoices	780
(e) Cash Payments Book	✓			350	Number of entries	900
(f) Purchase Ledger		✓		200	Number of accounts	80
(g) Petty Cash Book	✓			200	Number of entries	–
(h) Fixed Asset Register			✓	15	Number of assets	160
(i) Stock Ledger		✓		250	Number of lines	26
(j) Payroll		✓		7	Number of employees	55
(k) Nominal Ledger			✓			
(l) Management Accounts					Frequency	
(m) Financial Statements			✓			
(n) Other (specify):						

2 ***Sales system***
(Detail below the categories of income received and how a sale is first recorded.)

Shop sales - recorded through the till.
Credit sales - orders received and passed to warehouse. Goods despatched note drawn up when goods sent to customer. Invoices raised from GDN's

Client: Bright-a-Light Ltd		Prepared by: EAA	Date: 8.6.95	Ref: **C7**
Year/Period End: 31.3.95	File No:	Reviewed by: DGW	Date: 8.6.95	

SYSTEMS OVERVIEW (*cont.*)

3 *Purchases system*

(Detail below the way a liability is first recognised.)

Purchase orders raised which are matched against goods received notes. All invoices for goods are matched against grns, other invoices are sent, on receipt, to the relevant person for approval.

4 *Details of computer system*

Accounting ways software run through windows.

Conclusion

		Initials	Date
1	~~The above notes are an adequate record of the client's systems~~*. The above systems require further documentation which is filed on Permanent audit file*	EAA	8.6.95
2	These systems do/~~do not~~* provide a reliable basis for the preparation of statutory accounts (only when supplemented by our own accounts preparation work)*.	EAA	8.6.95

* Delete where not appropriate.

Client: Bright-a-Light Ltd		Prepared by: EAA	Date: 20.3.95	Ref: **C10**
Year/Period End: 31.3.95	File No:	Reviewed by: DGW	Date: 20.3.95	

ASSIGNMENT PLANNING – TIMETABLE

***Objective**: To plan and control the timing of the assignment.*

		Planned dates	Actual dates
1	Availability of accounting records	1.6.95	8.6.95
2	Staff bookings		
	(a) EAA	5.6.95 to 16.6.95	
	(b) KM	5.6.95 to 16.6.95	
	(c)	to	
	(d)	to	
	(e)	to	
	Stocktake attendance:		
	(f) KM	31.3.95 to	31.3.95
	(g)	to	
3	Information requests:		
	(a) Bank letter	20.3.95	20.3.95
	(b) Solicitor's letter	20.3.95	20.3.95
	(c) Debtor's circularisation	–	
	(d) Creditor's circularisation	–	
	(e) Paid cheques	20.3.95	20.3.95
	(f)		
	(g)		
4	Manager review	23.6.95	
5	Partner review	30.6.95	
6	Discussion of accounts with client	7.7.95	
7	Availability of final signed accounts	14.7.95	
8	Other details		

9 Comments

F TANGIBLE FIXED ASSETS

1	Lead schedule	✓
2	Audit programme	✓
3	Additions and disposals	✓
4	Depreciation basis/calculation	
5	Grants received/receivable	
6	Finance Lease adjustments	✓
7	Letter from bank	✓
8		

Client: Bright-a-Light		Prepared by: KM	Date: 15.9.95	Ref: **F**
Year/Period End: 31.3.95	File No:	Reviewed by: EAA	Date: 16.6.95	

SUMMARY SHEET – TANGIBLE FIXED ASSETS

Audit objectives	***Planning*** Number of tests which satisfy objective	Additional/ alternative tests to be carried out	***Final*** Are you satisfied that the objectives have been met?	Comments	Initials
1 To establish that tangible fixed assets exist.	1, 2, ~~3~~, 4, 7, 20		Yes/~~No~~		KM
2 To establish that tangible fixed assets are beneficially owned.	1, 2, ~~3~~, 4, 5, 6, 20		Yes/~~No~~		KM
3 To verify that tangible fixed assets are completely and accurately recorded at cost or valuation and that basis is acceptable.	1, 2, ~~3~~, 4, 8, 9, 10, 11, ~~12~~, 13, 14, ~~15~~, 18, 19, 20		Yes/~~No~~		KM
4 To confirm that depreciation is adequately provided over the estimated useful lives of the assets.	1, 2, ~~3~~, 4, 16, 17, 20		Yes/~~No~~		KM

Conclusion

From the audit work carried out I confirm that:

- nothing has occurred to necessitate changing the audit plan* ~~or the audit plan has been updated~~.*
- nothing has occurred to necessitate revising the risk assessment* ~~or the risk assessment has been revised~~.*
- nothing has occurred to necessitate revising the materiality level* ~~or the materiality has been revised~~.*
- ~~adjustments to the plan, risk assessment and materiality have been detailed on B5 or B8~~*
- the work has been performed in accordance with the audit programme.
- the work performed and the results obtained have been adequately documented.
- all necessary information has been collected for the preparation of the statutory accounts.
- in my opinion (subject to the matters highlighted on **B5** ~~or **B8**~~)* tangible fixed assets are fairly stated.

Prepared by EAA Date 16.6.95

Reviewed by DGW Date 3.7.95

*Delete if not applicable.

Alternative conclusion (*ANY* alternative conclusion *MUST* be referred to on **B5** or **B8**)

Prepared by ____________ Date ____________

Reviewed by ____________ Date ____________

Client: Bright-a-Light Ltd		Prepared by: KM	Date: 15/6/95	Ref: **F1**
Subject: Fixed assets	File No:	Reviewed by: EAA	Date: 16/6/95	
		Accounting dates: 31/3/95		

	Freehold property £	*Plant & equipment* £	*Motor vehicles* £	*Fixtures & fittings* £	*Total* £
Cost					
At 1 April 1994	β 143,902	β 4,500	β 16,975	β 1,753	β 167,130
Additions	–	–	16,345	326	16,671
Disposals (F3/1)	–	–	(5,000)	–	(5,000)
At 31 March 1995	143,902	4,500	28,320	2,079	178,801
	υ	υ	υ	υ	υ
Depreciation					
At 1 April 1994	960	1,650	6,207	451	9,268
Charge for the year	5,223	570	6,875	246	12,914
Eliminated on disposals (F3/1)	–	–	(2,388)	–	(2,388)
At 31 March 1995	6,183	2,220	10,694	697	19,794
	υ	υ	υ	υ	υ
Net book value					
At 31 March 1995	£137,719	£2,280	£17,626	£1,382	£159,007
	υ	υ	υ	υ	υ
At 1 April 1994	£142,942	£2,850	£10,768	£1,302	£157,862
	υ	υ	υ	υ	υ

Audit key

υ casts checked

β opening balances agreed to last year's accounts

Conclusion

Fixed assets are fairly stated

Client: Bright-a-Light Ltd		Prepared by: KM	Date: 15.6.95 Ref: **F2**
Year/Period End: 31.3.95	File No:	Reviewed by: EAA	Date: 16.6.95

AUDIT PROGRAMME – TANGIBLE FIXED ASSETS

Nature of test:	Test required Y/N	Covered by accountancy Y	Results satisfactory Y/N	Ref/ comments	Initials and date
General					
1 (a) Agree opening balances to last year's accounts.	Y		Y	F1	KM 15.6.95
(b) Obtain and check, or prepare, a lead schedule for the current year's figures.	Y		Y	F1	KM 15.6.95
(c) Enquire into and make notes of reasons for any major variations from expectations.	Y		Y	None	KM 15.6.95
2 Assess whether the initial materiality and/or risk assessment should be revised in view of the audit evidence obtained to date.	Y		Y	No revision needed	KM 15.6.95
3 Undertake detailed analytical review procedures and determine whether the results enable us to reduce our sample size.	N			—	EAA 8.6.95
4 Review for large and unusual items and verify.	Y		Y	None	KM 15.6.95
Ownership					
5 Inspect property title deeds/leases or obtain direct confirmation from bank or other custodian. Compare with detailed asset schedules and Permanent audit file.	Y		Y	F7.1	KM 15.6.95
6 Inspect vehicle registration documents. If the documents are not in the name of the company, obtain written confirmation from the registered holder that the vehicle is owned by the company.	Y		Y	F3	KM 15.6.95
Existence					
7 Carry out physical inspection of other assets including both current year additions and assets purchased in previous years.	Y		Y	F3	KM 15.6.95
Valuation					
8 Vouch additions to purchase invoices. Ensure that: (a) the cost is correctly recorded;	Y		Y	F3	KM 15.6.95
(b) they have been properly authorised;	N			—	EAA 8.6.95
(c) they are correctly classified;	Y		Y	F3	KM 15.6.95
(d) they are of a capital, not revenue nature;	Y		Y	F3	KM 15.6.95
(e) the value has been correctly computed where they represent the capitalisation of items made internally.	N	—	—	—	EAA 8.6.95

Client: Bright-a-Light		Prepared by: KM	Date: 15.6.95	Ref: **F2**
Year/Period End: 31.3.95	File No:	Reviewed by: EAA	Date: 16.6.95	

AUDIT PROGRAMME – TANGIBLE FIXED ASSETS (*cont.*)

	Test required Y/N	Covered by accountancy Y	Results satisfactory Y/N	Ref/ comments	Initials and date
9 Ensure that assets acquired were delivered prior to the balance sheet date.	Y		Y	F3	KM 15.6.95
10 Vouch disposal to available evidence. Ensure that: (a) sales proceeds have been correctly accounted for;	Y		Y	F3.1	KM 15.6.95
(b) profit/loss on disposal has been correctly calculated;	Y		Y	F3.1	KM 15.6.95
(c) they have been properly authorised;	N		—	—	EAA 8.6.95
(d) they have been removed from the fixed asset register/listing.	Y		Y	F3.1	KM 15.6.95
11 Enquire whether any assets were scrapped during the year.	Y		Y	None per directors	KM 15.6.95
12 For assets revalued during the year, inspect professional valuation or, if at directors' valuation, consider reasonableness.	N		—	—	EAA 8.6.95
13 Consider whether there are any known factors which might adversely affect the value of the assets.	Y		Y	F7	KM 15.6.95
14 Consider whether any diminution in value of an asset is appropriately classified between permanent and temporary, and that any necessary adjustment has been made.	Y		Y	Property value - permanent	EAA 16.6.95
15 Verify that government grants received/receivable in respect of fixed assets have been accounted for properly.	N		—	—	EAA 8.6.95
Depreciation					
16 (a) Compare bases and rates of depreciation with accounting policy note.	Y		Y	Rates agreed to accounts	KM 15.6.95
(b) Consider whether they are adequate to write assets off over their estimated useful lives.	Y		Y	F7	EAA 16.6.95
17 (a) Confirm that all assets are being depreciated in accordance with the company's accounting policy.	Y		Y	F3	KM 15.6.95
(b) Check calculations.	Y	Y	Y	F3	KM 15.6.95
(c) Ensure that no assets have been depreciated by more than cost.	Y	Y	Y		KM 15.6.95

Client: Bright-a-Light Ltd		Prepared by: KM	Date: 15.6.95	Ref: **F2**
Year/Period End: 31.3.95	File No:	Reviewed by: EAA	Date: 16.6.95	

AUDIT PROGRAMME – TANGIBLE FIXED ASSETS (*cont.*)

	Test required Y/N	Covered by accountancy Y	Results satisfactory Y/N	Ref/ comments	Initials and date
18 Enquire whether any assets are permanently not in use, and ensure that any such assets have been fully written off.	Y		Y	None per director	KM 15.6.95
19 Ensure that all necessary information has been collected for the preparation of the statutory accounts. (a) Enquire whether there are any capital commitments at the year end.	Y		Y	None per director (K Smith)	KM 15.6.95
(b) Prepare a schedule of any such commitments distinguishing between items 'contracted for but not provided' and 'authorised but not contracted for'.	Y		Y	None	KM 15.6.95
(c) Obtain details of all assets acquired during the year under a finance lease.	Y		Y	Peugeot now included	EAA 16.6.95
(d) Ensure that any items in (c) above have been correctly capitalised.	Y		Y		
(e) Calculate the NBV of all assets held under finance leases.	Y		Y		
(f) Ensure that any leases of less than 50 years have been correctly classified as short term.	N		—		EAA 8.6.95
(g) Where assets have been revalued ensure that the historical cost information, i.e., original cost and accumulated depreciation is available for disclosure purposes.	N		—		EAA 8.6.95
Conclusion 20 Consider whether there are any items which need to be included in a letter of representation or letter of comment and record on **A5** or **A6** as appropriate.	Y		Y	Std paras & split of land & buildings	EAA 16.6.95
21 Other tests:	N	—	—	—	EAA 8.6.95

Client: Bright-a-Light Ltd		Prepared by: KM	Date: 15/6/95	Ref: **F3**
Subject: Fixed asset register	File No:	Reviewed by: EAA	Date: 16/6/95	
		Accounting dates: P/E	31/3/95	

		COST				**DEPRECIATION**				**NBV**	
	Depreciation rate	*At 1.4.94* £	*Additions* £	*Disposals* £	*At 31.3.95* £	*At 1.4.94* £	*Charge* £	*Disposal* £	*At 31.3.95* £	*At 31.3.95* £	*At 1.4.94* £
Freehold land											
Buildings (1/3)	11.1% P	47,967	–	–	47,967	960	5,223	–	6,183	41,784	47,007
Land (2/3)	– P	95,935	–	–	95,935	–	–	–	–	95,935	95,935
		143,902	–	–	143,902	960	5,223	–	6,183	137,719	142,942
		υ			υ	υ	υ		υ	υ	υ
Plant & equipment	20%										
Pool (purchased in MBO)		4,000	–	–	4,000	1,600	480	–	2,080	1,920	2,400
Photocopier		500	–	–	500	50	90	–	140	360	450
		4,500	–	–	4,500	1,650	570	–	2,220	2,280	2,850
		υ			υ	υ	υ		υ	υ	υ
Motor vehicles	25%										
Pool (purchased in MBO)		7,000	–	5,000	2,000	3,343	261	2,388	1,216	784	3,657
Renault A 197 ODR		1,975	–	–	1,975	864	278	–	1,142	833	1,111
Lorry F845 ABC	PR	5,500	–	–	5,500	1,375	1,031	–	2,406	3,094	4,125
Lorry D870 JEP		2,500	–	–	2,500	625	469	–	1,094	1,406	1,875
Lorry G446 JAB	R√		2,600	–	2,600	–	650	–	650	1,950	–
Lorry G872 JRM	PR√		4,750	–	4,750	–	1,188	–	1,188	3,562	–
Peugeot K853 JCD F6	PR√		8,995	–	8,995	–	2,998	–	2,998	5,997	–
		16,975	16,345	5,000	28,320	6,207	6,875	2,388	10,694	17,626	10,768
		υ	υ	υ	υ	υ	υ	υ	υ	υ	υ
Fixtures & Fittings	15%										
Desks		499	–	–	499	170	50	–	220	279	329
Call connect system		924	–	–	924	256	100	–	356	568	668
Chairs		330	–	–	330	25	48	–	73	257	305
Display	√	–	326	–	326	–	48	–	48	278	–
		1,753	326	–	2,079	451	246	–	697	1,382	1,302
		υ	υ		υ	υ	υ		υ	υ	υ

Audit key

υ Casts checked
P Physically seen
R Vehicle registration documents inspected (all additions and one other item selected at random). All in name of company.
√ Additions agreed to purchase invoices and ensured item delivered prior to year end, that they are correctly treated as capital and have been correctly classified.

Client: Bright-a-Light Ltd		Prepared by: KM	Date: 15/6/95	Ref: **F3/1**
Subject: Disposals	File No:	Reviewed by: EAA	Date: 16/6/95	
		Accounting dates: 31.3.95		

	£	£
Disposals – proceeds		
Montego Estate J895 JTX		2,000
Ford Fiesta A579 HAB		400
		√ 2,400
NBV		
Purchased from Yorkshire Gas Ltd		
(joint cost)	5,000	
Depreciation 5/7 × £3,343	(2,388)	
		2,612
Loss – to be adjusted		(212)
		υ

υ Cast checked

√ Cash receipt agreed & traced to bank

Depreciation on motor vehicle pool has been incorrectly calculated per TB.

		£	
Cost of pool at 31.3.95		2,000	
Depreciation to 1.4.94 – BF	3,343		
Disposals in year	(2,388)		
		955	
NBV		1,045	
Depreciation at 25%		261	
Per TB		313	
Reduction in charge needed		(52)	Y2

Client: Bright-a-Light Ltd		Prepared by: KM	Date: 15·6·95	Ref: F3/2
Year/Period End: 31.3.95	File No:	Reviewed by: EAA	Date: 16.6.95	

SAMPLE SELECTION PLANNING – BALANCE SHEET

Objective: *To record the resources from which audit assurance has been obtained, and to assist in calculating sample sizes for tests of details.*

Audit area Fixed assets - existence

Approximate number of transactions in year	10

Inherent risk factor

Test of detail only = Table figure 1·2

OR

Test of detail and analytical review = Table figure × $\frac{2}{3}$ ______

Tolerable error = $\frac{\text{Materiality}}{\text{Inherent risk factor}} = \frac{15,000}{1·2} = 12,500$

Monetary value of population	(100%)	£ 159,007
Value of items above the tolerable error	(87%)	£(137,719)
Value of scheduled other 'key' items	(%)	£(______)
Value of residual population	(13%)	£ 21,288

Sample size =

$\frac{\text{Residual population} \times \text{Inherent risk factor}}{\text{Materiality}}$ $\frac{£\,21,288}{£\,15,000}$ ×1·2= 1·7 i.e 2

Plus: Number of items above the tolerable error = 1 Property

Number of other 'key' items = –

Actual sample size 3

Conclusion Three items [plus the property] selected at the stocktake

I am satisfied that the actual sample size will fairly test the population.

Prepared by KM Date 15·6·95

Reviewed by EAA Date 16.6.95

Client: Bright-a-Light Ltd		Prepared by: EAA	Date: 16/6/95	Ref: **F6**
Subject: Fixed assets – Finance lease adjustments	File No:	Reviewed by: DGW	Date: 3/7/95	
Car: Peugeot 405 SR – K853 JCD		Accounting dates: 31.3.95		

			£
Lease terms:	initial	1 @ £728.34	728.34
	monthly	35 @ £242.78	8,497.30
	final	1 @ £2,000.00	2,000.00
Total repayments			11,225.64
Cash value (i.e., capital value)			8,995.00
Total interest			£2,230.64

Allocation of interest over 36 months, using sum of digits method, commencing on date lease signed 19.6.94 (initial instalment paid then with no interest).

Sum of digits for 36 months $\frac{(36 + 1)}{2} \times 36 = 666$

	Proportion of interest	*Annual charge*
y/e 31.3.95 = 10 months (36 to 27) ∴ factor = $(37 + 27) \times \frac{10}{2} = 315$	315/666	1,055.03
y/e 31.3.96 = 12 months (26 to 15) ∴ factor = $(26 + 15) \times \frac{12}{2} = 246$	246/666	823.93
y/e 31.3.97 = 12 months (14 to 3) ∴ factor = $(14 + 3) \times \frac{12}{2} = 102$	102/666	341.63
y/e 31.3.98 = 3 months (but no interest on last instalment) ∴ factor = $(2 + 1) \times \frac{2}{2} = 3$	3/666	10.05
		£2,230.64

Therefore journals needed	*Dr*	*Cr*
1 to record the car as asset		
Dr Motor Vehicles	8,995.00	
Cr Finance lease liability		8,995.00
2 to charge depreciation over 3 years		
Dr Depreciation P & L	2,998.00	
Cr Motor vehicle accumulated depreciation		2,998.00
3 to record repayments in the year		
Dr Finance lease liability	1,858.33	
Dr Lease interest (P & L)	1,055.03	
Cr Repairs and renewals		2,913.36

Client: Bright-a-Light Ltd		Prepared by: EAA	Date: 16/6/95	Ref: **F7**
Subject: Land & Buildings	File No:	Reviewed by: DGW	Date: 2/7/95	
		Accounting dates: 30.6.95		

The freehold land and buildings are split on an arbitrary basis with 2/3 of the original cost being allocated to freehold land. The directors feel that this fairly reflects the value of the land. The buildings on the site are mostly poor quality storage sheds. It is therefore a reasonable allocation of the original cost of the site. This will be included in the letter of representation.

Following the move last year, the freehold buildings were depreciated at 2 per cent on cost in that year. This rate of depreciation seems very low, considering the poor quality of the buildings. I feel that the useful economic life of the buildings is more likely to be 10 years rather than 50 years. I have discussed the problem with Mr Strike and we agreed to adjust the depreciation figure accordingly.

The necessary adjustment to the accounts is set out below, based on the requirement in SSAP 12 to depreciate the remaining net book value of £47,007 over the remaining useful economoic life of 9 years.

Annual charge $= \frac{47,007}{9}$

$= £5,223$

Depreciation per TB $= £960$

∴ Adjustment needed is an increase in the depreciation charge of £4,263 Y2

F7/1

CAPITAL BANK

Messrs Jones Watson & Co
24 Barracks Square
Oldtown
Yorkshire

2 May 1995

17 Charter Way,
Oldtown
Yorkshire
Tel (01722) 127834
Fax (01722) 127849

Dear Sirs

BRIGHT-A-LIGHT LTD

Further to our telephone conversation of 28 April 1995, we can confirm that we are holding the title deeds to unit 12 Westend Industrial Estate, Oldtown, Yorkshire, and that these are in the above company's name.

Yours faithfully

G Roberts

G Roberts
Securities Officer

I STOCK AND WORK IN PROGESS

1	Lead schedule	✓
2	Audit programme	✓
3	Stock held by third parties	
4	Stocktake programme and report	
5		
6		
7		

Client: Bright-a-Light Ltd		Prepared by:	Date:	Ref: **I**
Year/Period End: 31.3.95	File No:	Reviewed by:	Date:	

SUMMARY SHEET – STOCK AND WORK IN PROGRESS

	Planning Number of tests which satisfy objective	Additional/ alternative tests to be carried out	***Final*** Are you satisfied that the objectives have been met?	Comments	Initials
Audit objectives					
1 To ensure that the company has good title to stock and work in progress.	1, 2, ~~3,~~ 4, 5, 6, ~~7,~~ 22		Yes/~~No~~		EAA
2 To ensure that all stock and work in progress exists.	1, 2, ~~3,~~ 4, 8, 9, 10, ~~13,~~ 22		Yes/~~No~~		EAA
3 To ensure that stock and work in progress have been valued correctly, consistently and in accordance with the Companies Act 1985, SSAP 9 and FRS 5.	1, 2, ~~3,~~ 4, ~~7,~~ 11, 12, ~~14,~~ ~~15,~~ ~~16,~~ 22		Yes/~~No~~		EAA
4 To ensure that full provision has been made for all damaged, obsolete or slow moving stock and work in progress.	1, 2, ~~3,~~ 4, 17, 18, 19, 20, 22		Yes/~~No~~		EAA
5 To ensure that cut-off has been strictly applied.	1, 2, 3, 4, 21, 22		Yes/~~No~~		EAA

Conclusion

From the audit work carried out I confirm that:

- nothing has occurred to necessitate changing the audit plan* ~~or the audit plan has been updated.~~*
- nothing has occurred to necessitate revising the risk assessment* ~~or the risk assessment has been revised.~~*
- nothing has occurred to necessitate revising the materiality level* ~~or the materiality has been revised.~~*
- ~~adjustments to the plan, risk assessment and materiality have been detailed on **B5** or **B8**.~~*
- the work has been performed in accordance with the audit programme.
- the work performed and the results obtained have been adequately documented.
- all necessary information has been collected for the preparation of the statutory accounts.
- in my opinion ~~(subject to the matters highlighted on **B5** or **B8**)*~~ stock and work in progress are fairly stated.

Prepared by EAA Date 19.6.95

Reviewed by DGW Date 3.7.95

*Delete if not applicable.

Alternative conclusion (*ANY* alternative conclusion *MUST* be referred to on **B5** or **B8**)

Prepared by ______________________ Date ____________

Reviewed by ______________________ Date ____________

Client	File No.	Ref.
Bright-a-Light Ltd		I1

Subject	Prepared by	Date
Stock	KM	15/6/95
	Reviewed by: EAA	Date: 19/6/95
	Accounting Dates	31·3·95

Type	*Area*	*£*	*1995* *£*	*1994* *£*
Solid fuel	Gate 3	√3,524.57		
	Gate 4	√1,208.91		
	Gate 12	√6,818.92		
			11,552.40	3,883.00
Gas packed	Gate 5	√2,678.80		
	Gate 6	√3,635.38		
	Gate 7	√1,092.62		
			7,406.80	6,247.00
Gas equipment	Gate 8	√ 40.50		
	Gate 9	√ 656.95		
	Gate 10	√ 754.77		
	Gate 11	√1,319.17		
			2,771.39	4,551.00
Leisure products	Gate 13	√1,468.91		
	Gate 14	√ 686.37		
	Gate 15	√ 647.36		
			2,802.64	7,440.00
Diesel	Gate 17	√ 547.45		
			547.45	739.00
Solvents	Gate 16	√ 922.77		
			922.77	—
Finished goods		TB	£26,003.45	£22,860.00
			v	v

Key

- v Casts checked.
- √ Agreed to stock valuation report I7.
- TB Agreed to trial balance.

Fluctuations

Client is holding about the same overall level of stock, but is now holding more solid fuel this year. This is a result of the increased volume of trading, and subsequent need to hold higher levels of the popular stock items. Client has cut levels of less popular items, particularly leisure products. The increase in solid fuels corresponds to the increase in turnover.

Conclusion

I am satisfied that stocks are fairly stated.

Client: Bright-a-Light Ltd		Prepared by: KM	Date: 16.6.95	Ref: **I2**
Year/Period End: 31.3.95	File No:	Reviewed by: EAA	Date: 19.6.95	

AUDIT PROGRAMME – STOCK AND WORK IN PROGRESS

Nature of test:	Test required Y/N	Covered by accountancy Y	Results satisfactory Y/N	Ref/ comments	Initials and date
General					
1 (a) Agree opening balances to last year's accounts.	Y		Y	I1	KM 16.6.95
(b) Obtain and check, or prepare, a lead schedule for the current year's figures.	Y		Y	I1	KM 16.6.95
(c) Enquire into and make notes of reasons for any major variations from expectations.	Y		Y	I1	KM 16.6.95
2 Assess whether the initial materiality and/or risk assessment should be revised in view of the audit evidence obtained to date.	Y		Y	No revision needed	KM 16.6.95
3 Undertake detailed analytical review procedures and determine whether the results enable us to reduce our sample size.	N		—	—	EAA 8.6.95
4 Review for large and unusual items and verify.	Y		Y	None	KM 16.6.95
Ownership					
5 Enquire if any of the stock is held on behalf of third parties and ensure that such items are excluded from stock. Where material, obtain confirmation from the third party.	Y		Y	None per K Strike	KM 16.6.95
6 Where stock is held by third parties on behalf of the company, obtain certificates where amounts are material.	Y		Y	None per K Strike	KM 16.6.95
7 Consider whether any consignment stock has been accounted for in accordance with FRS 5.	N		—	—	EAA 8.6.95
Existence					
8 Complete the stocktake attendance programme, **I4**. Trace all items selected at the stocktake to the final stock sheets, and, where appropriate, internal stock records. Obtain explanations for any differences.	Y		Y	I5.1	KM 16.6.95
9 Select a sample of items from the final stock sheets and trace to the copies of the rough stock sheets taken during the stocktake.	Y		Y	I6	KM 16.6.95

Client: Bright-a-Light Ltd		Prepared by: KM	Date: 16.6.95	Ref: **I2**
Year/Period End: 31.3.95	File No:	Reviewed by: EAA	Date: 19.6.95	

AUDIT PROGRAMME – STOCK AND WORK IN PROGRESS (*cont.*)

	Test required Y/N	Covered by accountancy Y	Results satisfactory Y/N	Ref/ Comments	Initials and date
10 Ensure that all sheets in the sequence recorded at the stocktake are available (obtain explanations for any numbers missing from the sequence).	Y		Y	I5.2	KM 16.6.95
Valuation 11 Test the additions and extensions of the final stock sheet.	Y		Y	I7	KM 16.6.95
12 Ascertain the method used for valuing stock and consider whether: (a) it has been correctly applied: (i) *Actual* Agree prices used to purchase invoices on costing records.	Y		Y	I5.1	KM 16.6.95
(iii) *Selling price less mark-up* Agree a selection of items to current price lists and also prices noted at the stock attendance. Consider whether the gross margin used to reduce selling price to cost is reasonable and has been correctly applied.	N		—	—	EAA 8.6.95
(iii) *Standard cost* Confirm that standard costs are updated only during an annual review of all standards. Enquire whether large variances from standard are investigated on a regular basis. Select a sample of purchase invoices and ensure that details have been entered correctly in the nominal ledger.	N		—	—	EAA 8.6.95
(iv) *FIFO* Check back through purchase invoices for a selection of items until sufficient invoices have been identified to account for the items in stock at the year end. Ensure that costs have been allocated correctly.	N		—	—	EAA 8.6.95

Client: Bright-a-Light Ltd		Prepared by: KM	Date: 16.6.95	Ref: **I2**
Year/Period End: 31.3.95	File No:	Reviewed by: EAA	Date: 19.6.95	

AUDIT PROGRAMME – STOCK AND WORK IN PROGRESS (*cont.*)

	Test required Y/N	Covered by accountancy Y	Results satisfactory Y/N	Ref/ comments	Initials and date
12 (b) It is an acceptable basis of valuation under SSAP 9 and Companies Act 1985.	Y		Y		KM 16.6.95
(c) It is consistent with previous years and with the company's accounting policy.	Y		Y		KM 16.6.95
Work in progress 13 Where there is material work in progress that has not been physically verified at the stocktake attendance, specify below the audit work required to verify existence:	N		—		EAA 8.6.95
14 Review work in progress and manufactured finished goods and ensure that: (a) the material costs have been correctly recorded;	N		—		EAA 8.6.95
(b) the allocation of labour costs has been applied correctly, consistently and is reasonable;	N		—		EAA 8.6.95
(c) the allocation of overheads has been applied correctly, consistently and is reasonable.	N		—		EAA 8.6.95
15 Review long-term work in progress and: (a) ensure that costs have been recorded accurately;	N	—	—	—	EAA 8.6.95
(b) review any profit taken in the light of work carried out (i.e., stage of completion), costs to date, expected costs to complete and total contract value;	N	—	—	—	EAA 8.6.95
(c) ensure that adequate provision has been made for any anticipated losses;	N		—		EAA 8.6.95

Client: Bright-a-Light Ltd		Prepared by: KM	Date: 16.6.95	Ref: **I2**
Year/Period End: 31.3.95	File No:	Reviewed by: EAA	Date: 19.6.95	

AUDIT PROGRAMME – STOCK AND WORK IN PROGRESS (*cont.*)

	Test required Y/N	Covered by accountancy Y	Results satisfactory Y/N	Ref/ Comments	Initials and date
15 (d) ensure that the accounting treatment and disclosure of each project is in accordance with SSAP 9.	N		—	—	EAA 8.6.95
16 Ensure that any internal profits on inter-departmental transfers are eliminated.	N		—	—	EAA 8.6.95
Provisions 17 Obtain details of the basis for making provisions and determine if it is both adequate and consistent. (a) Where the client determines the position on the basis of a formula consider whether: – it is appropriate for the nature of business; – it is consistent; – it has been accurately applied; – where the formula relies on the age of the stock, check to ensure that the ageing is accurate.	N		—	—	EAA 8.6.95
(b) Where the provision is determined on an item-by-item basis: – consider whether the procedures are adequate to identify all stocks needing a provision; – test a sample of items both provided for and not provided for and ensure that they have been treated correctly.	Y		Y	I6	KM 19.6.95
18 Review the stock sheets and ensure that any items identified as damaged, slow moving or obsolete have been correctly written down.	Y		Y	I4.1	KM 19.6.95
19 Review all items of stock and work in progress and consider whether any further provision is necessary. (a) Review WIP and ensure that provision has been made against any 'old' jobs.	N		—	—	EAA 8.6.95

Client: Bright-a-Light Ltd		Prepared by: KM	Date: 16.9.95	Ref: **I2**
Year/Period End: 31.3.95	File No:	Reviewed by: EAA	Date: 19.6.95	

AUDIT PROGRAMME – STOCK AND WORK IN PROGRESS (*cont.*)

	Test required Y/N	Covered by accountancy Y	Results satisfactory Y/N	Ref/ comments	Initials and date
19 (b) When assessing the need for any further provision consider the following: – whether production levels are falling; – whether stock levels are high in comparison to orders received and anticipated demand; – any fluctuations in cost or selling price; – any likely change in technology or market demands.	Y		Y	I6	KM 19.6.95
20 Select a sample of stock items and compare costs to the selling price less expenditure necessary for realisation. (a) Stock lines need to be examined individually. Losses on one line cannot be set off against profits on another.	Y		Y	I5.1	KM 19.6.95
(b) Where a provision is made on a finished product consider whether any provision should be made against WIP and materials used in the process.	N		—	—	EAA 8.6.95
(c) Expenditure necessary for realising stock should include a proportion of marketing, selling and distribution expenses as well as an allowance for scrap and reworking costs.	N		—	—	EAA 8.6.95
Cut-off 21 Review the results of the tests on cut-off carried out on debtors and creditors and ensure they provide adequate assurance as to the accuracy of the year end cut-off.	Y		Y	J8 + L3.6	EAA 20.6.95
Conclusion 22 Consider whether there are any points which need to be included in a letter of representation or letter of comment and record on **A5** or **A6** as appropriate.	Y		Y	None	EAA 20.6.95
23 Other tests:	N	—	—	—	EAA 8.6.95

Client: Bright-a-Light Ltd		Prepared by: KM	Date: 31.3.95	Ref: **I4**
Year/Period End: 31.3.95	File No:	Reviewed by: EAA	Date: 19.6.95	

AUDIT PROGRAMME – STOCKTAKE ATTENDANCE

Nature of test:	Test required Y/N	Covered by accountancy Y	Results satisfactory Y/N	Ref/ comments	Initials and date
General					
1 Record the following details for each location visited:					
(a) location(s) being counted;	Y		Y		
(b) date(s) of count and attendance;	Y		Y		
(c) types of stock held at location;	Y		Y		
(d) approximate value of stock by category at location;	Y		Y	See	
(e) details of any stocks at locations not covered by the count and any alternative method used to verify their existence;	Y		Y	Report I4.1	KM 31.3.95
(f) brief description of the procedures adopted;	Y		Y		
(g) names of client staff counting;	Y		Y		
(h) names of audit staff taking part.	Y		Y		
2 Ascertain and note whether:					
(a) the stocktake teams were properly briefed prior to commencing the count;	Y		Y	Have done it for several years	KM 31.3.95
(b) the teams only include people who are not responsible for the storing and recording of stock and work in progress;	Y		Y	Client staff small ∴ tests by MD	KM 31.3.95
(c) stock was counted by teams of two (one counting and one checking and recording);	Y		Y		KM 31.3.95
(d) the teams were asked to identify damaged, slow moving or obsolete stock;	Y		Y		KM 31.3.95
(e) the teams were made aware of any stocks held on behalf of third parties and these were excluded from the count.	Y		Y	None	KM 31.3.95
Stock counting					
3 Determine whether:					
(a) the teams were counting and recording accurately;	Y		Y	Test checks done	KM 31.3.95
(b) the counts were being controlled to ensure that all stock was counted and only once;	Y		Y	See report I4.1	KM 31.3.95

Client: Bright-a-Light Ltd		Prepared by: KM	Date: 31.3.95	Ref: **I4**
Year/Period End: 31.3.95	File No:	Reviewed by: EAA	Date: 19.6.95	

AUDIT PROGRAMME – STOCKTAKE ATTENDANCE (*cont.*)

	Test required Y/N	Covered by accountancy Y	Results satisfactory Y/N	Ref/ comments	Initials and date
3 (c) there was adequate control over stock sheets to ensure that they are all accounted for (e.g., pre-numbered).	Y		Y	See report	KM 31.3.95
4 Where serially numbered sheets are used, record the numbers of all sheets used at the end of the count.	Y		Y	I4.1	KM 31.3.95
5 Select a sample of items from completed stock sheets and check to ensure that the number has been recorded properly. (These should be followed through to final stock sheets at the final audit – see **I2**, Test 8.)	Y		Y	I4.2	KM 31.3.95
6 Count a sample of stock items and ensure that they have been recorded properly on the final stock sheets.	Y		Y	I4.3	KM 31.3.95
7 Where possible, copy or extract details of a sample of rough stock sheets for checking at the final audit.	Y		Y		KM 31.3.95
8 Where stocks are valued at selling price less mark-up, record the shelf price of a number of stock items.	N		—	N/A —	KM 31.3.95
9 Ascertain whether any stock is held on behalf of a third party. Where applicable ensure that it has been separately identified and excluded from the count.	Y		Y		KM 31.3.95
10 Ascertain whether any consignment stock is held. Ensure, where appropriate, a full record is made.	Y		Y	None	KM 31.3.95
11 Note any old or damaged stock during the count. Ensure that it is marked as such on the final stock sheets.	Y		Y	See report	KM 31.3.95
Cut-off					
12 Ensure that no movements in or out took place during the stocktake.	Y		Y	None	KM 31.3.95
13 Record details of the last goods despatch number and the last goods received note number to follow up at the final audit.	Y		Y	I4.1	KM 31.3.95

Client: Bright-a-Light Ltd		Prepared by: KM	Date: 31.3.95	Ref: **I4**
Year/Period End: 31.3.95	File No:	Reviewed by: EAA	Date: 19.6.95	

AUDIT PROGRAMME – STOCKTAKE ATTENDANCE (*cont.*)

	Test required Y/N	Covered by accountancy Y	Results satisfactory Y/N	Ref/ comments	Initials and date
Other work					
14 Perform any other procedures that would normally be carried out at the stocktake attendance, such as physical inspection of fixed assets and/or cash counts.	Y		Y	Property C845 ABC D872 JRM K855 JCD seen	KM 31.3.95
Conclusion					
15 Write a report on the stocktake concluding on its accuracy and the ability to rely on it.	Y		Y	I4.1	KM 31.3.95
16 Other tests:	N	—	—	—	KM 31.3.95

BRIGHT-A-LIGHT LIMITED

STOCKTAKE ATTENDANCE VISIT
FRIDAY 31 MARCH 1995

I visited the clients only premises at Westend Industrial Estate, Oldtown on Friday 31 March 1995.

The count had been virtually completed by the time I arrived, with the exception being the gas cylinders. The client holds about £25,000 of stock of various fuels and leisure products at this site, of which most comprises prepacked solid fuel and bottled gas containers.

Stocktaking procedures

The stock was counted by Mr Sargeant and Mr Flowers. Mr Flowers did the counting and Mr Sargeant checked the counts and recorded them, on pre-numbered sheets. Some test counts had been done by Mr Strike, the Managing Director. Mr Strike also came with me to perform further test counts on the gas cylinder stock.

Once items had been counted, stock was marked with a red star-shaped sticker to prevent double-counting.

Damaged stock was not counted – it is kept separately from the main storate site. Slow moving or obsolete lines were marked on the rough stock sheets.

The client does not hold any third party stocks.

Stock sheet numbers issued and returned, numbered 1–12.

Copies were taken for later use. (Note for readers: rough sheets not included.)

Cut-off details

Last GDN – 31.3.95 despatch note 3381: ABC Solid Fuel for 5 × 25 kg anthracite.
Last GRN – 31.3.95 number 1062: 200 × 25 kg bags coalite.

Detailed tests

Assume stock value £25,000

Risk	Low	(as last year)	Interest risk factor = 1.2
Materiality	£12,000	(as last year)	

Therefore no. of items $= \frac{25,000}{12,000} \times 1.2 = 2.5$ (say 3 items)

As the sample size is based on draft figures, five items were picked for detailed tests, to avoid possibility of not doing enough items.

Results of detailed testing

See I4.2 and I4.3. All tests satisfactory.

Conclusion

On the basis of the audit work performed, I am satisfied that the clients stocktake has been performed properly and that it forms an accurate basis for the final stock valuation.

K Martin

Client Bright-a-Light Ltd	File No.	Ref. 14.2	
Subject Stocktake Attendance	Prepared by KM		Date 31/3/95
Test 5 – Sample selected from sheets	Reviewed by EAA		Date 19/6/95
	Accounting Dates 31·3·95		

Work done

A sample of five items were selected from the stock sheets and agreed to the physical stock and the stock ledger balances.

	Description	*Sheet*	*No per sheet*	*Physical count*	*Agreed to stock ledger*	*Satisfactory*
1.	10 kg bags Coalite	1	366	366	√	Yes
2.	10 kg bag lumpwood charcoal	5	637	637	√	Yes
3.	Case (12) of lighter fluid	8	84	84	√	Yes
4.	15 kg Shellgas refill	12	204	204	√	Yes
5.	46 kg Shellgas refill	12	46	46	√	Yes

Results

Satisfactory.

Conclusion

Physical quantities of stock are not materially mis-stated.

Client		File No.	Ref.
Bright-a-Light Ltd			I4.3
Subject		Prepared by	Date
Stocktake Attendance		KM	31/3/95
		Reviewed by	Date
Test 6 – Sample selected from physical stock		EAA	19/6/95
		Accounting Dates	31·3·95

Work done

A sample of five items were selected from the physical stock and agreed to the client's stocktaking sheets and the computerised ledger.

	Description	*Physical count*	*Per sheet*	*Sheet No*	*Agreed to stock ledger*	*Satisfactory*
1.	Gimeg 200 gas cartridge	540	540	3	√	Yes
2.	18.5 kg Shellgas refills	41	41	12	√	Yes
3.	25 kg bags Dry Steam Large Nuts	37	37	1	√	Yes
4.	6 × 3 kg Lumpwood charcoal	245	245	5	√	Yes
5.	Thermos, portable gas barbecue	33	33	7	√	Yes

Results

Satisfactory.

Conclusion

Physical quantities of stock are not materially mis-stated.

Client	File No.	Ref.
Bright-a-Light Ltd		I5.1

Subject	Prepared by	Date
Stock – detailed testing	KM	19/6/95
Follow up of stock take – test 8 Valuation of stock – test 12	Reviewed by: EAA	Date: 20/6/95
NRV of stock – test 20	Accounting Dates: 31·3·95	

Method: Stock is valued at lower of cost and NRV.

Sample: Items selected at stocktake were traced to the stock valuation report, agreeing amounts (test 8). All items traced and tested, even though test samples only need 2 items.
Cost was tested by agreeing to purchase invoices (test 12). NRV was reviewed by agreeing to sales prices less bulk discount 5% (not always given) (test 20).

	Description	*Agreed to stock valuation*	*Unit cost*	*Agreed to invoice*	*Sales price*	*NRV*	*Cost < NRV*
1.	10 kg Coalite	√	1.52	√	1.99	1.89	√
2.	10 kg lumpwood charcoal	√	2.78	√	3.30	3.14	√
3.	Case (12) lighter fluid	√	5.04 (42p each)	√	6.00 (50p each)	5.70	√
4.	15 kg Shellgas refill	√	9.00	√	11.45	10.87	√
5.	46 kg Shellgas refill	√	19.50	√	22.95	21.80	√
6.	Gimeg 200 gas cartridge	√	0.44	√	0.50	0.47	√
7.	18.5 kg Shellgas	√	10.64	√	12.75	12.11	√
8.	25 kg Dry Steam Large Nuts (DSLN)	√	2.72	√	3.15	2.99	√
9.	6 × 3 kg lumpwood charcoal	√	5.28	√	6.00	5.70	√
10.	Thermos portable gas barbecue	√	17.73	√	21.95	20.85	√

Results – Tests 8, 12 and 20 are satisfactory.

Client	File No.	Ref.
Bright-a-Light Ltd		I5.2

Subject	Prepared by	Date
Review of stock-take sheets – test 9 and 10	KM	17/6/95
	Reviewed by: EAA	Date: 19/6/95
	Accounting Dates: 31·3·95	

Test 9

Sample: Two items were selected at random from the final sheets and agreed to the copies of the rough sheets taken in the stock-take.

	Description	*Quantity per final sheet*	*Quantity per rough sheet*	*Test satisfactory*
(1)	25 kg anthracite large nuts	95	95	√
(2)	15 kg Shellgas refill	204	204	√

Test 10

During the stocktake, 12 sheets were issued, numbers 1 to 12. All were used and returned – see I4.1. These sheets were reviewed to ensure that all of the gates had been included on the final stock valuation report. No missing items were seen.

Conclusion

Stock has not been materially mis-stated.

Client		File No.	Ref.
Bright-a-Light Ltd			I6
Subject Stock Provisions		Prepared by KM	Date 17/6/95
		Reviewed by EAA	Date 19/6/95
		Accounting Dates	31·3·95

Basis: Items identified at the stocktake as being obsolete/slow moving are not valued – see I4.1. Damaged items are not counted.

Review of provision

The computerised ledger printouts were reviewed and slow moving items were identified from the last sale date. These were traced to the stock valuation report to ensure that no value had been placed on them. The accuracy of the stock valuation report was reviewed during cut off tests on debtors J8 and creditors L3.6.

Description	*Date of last sale*	*Value per report*	*Comments*	*Satisfactory*
Cosyhome fire – delivered 1.7.93 – demo	—	nil		√
Infravector gas heater	15.9.93	nil		√
Wonderfire 16 gas fire and Spanish grate delivered 11.3.92 –demo	—	nil		√
Weber wok	11.12.93	nil		√
Weber roast holder	11.12.93	nil		√

Also reviewed obsolete/slowmoving items identified at stock take – all shown at £nil.

Results

Adequate provision has been made for obsolete and slow moving stock.

BRIGHT-A-LIGHT LIMITED

STOCK VALUATION REPORT

31 MARCH 1995

CODE	DESCRIPTION	QUANTITY	UNIT COST	VALUE
10 KG	HOUSECOAL GROUP B	51	0.93	47.43
10 KG	HOUSECOAL GROUP C	106	0.89	94.34
10 KG	COALITE	366γ	1.52	556.32 <
20 KG	HOUSECOAL GROUP C	87	1.77	153.99
20 KG	COALITE	83	3.01	249.83
25 KG	HOUSECOAL GROUP A	47	2.51	117.97
25 KG	HOUSECOAL GROUP B	39	2.31	90.09
25 KG	HOUSECOAL GROUP C	24	2.21	53.04
25 KG	COALITE	44	3.72	163.68
25 KG	HOMEFIRE	29	4.11	119.19
25 KG	WARMACITE	39	2.66	103.74
25 KG	ANTHRACITE BEANS	29	3.21	93.09
25 KG	ANTHRACITE GRAINS	18	2.89	52.02
25 KG	ANTHRACITE IMPORTED NUTS	31	3.39	105.09
25 KG	ANTHRACITE LARGE NUTS	95β	3.41	323.95
25 KG	ANCIT	22	3.73	82.06
25 KG	DRY STEAM LARGE NUTS	37γ	2.72	100.64 <
25 KG	DRY STEAM SMALL NUTS	33	2.99	98.67
25 KG	EXTRACITE	19	3.73	70.87
25 KG	FIREGLO	29	3.69	107.01
25 KG	MAXIBRITE	50	2.89	144.50
25 KG	SUNBRITE	1	3.31	3.31
BATER	HOUSECOAL GROUP B	61	2.31	140.91
BATER	COALITE	32	3.72	119.04
BATER	EXTRACITE	25	3.65	91.25
BATER	FIREGLO	34	3.62	123.08
BATER	MAXIBRITE	17	3.41	57.97
BATER	PHURNACITE	1	3.11	3.11
BATER	UNION BRIKETTE	14	1.95	27.30
BATER	WARMACITE	12	2.59	31.08
	GATE 3 SOLID FUEL	TOTAL		£3,524.57 ✓
				v
	CHOPPED WOOD	2,030	0.25	507.50
	FIRELIGHTERS 24'S	37	3.83	141.71
	LOGS (BAG)	413	0.82	338.66
10 KG	PEAT BLOCKS	105	1.30	136.50
	COMET BLOCKS	44	0.50	22.00
24 KG	COSY COAL	26	2.35	61.10
	COSYHOME FIRE	1	0.00	0.00
	FIRELIGHTER	9	0.16	1.44
	FLUE FREE CHIMNEY CLEANER	16	0.00	0.00
	GATE 4 SOLID FUEL			£1,208.91
				v
	SHELLGAS LOAN STOCK	988	0.00	0.00
	SHELLGAS HIRECHARGE	740	3.63	2,678.80

BRIGHT-A-LIGHT LIMITED

STOCK VALUATION REPORT
31 MARCH 1995

CODE	DESCRIPTION	QUANTITY	UNIT COST	VALUE
	SHELLGAS RESERVE	739	0.00	0.00
	MISCELLANEOUS CYLINDERS	106	0.00	0.00
	GATE 5 GAS CYLINDERS			£2,678.80√
				v
5.5 KG	SHELLGAS REFILL	16	5.36	85.76
15 KG	SHELLGAS REFILL	204β	9.00	1,836.00
4.7 KG	SHELLGAS REFILL	35	4.62	161.70
11 KG	SHELLGAS REFILL	12	6.58	78.96
18.5 KG	SHELLGAS REFILL	41γ	10.64	436.24 <
46 KG	SHELLGAS REFILL	46γ	19.50	897.00 <
18 KG	SHELLGAS REFILL	9	10.15	91.35
4.7 KG	CONTRACTED	4	4.62	18.48
11 KG	CONTRACTED	3	6.58	19.74
18 KG	CONTRACTED	1	10.15	10.15
	GATE 6 PACKED SHELLGAS			£3,635.38√
				v
901	CAMPING GAS REFILL	7	1.67	11.69
904	CAMPING GAS REFILL	3	3.98	11.94
907	CAMPING GAS REFILL	11	1.46	16.06
	CAMPING GAS CYLINDER	29	10.41	301.89
2000	PRIMUS REFILL	16	1.33	21.28
2005	PRIMUS REFILL	1	2.54	2.54
2012	PRIMUS REFILL	2	3.97	7.94
	PRIMUS CYLINDER	57	7.16	408.12
200	GIMEG GAS CARTRIDGE	540γ	0.44	237.60 <
200	MISC GAS CARTRIDGE	26	0.00	0.00
200	PRIMUS GAS CARTRIDGE	43	0.49	21.07
2201	PRIMUS GAS CARTRIDGE	55	0.89	48.95
40/60	PRIMUS GAS CARTRIDGE	2	0.98	1.96
	LIGHTER CARTRIDGE	2	0.79	1.58
	GATE 7 PACKED GAS MISC			£1,092.62√
				v
F120	SUPER SERIES F120	1	40.50	40.50
	GATE 8 GAS HEATERS			£40.50√
				v
BOILER	VALIANT WATER HEATER	1	96.96	96.96
	AUTOSELECT 125 HOT AIR UNIT	3	73.33	219.99
	AUTOSELECT 300 HOT AIR UNIT	2	82.50	165.00
MAJOR	JETAIRE HOT AIR UNIT	2	50.00	100.00
MINOR	JETAIRE HOT AIR UNIT	1	75.00	75.00
	INFRAVECTOR GAS HEATER	1	0.00	0.00

BRIGHT-A-LIGHT LIMITED

STOCK VALUATION REPORT
31 MARCH 1995

CODE	DESCRIPTION	QUANTITY	UNIT COST	VALUE
	WONDER AIR FLAME	1	0.00	0.00
	WONDERFIRE 16″ GAS FIRE	1	0.00	0.00
	WONDERFIRE SPANISH GRATE	1	0.00	0.00
	GATE 9 GAS APPLIANCES			656.95✓
				v
	PRIMUS CROFTER T/SET	7	11.52	80.64
	PRIMUS DIY–MAN T/SET	4	11.08	44.32
	CYCLONE 2000 T/SET	1	0.00	0.00
	HANDLE 3466 (SIEVERMATIC)	1	15.88	15.88
	BURNER 3533 (SIEVERMATIC)	2	7.61	15.22
	BURNER 3534 (SIEVERMATIC)	2	7.61	15.22
	BURNER 3535 (SIEVERMATIC)	1	7.61	7.61
	BURNER 2940	2	4.50	9.00
	BURNER 2941	2	3.93	7.86
	BURNER 2942	5	3.68	18.40
	BURNER 2943	5	3.68	18.40
	BURNER 2944	1	4.85	4.85
	BURNER 2954	1	5.81	5.81
	ADJUST REG 3065	1	8.40	8.40
	VALVE 3084	4	6.63	26.52
3485	HANDLE	3	7.74	23.22
3487	HANDLE	2	13.18	26.36
350 mm	NECK TUBE	1	6.45	6.45
3511	NECK TUBE (SHORT)	5	3.40	17.00
3517	BURNER	1	8.11	8.11
3523	BURNER	1	5.95	5.95
3524	BURNER	1	6.91	6.91
3537	BURNER	3	5.50	16.50
3546	BURNER	1	0.00	0.00
3757	FURNACE	2	0.00	0.00
3938	BURNER	1	3.48	3.48
3939	BURNER	1	3.65	3.65
3941	BURNER	2	3.48	6.96
7015	HOSE 2m	6	5.60	33.60
2172	PRIMUS LANTERN	1	9.32	9.32
2269	PRIMUS LANTERN	3	11.48	34.44
2281	PRIMUS CAMPING STOVE	1	7.94	7.94
2289	PRIMUS LANTERN	12	12.74	152.88
2328	PRIMUS CAMPING HEATER	3	5.37	16.11
7157	PRIMUS GAS MATCH	2	3.94	7.88
	STANDARD GLOBE	19	0.97	18.43
	PRIMUS SERIES 8000 FITTING	11	1.55	17.05
	BULLFINCH TORCH SYSTEM	1	25.00	25.00
	BULLFINCH TORCH SET	2	14.70	29.40
	GATE 10 VARIOUS GAS PARTS			£754.77✓
				v

BRIGHT-A-LIGHT LIMITED

STOCK VALUATION REPORT
31 MARCH 1995

CODE	DESCRIPTION	QUANTITY	UNIT COST	VALUE
1000Btu	AUTOMATIC C/OVER	1	94.80	94.80
400Btu	AUTOMATIC C/OVER	1	31.29	31.29
2 PACK	AUTOMATIC C/OVER	2	25.10	50.20
4 PACK	AUTOMATIC C/OVER	8	37.65	301.20
	FNS/POL PIGTAIL	4	2.93	11.72
	MNS/POL PIGTAIL	1	2.25	2.25
	POL/POL PIGTAIL	6	3.10	18.60
	Y-PIECE	6	3.98	23.88
1/2″	BALL VALVE	7	3.08	21.56
3/8″	BALL VALVE	1	2.50	2.50
3/4″	BALL VALVE	2	4.20	8.40
	GAS HEATER FIREGUARD	5	8.71	43.55
	GAS FITTINGS	118	0.82	96.76
	GAS POKER	1	11.50	11.50
	2ND STAGE TANK UNIT	1	0.00	0.00
	GAS VALVE/REGULATOR	1	13.23	13.23
	GAS RACK	6	2.14	12.84
3/8	COPPER GAS TUBE	46	0.91	41.86
	GAS WHEELS	4	0.00	0.00
	ALPHA 2000 2-BURNER HOTPLATE	1	15.60	15.60
	GIMEG PIEZO TORCH	1	15.75	15.75
5 mm	HIGH PRESSURE LPG HOSE	8	0.65	5.20
8 mm	HIGH PRESSURE LPG HOSE	8	1.24	9.92
	LOW PRESSURE LPF HOSE	45	0.57	25.65
	VERITAS MANTLES NO. 3	241	0.00	0.00
21 mm	CALOR REGULATOR	35	1.85	64.75
27 mm	SHELL REGULATOR	19	2.80	53.20
	ADJUSTABLE 0–2 BAR REGULATOR	4	5.21	20.84
	CAMPING GAS REGULATOR	3	2.03	6.09
	REGULATOR/HODD CONTROLLER	17	0.00	0.00
	PROPANE 50–150Mb ADJ. REG.	3	3.29	9.87
	SITE HEATER	1	32.75	32.75
	CAMPING GAS TAP	5	0.28	1.40
	IN–LINE GAS TAP	2	1.26	2.52
	TAP ADAPTOR CAMPING GAS	2	0.00	0.00
	TAP ADAPTOR SHELL	5	1.20	6.00
	CALORTITE	8	1.11	8.88
	GAS TROLLEY 3–PLAQUE	1	0.00	0.00
25 mm	WAVIN GAS PIPE	100	0.61	61.00
	WAVIN PIPE FITTING	3	9.85	29.55
	CAMPING GAS BELVEDERE GLOBE	39	0.00	0.00
	CAMPING GAS B300 FINE BURNER	1	5.30	5.30
	CAMPING GAS B300 TURBO BURNER	1	5.80	5.80
	GAS MANTLE SINGLE	67	0.24	16.08
	GAS FLOODLIGHT	1	0.00	0.00
	HEATER SPARES	116	1.18	136.88
	JUBILEE CLIPS	115	0.00	0.00
	GATE 11 MISC GAS EQUIP			£1,319.17√

v

BRIGHT-A-LIGHT LIMITED

STOCK VALUATION REPORT
31 MARCH 1995

CODE	DESCRIPTION	QUANTITY	UNIT COST	VALUE
6 × 3 KG	OUTER LUMPWOOD CHARCOAL	245γ	5.28	1,293.60 <
4 × 5 KG	OUTER LUMPWOOD CHARCOAL	84	5.68	477.12
6 × 3 KG	OUTER BRIKETTE CHARCOAL	124	5.29	655.96
4 × 5 KG	OUTER BRIKETTE CHARCOAL	55	5.68	312.40
3 KG	LUMPWOOD CHARCOAL	191	0.88	168.08
5 KG	LUMPWOOD CHARCOAL	132	1.44	190.08
10 KG	LUMPWOOD CHARCOAL	637γ	2.78	1,770.86 <
3 KG	BRIKETTE CHARCOAL	1	0.98	0.98
5 KG	BRIKETTE CHARCOAL	347	1.80	624.60
10 KG	BRIKETTE CHARCOAL	266	2.62	696.92
12 KG	CATERING CHARCOAL	187	3.36	628.32
	GATE 12 CHARCOAL			£6,818.92 ✓
				v
	CHAMP GAS	2	6.25	12.50
	THERMOS PORTABLE	33γ	17.73	585.09 <
WG47	THERMOS GAS	2	134.49	268.98
WG87	THERMOS GAS	1	0.00	0.00
	BISTRO	1	0.00	0.00
	BOLERO	1	16.25	16.25
	CANADIAN	1	0.00	0.00
	CAST IRON	1	0.00	0.00
	HAPPY COOKER	1	54.74	54.74
	HIBACHI DOUBLE	152	2.55	387.60
	HIBACHI TREBLE	11	5.15	56.65
	SMALL KETTLE	5	17.42	87.10
	ROUND	1	0.00	0.00
	GATE 13 BARBECUES			£1,468.91
				v
	CASE (12) LIGHTER FLUID 1L	84γ	5.04	423.36
	CASE (24) BBQ LIGHTER BLOCKS	31	5.04	156.24
	SINGLE LIGHTER FLUID 1 LTR	22	0.42	9.24
	SINGLE BBQ BLOCKS	14	0.22	3.08
	BELLOWS	3	0.00	0.00
	COOKBOOK – SUNSET	68	0.00	0.00
	BOOKS VARIOUS	8	0.00	0.00
CANDLES	TULIP	23	0.00	0.00
CANDLES	TERRACOTTA DISH	5	0.00	0.00
CANDLES	FLOWER POT	7	0.00	0.00
CANDLES	FLARES	9	0.00	0.00
	CHARLITE TUBES	33	0.00	0.00
	CHARCOAL CHEST	2	0.00	0.00
	DORSET LANTERN	6	1.33	7.98
	GAS FIRELANCE	3	0.00	0.00
	HICKORY CHIPS	10	0.00	0.00
	LAVA ROCK	10	3.88	38.80

BRIGHT-A-LIGHT LIMITED

STOCK VALUATION REPORT
31 MARCH 1995

CODE	DESCRIPTION	QUANTITY	UNIT COST	VALUE
	KETTLE STARTER SET	9	0.00	0.00
	THERMOS BBQ COVER	2	0.00	0.00
	VINEWOOD	5	0.00	0.00
	GRILL BRUSH	16	0.80	12.80
	BATTERY MOTOR	7	0.43	3.01
	BASTING BRUSH	9	0.30	2.70
	7 IN 2 TOOL SET	6	4.86	29.16
	HAMBURGER MOLD	2	0.00	0.00
	GATE 14 BARBECUE ACCESSORIES			£686.37√
				v
	POTATOES 25 KG	12	2.50	30.00
	CAMPING GAS INSTALUX TORCH	2	0.00	0.00
	DORSET PEBBLES	1	0.00	0.00
	PARTY TRAY PACK	14	0.00	0.00
	POTATOES 25 KG	1	2.10	2.10
	MIXED CORN	7	5.27	36.89
	LAYERS MEAL	2	6.84	13.68
	SUPERBEET SHREDS/PELLETS	10	5.30	53.00
STAMPS	1ST CLASS × 4 PACK	91	0.76	69.16
STAMPS	1ST CLASS × 10 PACK	51	2.09	106.59
STAMPS	2ND CLASS × 10 PACK	50	1.62	81.00
	CASE (6) DISINFECTANT 4 LTR	1	4.50	4.50
	DETERGENT 4 LTR	3	0.75	2.25
	PVC TAPE 50 mm	16	0.73	11.68
19 mm	MASKING TAPE	20	0.38	7.60
25 mm	MASKING TAPE	4	0.40	1.60
	DISINFECTANT 4 LTR	6	0.75	4.50
	SPIRITS OF SALT 4 LTR	12	0.00	0.00
	DRIPTRAY × 10	40	0.00	0.00
	FREEZER BAGS	76	0.08	6.08
	HOSE TROLLEY	1	0.00	0.00
	MATCHES × 10	4	4.00	16.00
	MATCHES SINGLE	12	0.04	0.48
	LITTLE PLAYMATE COOLER	1	0.00	0.00
	ROCK SALT × 25 KG	90	0.00	0.00
	SANIPOTTI PORTABLE LOO	1	0.00	0.00
	THERMOS COFFEE BUTLER	17	6.87	116.79
	THERMOS BOTTLE COOLER	2	3.28	6.56
	THERMOS FLASKS	3	2.38	7.14
	THERMOS ICE BUCKET	8	3.28	26.24
	THERMOS ROUGHNECK FLASKS	17	2.56	43.52
LARGE	WALL TRAY	24	0.00	0.00
SMALL	WALL TRAY	30	0.00	0.00
WEBER	CHARCOAL RAILS	3	0.00	0.00
WEBER	COVER	5	0.00	0.00
WEBER	GRIDDLE	2	0.00	0.00
WEBER	RIB RACK	4	0.00	0.00

BRIGHT-A-LIGHT LIMITED

STOCK VALUATION REPORT
31 MARCH 1995

CODE	DESCRIPTION	QUANTITY	UNIT COST	VALUE
WEBER	ROAST HOLDER	2	0.00	0.00
WEBER	WOK	2	0.00	0.00
	GATE 15 MISC			£647.36√
				ν
CASE	PARAFFIN 4 LTR × 4	21	5.68	119.28
CASE	WHITE SPIRIT 2 LTR × 10	75	5.95	446.25
CASE	WHITE SPIRIT 1 LTR × 12	21	5.28	110.88
CASE	WHITE SPIRIT 750 ml × 12	6	4.32	25.92
CASE	METHYL SPIRIT 2 LTR × 10	2	13.30	26.60
CASE	METHYL SPIRIT 750 ml × 12	4	7.44	29.76
CASE	METHYL SPIRIT 250 ml × 24	3	7.92	23.76
CASE	BOILED LINSEED 500 ml × 12	2	10.08	20.16
CASE	BRUSH CLEANER 500 ml × 12	2	5.64	11.28
CASE	GOLDEN CREOSOTE 4 LTR × 4	1	5.96	5.96
CASE	DARK CREOSOTE 4 LTR × 4	1	5.96	5.96
CASE	TURPENTINE 500 ml × 12	1	8.28	8.28
CASE	TURPENTINE 750 ml × 12	2	11.64	23.28
CASE	LAMP OIL 1 LTR × 12	2	6.00	12.00
CASE	RAW LINSEED 500 ml × 12	2	9.60	14.40
4 LTR	PARAFFIN	4	1.29	5.16
750 ml	WHITE SPIRIT	3	0.32	0.96
1 LTR	WHITE SPIRIT	33	0.44	14.52
2 LTR	WHITE SPIRIT	9	0.60	5.40
750 ml	METHYL SPIRIT	4	0.49	1.96
4 LTR	DARK CREOSOTE	1	0.00	0.00
1 LTR	LAMP OIL	22	0.50	11.00
	GATE 16 SOLVENTS & KEROSENE			£922.77√
				ν
	DERV	105	3.49	366.45
	GASOIL	100	1.81	181.00
	GATE 17 DIESEL			£547.45√
				ν

ν = extensions checked (qty & cost)
√ = additions checked
< = costs checked, I5.1
γ = existence confirmed at stocktake, I4.2 & I4.3
β = tested on I5.2

J DEBTORS AND PREPAYMENTS

1	Lead schedule	✓
2	Audit programme	✓
3	List of debtor balances — credit balances	✓
4	Bad and doubtful debts	✓
5	Prepayments	
6	Results of confirmation	
7	Certificates/confirmation replies	
8	Cut off tests	✓
9		
10		

Client: Bright-a-Light		Prepared by: KM	Date: 16.6.95	Ref: **J**
Year/Period End: 31.3.95	File No:	Reviewed by: EAA	Date: 19.6.95	

SUMMARY SHEET – DEBTORS AND PREPAYMENTS

Audit objectives	***Planning*** Number of tests which satisfy objective	Additional/ alternative tests to be carried out	***Final*** Are you satisfied that the objectives have been met?	Comments	Initials
1 To ensure that debtors are due at the value recorded.	1, 2, ~~3,~~ 4, 5, 6, 7, ~~8, 9, 10,~~ 11, 12, 22, 23	24	Yes/~~No~~		EAA
2 To ensure that adequate provision has been made for all bad and doubtful debts.	1, 2, ~~3,~~ 4, 18, 16, 17, 22, 23		Yes/~~No~~	If additional Provision made	EAA
3 To ensure that all debts are adequately supported and properly disclosed.	1, 2, ~~3,~~ 4, 5, ~~10,~~ 12, 22, 23	24	Yes/~~No~~		EAA
4 To ensure that proper cut-off has been made.	1, 2, ~~3,~~ 4, 13, 14, ~~15,~~ 23		Yes/~~No~~		EAA
5 To ensure that prepayments and loan debtors (including staff and directors) are properly classified, verified and disclosed.	1, 2, ~~3,~~ 4, 19, 20, 21, 23		Yes/~~No~~		EAA
6 To ensure that income is not over recorded.	1, 2, ~~3,~~ 4, 5, 6, 7, ~~8, 9, 10,~~ 11, 12, 13, 14, ~~15,~~ 16, 17, 18, 23	24	Yes/~~No~~		EAA

Conclusion

From the audit work carried out I confirm that:

- nothing has occurred to necessitate changing the audit plan* ~~or the audit plan has been updated*~~
- nothing has occurred to necessitate revising the risk assessment* ~~or the risk assessment has been revised.~~*
- nothing has occurred to necessitate revising the materiality level* ~~or the materiality has been revised.~~*
- ~~adjustments to the plan, risk assessment and materiality have been detailed on **B5** or **B8**.*~~
- the work has been performed in accordance with the audit programme.
- the work performed and the results obtained have been adequately documented.
- all necessary information has been collected for the preparation of the statutory accounts.
- in my opinion (subject to the matters highlighted on **B5** ~~or **B8**~~)* debtors and prepayments are fairly stated.

Prepared by EAA Date 19.6.95

Reviewed by DGW Date 3.7.95

*Delete if not applicable.

***Alternative conclusion** (ANY alternative conclusion MUST be referred to on **B5** or **B8**)*

Prepared by ______ Date ______

Reviewed by ______ Date ______

Client: Bright-a-Light Ltd	File No.	Ref. J1
Subject: Debtors	Prepared by KM	Date 16/6/95
	Reviewed by EAA	Date 19/6/95
	Accounting Dates 31·3·95	

				1995 £	*1994* £
Trade debtors					
per sales ledger listing			W13.1	128,398	
less provision			J4.2	(2,501)	
add credit balances	L1		J3	1,218	
				127,115	73,196β
Other debtors – VAT			U1	4,773	940β
Prepayments					
Advertising 11/12 × £1,242		1,138			
Computer		439			
				1,577√	1,036β
				£133,465	£75,172
					β

Audit key

ν Casts checked.
√ Prepayments agreed to invoices during accountancy work.
β Agreed to 1994 financial statements.

See above references for detailed work.

Fluctuations

Trade debtors have risen from £73,196 to £128,398 (before any provision for bad debts). This increase is higher than might be anticipated in relation to the increased turnover. The client appears to be having problems collecting debts, and an extensive review of potential bad debts was performed (see J4.2).

Total – as above	133,465
Adjustment for additional provision (B7)	(5,923)
Per final accounts.	£127,542
Revised trade debtors 127,115 − 5,923 =	£121,192

Client: Bright-a-Light Ltd		Prepared by: KM	Date: 16.6.95	Ref: **J2**
Year/Period End: 31.3.95	File No:	Reviewed by: EAA	Date: 19.6.95	

AUDIT PROGRAMME – DEBTORS AND PREPAYMENTS

Nature of test:	Test required Y/N	Covered by accountancy Y	Results satisfactory Y/N	Ref/ comments	Initials and date
General					
1 (a) Agree opening balances to last year's accounts.	Y		Y	J1	KM 16.6.95
(b) Obtain and check, or prepare, a lead schedule for the current year's figures.	Y		Y	J1	KM 16.6.95
(c) Enquire into and make notes of reasons for any major variations from expectations.	Y		Y	J1	KM 16.6.95
2 Assess whether the initial materiality and/or risk assessment should be revised in view of the audit evidence obtained to date.	Y		Y	No revision needed	KM 16.6.95
3 Undertake detailed analytical review procedures and determine whether the results enable us to reduce our sample size.	N		—	—	EAA 8.6.95
4 Review for large and unusual items and verify.	Y		Y	None	KM 16.6.95
Trade debtors					
5 Obtain ~~or prepare an aged~~ list of balances. ~~Check a sample to the underlying records and vice versa. Ensure that the ageing on the items selected has been correctly applied.~~	Y		Y	J1	KM 16.6.95
6 Test the casts. EAA 8.6.95	Y		Y	Casts agreed	KM 16.6.95
7 Agree the list of balances to the control account. Obtain explanations for all material adjustments to the control account.	Y	Y	Y	W13.1	KM 16.6.95

Client: Bright-a-Light Ltd		Prepared by: KM	Date: 16.6.95	Ref: **J2**
Year/Period End: 31.3.95	File No:	Reviewed by: EAA	Date: 19.6.95	

AUDIT PROGRAMME – DEBTORS AND PREPAYMENTS (*cont.*)

	Test required Y/N	Covered by accountancy Y	Results satisfactory Y/N	Ref/ comments	Initials and date
8 Perform a debtors circularisation.					
(a) Select a sample of accounts for confirmation from a complete list of balances (include nil and credit balances where applicable). Record the details on the standard working paper.	N				
(b) Confirm with client the debtors you wish to circularise. Obtain explanations where they do not want you to circularise.	N				
(c) Send the confirmation requests. Enclose a prepaid envelope for return to the firm. Ensure the reply part of the letter is properly referenced.	N				
(d) Record replies on the control sheet.	N				
(e) Where replies are not received within a reasonable period send a follow-up letter.	N		See		
(f) Follow the alternative procedures for any unfavourable responses or where no response obtained.	N		test 24		EAA 8.6.95
(g) Summarise the results and consider whether adequate audit comfort has been obtained for trade debtors.	N				
9 Where circularisation has not been carried out or unsatisfactory results obtained carry out alternative procedures.	N				
(a) Examine the ledger for cash after date.					
(b) For unpaid items inspect the sales invoice supporting them.	N				
(c) Review correspondence files for items in (b) to determine whether any disputes exist.	N				
10 For each account selected in steps 8 or 9:					
(a) ensure that it is made up of specific items; investigate any payments on account;	N				
(b) verify all contra entries;	N				
(c) ensure that discounts and allowances are in accordance with company policy;	N				
(d) check casts.	N				

Client: Bright-a-Light Ltd		Prepared by: KM	Date: 16.6.95	Ref: **J2**
Year/Period End: 31.3.95	File No:	Reviewed by: EAA	Date: 19.6.95	

AUDIT PROGRAMME – DEBTORS AND PREPAYMENTS (*cont.*)

	Test required Y/N	Covered by accountancy Y	Results satisfactory Y/N	Ref/ comments	Initials and date
11 List all credit balances over £— and obtain explanations. for any major items	Y		Y	J3	KM 16.6.95
12 Ensure that any factored debts have been accounted for in accordance with FRS 5.	Y		Y	None	KM 16.6.95
Cut-off					
13 Review credit notes after the year end and consider whether these have been accounted for in the correct period.	Y		Y	Two C/NS raised after YE. Both relate to 95/96	KM 16.6.95
14 If the company has despatch records, examine sales and despatch records before and after the year end and ensure that: (a) all goods despatched before the year end are excluded from stock and included in sales and debtors where appropriate;	Y		Y	J8	KM 16.6.95
(b) all goods despatched after the year end are included in stock and excluded from sales and debtors, where appropriate. (Refer to stock attendance notes.)	Y		Y	J8	KM 16.6.95
15 If the company does not have despatch records, specify below the audit work to ensure that cut-off has been correctly applied:	N		—		EAA 8.6.95
Bad and doubtful debts					
16 Review ledger accounts and obtain a list of any debts with balances not paid at date of report obtained in test 24 ~~(a) not paid within months of the period end; (b) in excess of their credit limit; (c) in the hands of liquidators or receivers; (d) in the hands of solicitors for collection.~~	Y		N	J4.2 Debtors overstated by £5923. On B7 unadjusted errors	EAA 19.6.95
17 Compare the client's provision with the list completed under 16 above and consider its adequacy. Obtain explanations for any material accounts omitted from the client's list.	Y		N	J4.2	EAA 19.6.95

Client: Bright-a-Light Ltd		Prepared by: KM	Date: 16.6.95	Ref: **J2**
Year/Period End: 31.3.95	File No:	Reviewed by: EAA	Date: 19.6.95	

AUDIT PROGRAMME – DEBTORS AND PREPAYMENTS (*cont.*)

	Test required Y/N	Covered by accountancy Y	Results satisfactory Y/N	Ref/ comments	Initials and date
18 Examine debts written off during the year and ensure that they were authorised and the write off was valid.	Y		Y	None	KM 16.6.95
Prepayments					
19 Obtain or prepare a list of items included as prepayments. (a) Vouch all items over £ by reference to the cash book and invoices.	Y	Y	Y	J1	KM 16.6.95
(b) Compare the list in detail to last year's and enquire into any major differences.	Y		Y	None	KM 16.6.95
(c) Review the cash book, nominal ledger and profit and loss account to ensure all likely prepayments are included.	Y	Y	Y	—	KM 16.6.95
Other debtors					
20 Obtain or prepare a list of other debtors. (a) Vouch material items to supporting documentation.	Y	Y	Y	None	KM 16.6.95
(b) Compare with previous year's and enquire into major differences.	Y		Y	None	KM 16.6.95
(c) Obtain confirmation of all staff loans, and ensure that: – repayment instalments are being received; – repayments are being made in accordance with the agreement.	Y		Y	None	KM 16.6.95
Loans					
21 Ensure that no loans have been made to directors unless within the provisions of the Companies Act 1985. (*NB* where loans exist, either debit or credit, calculate the balance at the end of each month. The highest amount due to the company should be disclosed in the accounts.)	Y		Y	None	KM 16.6.95

Client: Bright-a-Light Ltd		Prepared by: KM	Date: 16.6.95	Ref: **J2**
Year/Period End: 31.3.95	File No:	Reviewed by: EAA	Date: 19.6.95	

AUDIT PROGRAMME – DEBTORS AND PREPAYMENTS (*cont.*)

	Test required Y/N	Covered by accountancy Y	Results satisfactory Y/N	Ref/ comments	Initials and date
Long-term debts/retentions 22 Where a debt, or portion thereof is recoverable after more than one year, consider: (a) whether any provision is necessary; (b) whether adequate disclosure has been made.	Y		Y	None	KM 16.6.95
Conclusion 23 Consider whether there are any items which need to be included in a letter of representation or letter of comment and record on **A5** or **A6**, as appropriate.	Y		Y	Possibly need for more Provision	EAA 19.6.95
24 Other tests:	Y		Y	J4.1 & J4.2	KM 16.6.95

(a) Ask for an aged sales ledger listing to be produced as at the date of the test having first ensured that all cash received has been posted and allocated.

(b) Select a sample of accounts as at the year end and check to see what cash has been received, relating to the year end balance.

(c) Compare the calculated outstanding year end balance to that on the report obtained in (a) above

(d) Check that no debtors have been written off since the year end.

Client	File No.	Ref.
Bright-a-Light Ltd		J3

Subject	Prepared by	Date
Credit balances on sales ledger	KM	16/6/95
	Reviewed by EAA	Date 19/6/95
	Accounting Dates	31·3·95

No	Name	Balance £	
AS0171	Mr J Ashby	52.00	
CL0678	Mr Clare	2.00	β
EW1079	J R Ewing	15.00	
MA0639	Mr Martin	9.60	
MC0739	Mrs McArthur	9.75	
MO0722	Mount School	50.00	
MU0337	Mr Munter	6.00	
NI0213	Nicholas Garage	98.56	
PA1181	Mr A Paris	3.80	
PI0910	Pipers	5.35	
PI0718	Mr Piggot	2.00	
PR0093	Puddletown Supermarket	139.60	
RO0083	Mrs S Rogers	88.00	
SI0966	Mr & Mrs Simmonds	63.42	β
ST0047	Standard Service Station	4.15	
ST0868	Mr Stephens	32.00	β
SUS	Suspense	368.92	γ
UN0065	Mr T Underhill	268.04	β
		£1,218.19	
		ν	

ν Casts checked.

β Budget accounts – expected to be in credit occasionally because people pay a set monthly rate and order coal when necessary. Usually have to pay for one or two months before coal or gas is delivered.

γ Suspense = unallocated cash, when cheques received from people that can not be identified on the ledger.

Conclusion

Credit balances on S/L adjusted, as post TB journal. Debtors fairly stated.

Client		File No.	Ref.
Bright-a-Light Ltd			J4.1
Subject	Prepared by KM		Date 16/6/95
Trade debtors – Outstanding balances at 16 June 95	Reviewed by EAA		Date 19/6/95
	Accounting Dates	31·3·95	

An aged debtors listing was obtained as at 16 June 1995, with the 'current' period being set to 1 June–16 June. The ledger totals were:

No. of accounts	*Balance*	*Current (1 June–16 June)*	*>30 (May)*	*>60 (April)*	*>90 (March)*	*>120 (Feb & earlier)*
	£	£	£	£	£	£
326	114,326.71	36,074.24	58,439.15	11,248.73	972.72	7,591.87
					£8,564.59	

$$\text{sample size} = \frac{£128{,}398}{£15{,}000} \times 1.8 = 15.4 \text{ say } 16$$

A sample of 16 balances was selected from the year end debtors listing and the accounts reviewed for cash received after the year end. The amount outstanding as at 16 June 95 was calculated and compared with the amount outstanding in the >90 day and >120 day columns (March and earlier). The sample started on the 3rd account and every 21st was selected.

Account No.	*Name*	*Balance at year end*	*Cash received*	*Calculated outstanding balance*	*March and earlier bal. per report*	*Report dated 16 June 95 agreed*
		£	£	£	£	£
AB1732	Abbot Oil	1,421.76	1,421.76	NIL	NIL	√
BI2439	Binns Motors	78.42	78.42	NIL	NIL	√
DA7117	Daytime Heating	143.61	143.61	NIL	NIL	√
DU0329	Dudley Garages Ltd	2,139.62	2,139.62	NIL	NIL	√
GE1521	George C.L.	62.41	62.41	NIL	NIL	√
HI1202	Highfield Motors	921.18	921.18	NIL	NIL	√
JA3202	Jacobs Garages	123.47	123.47	NIL	NIL	√
KI3204	Kirkwood Service Station	187.41	187.41	NIL	NIL	√
LA4209	Lamont Stores	246.88	246.88	NIL	NIL	√
LI7132	Lizzards	1,026.60	1,026.60	NIL	NIL	√
MO8715	Morris P.A.	180.00	40.00	140.00	140.00	√
RA2169	Rayleigh Heating	1,732.21	1,732.21	NIL	NIL	√
RO2245	Roche Shoe Shop	714.75	—	714.75	714.75	√
SA3396	Sanders Oil and Gas	93.70	93.70	NIL	NIL	√
VA1179	Valley Garages	148.52	148.52	NIL	NIL	√
WI1892	Willson Motors	1,593.45	1,593.45	NIL	NIL	√

All cash received after the year end on the accounts selected was verified to the remittance advice and was checked as correctly posted to the sales ledger. The ageing of the report dated 16 June 95 was agreed in respect of these balances. The report dated 16 June 95 can therefore be accepted as an accurate record of the year end debtors still unpaid as at 16 June 95. This age analysis can therefore be used to determine whether the provision for bad debts is adequate. See J4.2.

Client Bright-a-Light Ltd	File No.	Ref. J4.2	
Subject Testing of bad debt provision	Prepared by KM		Date 16/6/95
	Reviewed by EAA		Date 19/6/95
	Accounting Dates	31·3·95	

Audit work

The aged debtors listing at 16.6.95 was used to identify debtors at 31.3.95 that have not yet paid. The accuracy of this report was tested when reviewing post year end receipts J4.1. Each balance was then discussed with the client to see whether or not any provision was necessary (NB client had not made any provisions to date against any of the balances at 31.3.95).

A/C No	*Name*	*Balance unpaid* £	*Reason*	*Provision needed* £
BA0837	Mr & Mrs F Barber	257.97	Unable to trace them	257.97
CR1157	Mr Creeper	461.48	In court, client feels that it is recoverable	461.48
FI0101	Fitroys	394.32	" " " " " " "	394.32
MO8715	Morris	140.00	Is paying £20 p.w.	—
JA0103	J Austins Distributor	5,923.43	See below	—
SP0375	AJ Spratts	295.89	Has gone bust	295.89
VA1179	Valley Garage	143.75	Unlikely to pay	143.75
SA0893	Saveheat Insulation	100.00	Will not pay	100.00
RO2245	Roche Shoe Shop	714.75	In liquidation	714.75
CO2843	Connollys Garage	133.00	In court, outcome uncertain	133.00
		£8,564.59		£2,501.16

Results

Client has agreed to make provision of £2,501.16. However, Mr Strike feels that the debt of £5,923.43 with J Austins Distributors is collectable as it is owed by his brother-in-law. However, it seems that his brother-in-law is having severe cash flow problems.

Conclusion

An additional provision appears to be required in respect of the sales ledger balance relating to J Austins Distributor. Recorded on schedule of unadjusted errors B7 and on audit highlights, B5.

Client		File No.	Ref.
Bright-a-Light Ltd			J8
Subject		Prepared by	Date
Cut off – Debtors – test 14		KM	16/6/95
		Reviewed by	Date
		EAA	19/6/95
		Accounting Dates	31·3·95

Work done

16 goods despatch notes (8 just before the year end and 8 after) were selected from the GDN file in the warehouse for one month either side of the year end.

$$\frac{858\text{K (turnover)}}{15\text{K (materiality)}} \times \underset{\substack{\text{medium}\\ \text{P \& L}}}{1.8} \times \frac{1}{2} \times \frac{2}{12} = 8.5 \quad \therefore \text{selected 8 each way}$$

The following tests were carried out:
(a) Trace to sales and debtors (if before year end).
(b) Ensure item is not in stock (if before year end) per stock ageing.
(c) Ensure no sale or debtor (if after year end).
(d) Ensure item is in stock (if after year end) per stock ageing.

Results

Date	*GDN No*	*Stock details*	*Customer*	*Invoice date*	*In debtors*	*In stock*
(a) before year end						
27.3.95	3347	5 × 25 kg Warmacite	Mr Stackhouse	27.3.95	✓	NO
27.3.95	3350	5 × 20 kg Coalite	Mr McPherson	27.3.95	✓	NO
28.3.95	3359	20 × 25 kg Fireglo	Freds Coals	28.3.95	✓	NO
28.3.95	3361	2 × 46 kg Shellgas	Mr P Newman	28.3.95	✓	NO
29.3.95	3363	2 × 46 kg Shellgas	Mr I Rush	30.3.95	✓	NO
30.3.95	3370	5 × Maxibrite 25 kg	Mr T Edwards	30.3.95	✓	NO
31.3.95	3379	4 × Shellgas 18.5 kg	Mr Barber	31.3.95	✓	NO
31.3.95	3381	5 × 25 kg Anthracite beans	ABC Solid Fuel	31.3.95	✓	NO
(b) after year end						
1.4.95	3382	Valiant water heater	New Hotel	3.4.95	NO	✓
1.4.95	3383	2 × Jetaire units (major)	New Hotel	3.4.95	NO	✓
3.4.95	3386	105 × 10 kg peat	Bow Garage	3.4.95	NO	✓
3.4.95	3392	200 × 10 kg Coalite	Edwards Garage	3.4.95	NO	✓
3.4.95	3393	Super F120 Gas Heater	Mr Jordan	3.4.95	NO	✓
4.4.95	3394	1 × Primus 2005 Refill	Mr Smith	4.4.95	NO	✓
4.4.95	3399	1 × 1000Btu Automatic	DEF Plumbing	4.4.95	NO	✓
4.4.95	3403	4 × Shellgas 46 kg	Mr C Allen	4.4.95	NO	✓

Conclusion

Cut off has been correctly applied.

K BANK BALANCES AND CASH

1 Lead schedule ✓

2 Audit programme ✓

3 Bank reconciliations ✓

4 Bank certificates ✓

5 Cash counts ☐

6 Bank account No. 2 ✓

7 Bank account No. 3 ✓

8 Bank vehicle loan ✓

Client: Bright-a-Light Ltd		Prepared by:	Date:	Ref: **K**
Year/Period End: 31.3.95	File No:	Reviewed by:	Date:	

SUMMARY SHEET – BANK BALANCES AND CASH

Audit objectives	***Planning*** Number of tests which satisfy objective	Additional/ alternative tests to be carried out	***Final*** Are you satisfied that the objectives have been met?	Comments	Initials
1 To establish that all bank balances and overdrafts have been included at the correct amount.	1, 2, ~~3,~~ 4, 5, 6, 7, 8, 9, 14		Yes/~~No~~		KM
2 To ensure that only genuine items are included in the reconciliations.	1, 2, ~~3,~~ 4, 6, 9, 14		Yes/~~No~~		KM
3 To ensure that cash balances are genuine and have been included at the correct amount.	1, 2, ~~3,~~ 4, 10, 11, ~~12,~~ ~~13,~~ 14		Yes/~~No~~	not material	KM
4 To ensure that cash sales are not overstated	1, 2, ~~3,~~ 4, 10, 11, 14		Yes/~~No~~	not material	KM

Conclusion

From the audit work carried out I confirm that:

- nothing has occurred to necessitate changing the audit plan* ~~or the audit plan has been updated~~*
- nothing has occurred to necessitate revising the risk assessment* ~~or the risk assessment has been revised.~~*
- nothing has occurred to necessitate revising the materiality level* ~~or the materiality has been revised~~.*
- ~~adjustments to the plan, risk assessment and materiality have been detailed on **B5** or **B8**~~.*
- the work has been performed in accordance with the audit programme.
- the work performed and the results obtained have been adequately documented.
- all necessary information has been collected for the preparation of the statutory accounts.
- in my opinion (~~subject to the matters highlighted on **B5** or **B8**~~)* bank balances and cash are fairly stated.

Prepared by KM Date 16.6.95

Reviewed by EAA Date 19.6.95

*Delete if not applicable.

Alternative conclusion (*ANY* alternative conclusion *MUST* be referred to on **B5** or **B8**)

Prepared by ______ Date ______

Reviewed by ______ Date ______

Client	File No.	Ref.
Bright-a-Light Ltd		K1

Subject	Prepared by	Date
Bank & cash	KM	16/6/95
	Reviewed by	Date
	EAA	19/6/95
	Accounting Dates	31·3·95

		Ref	*1995*	*1994*
			£	*£*
Cash in hand – cash held		W9	£ 461	£ 123
			ν	ν √
Bank loans & overdrafts				
Current Account	W1	K3.1	41,605	27,776
Business Development loan – No 2		K6	40,000	45,000
Business Development loan – No 3		K7	80,697	87,867
Vehicle loan		K8	2,827	4,542
			176,515	165,185
less: due after 1 year		K1.1	(109,000)	√ (123,524)
		L1	£56,129	£41,661
			ν	ν √

Key

ν Casts checked.
√ Agreed to 1994 financial statements.

Conclusion

Bank and cash balances are fairly stated.

Client	File No.	Ref.
Bright-a-Light Ltd		K1.1

Subject	Prepared by	Date
Bank & Cash – Amounts due in more than one year	KM	16/6/95
	Reviewed by EAA	Date 19/6/95
	Accounting Dates	31·3·95

				1995 £	*1994* £
Business development loans					
	0465212509	No 2	K6	35,000	40,000
	0465212510	No 3	K7	72,965	80,697
Vehicle loan	0465025517		K8	1,035	2,827
				£109,000	£123,524
				v	

v Casts checked.

The split between amounts due within one year and more than one year was calculated by us, and the appropriate figures put into the accounts.

Amounts due after five years – all instalments				*1995* £	*1994* £
BDL	0465212509	No 2	K6	15,000	20,000
	0465212510	No 3	K7	42,037	49,207
Vehicle loan	0465025517			—	—
				57,037	69,207

Amounts due 2–5 years – all instalments				
BDL	No 2	K6	15,000	15,000
	No 3	K7	23,196	23,758
Vehicle loan		K8	—	1,035
			38,196	39,793

Amounts due 1–2 years – all instalments				
BDL	No 2	K6	5,000	5,000
	No 3	K7	7,732	7,732
Vehicle loan		K8	1,035	1,792
			13,767	14,524
		Total	£109,000	£123,524
			K1	

Client: Bright-a-Light Ltd		Prepared by: KM	Date: 16.6.95	Ref: **K2**
Year/Period End: 31.3.95	File No:	Reviewed by: EAA	Date: 19.6.95	

AUDIT PROGRAMME – BANK BALANCES AND CASH

Nature of test:	Test required Y/N	Covered by accountancy Y	Results satisfactory Y/N	Ref/ comments	Initials and date
General					
1 (a) Agree opening balances to last year's accounts.	Y	Y	Y	K1	KM 16.6.95
(b) Obtain and check, or prepare, a lead schedule for the current year's figures.	Y	Y	Y	K1	KM 16.6.95
(c) Enquire into and make notes of reasons for any major variations from expectations.	Y		Y	None	KM 16.6.95
2 Assess whether the initial materiality and/or risk assessment should be revised in view of the audit evidence obtained to date.	Y		Y	No revision needed	KM 16.6.95
3 Undertake detailed analytical review procedures and determine whether the results enable us to reduce our sample size.	N		—		EAA 8.6.95
4 Review for large and unusual items and verify.	Y		Y	None	KM 16.6.95
5 Obtain bank letter for all bank accounts open at any time during the year.	Y		Y	K4	KM 16.6.95
6 Obtain or prepare bank reconciliations for all accounts and verify. (a) Check bank balances to bank statement and bank letter.	Y	Y	Y	K3.1	KM 16.6.95
(b) Check cash book balance to nominal ledger.	Y	Y	Y	K3.1	KM 16.6.95
(c) Check casting of the reconciliations.	Y	Y	Y	K3.1	KM 16.6.95
(d) Vouch a sample of transactions from the bank statements to cash book – ensure all items have been dealt with correctly. (*NB* use the sample selection planning – profit and loss form).	Y		Y	K3.3	KM 16.6.95
(e) Check uncleared items through to the new period (noting dates). Obtain reason where any item has taken longer than expected to clear.	Y		Y	K3.2	KM 16.6.95
(f) Obtain explanations and substantiate all adjustments on the bank reconciliations.	Y		Y	No adjustments	KM 16.6.95
(g) Ensure receipts have been accounted for in the correct period by reviewing the paying-in book before and after the period end and ensuring items have been treated correctly.	Y		Y		KM 16.6.95

Client: Bright-a-Light Ltd		Prepared by: KM	Date: 16.6.95	Ref: **K2**
Year/Period End: 31.3.95	File No:	Reviewed by: EAA	Date: 19.6.95	

AUDIT PROGRAMME – BANK BALANCES AND CASH (*cont.*)

	Test required Y/N	Covered by accountancy Y	Results satisfactory Y/N	Ref/ comments	Initials and date
7 Ensure that all matters dealt with in the bank letters have been referenced to the relevant schedule/sections.	Y		Y	K4	KM 16.6.95
8 Ensure that bank balances and overdrafts are only netted off where a formal right of set-off exists.	Y		Y	No set-off exists	KM 16.6.95
9 Confirm that cash 'window dressing' has not taken place by: (a) ensuring that all payments recorded in the cash book before the period end were despatched before that date;	Y	Y	Y	K3.1	KM 16.6.95
(b) noting any 'artificial' movement between accounts;	Y		Y	None	KM 16.6.95
(c) obtaining explanations of any material items cancelled in the cash book in the new period.	Y		Y	None	KM 16.6.95
10 For businesses receiving cash income, ensure unbanked takings before and after the year end have been accounted for in the correct period.	Y		Y	K3.3	KM 16.6.95
11 For businesses receiving cash income, ensure that all unbanked takings at the year end have been timeously banked in the new period.	Y		Y	No unbanked receipts	KM 16.6.95
Cash					
12 Count all material cash balances, record details and reconcile. (a) Count cash in the presence of a member of the client's staff. Ask him/her to confirm the amount counted.	N	—		Not Material	EAA 8.6.95
(b) Ensure all cash, etc., is received at the same time to avoid substitution.	N	—	—	—	
(c) Prepare a list of IOUs and obtain confirmation from the individuals.	N		—	—	
(d) Discuss any staff IOUs with management and ensure that they are properly authorised.	N			—	
(e) Agree balances to the nominal ledger.	N	—	—	—	
(f) Where the count takes place after the year end reconcile movements since the year end.	N	—	—	—	
(g) Obtain explanations of all material differences.	N			—	

Client: Bright-a-Light Ltd		Prepared by: KM	Date: 16.6.95	Ref: **K2**
Year/Period End: 31.3.95	File No:	Reviewed by: EAA	Date: 19.6.95	

AUDIT PROGRAMME – BANK BALANCES AND CASH (*cont.*)

	Test required Y/N	Covered by accountancy Y	Results satisfactory Y/N	Ref/ comments	Initials and date
13 Obtain certificates for all cash balances not counted.	N		—	—	EAA 8.6.95
Conclusion					
14 Consider whether there are any items which need to be included in a letter of representation or letter of comment and record on **A5** or **A6** as appropriate.	Y		Y	None	KM 16.6.95
15 Other tests:	N	—	—	—	EAA 8.6.95

Client		File No.	Ref.
Bright-a-Light Ltd			K3.1
Subject		Prepared by KM	Date 9/6/95
Bank Account & Reconciliation Statement			
Current A/c No. 05212509		Reviewed by EAA	Date 19/6/95
		Accounting Dates	31·3·95

Balance per bank statement	K4	β	✓̸	62,728.83
Add: o/s bankings	K3.2			15,320.60
Less: o/s cheques	K3.2			(119,654.60)
Balance per accounts	K1			41,605.17
				ν

Audit key

ν Casts checked.
√ Agreed to last year's working papers.
β Agreed to bank statement.
✓̸ Agreed to bank confirmation letter. K4

Client still has uncleared cheques of £246.87 @ 5.6.95. There is no real indication of window dressing by holding onto cheques once they have been written. Larger payments to major suppliers clear quickly.

Results and conclusion

See K1.

Client		File No.	Ref.
Bright-a-Light Ltd			K3.2
Subject: Schedule of o/s cheques and bankings		Prepared by: KM	Date: 9/6/95
		Reviewed by: EAA	Date: 19/6/95
		Accounting Dates: 31·3·95	

Cheque No	*Date written*	*Amount*	*Date cleared*
1251	2/1	60.00	*
1391	30/1	186.87	*
1420		110.14	3/4
1422		171.22	3/4
1424		212.29	6/4
1425		118.30	3/4
1426		548.53	3/4
1427		302.24	3/4
1428		73.21	7/4
1429		32.00	6/4
1430		500.00	6/4
1431		138.00	7/4
1433		342.58	3/4
1434		131.10	21/4
1435		95.55	28/4
1436		30.38	3/4
1437		914.33	7/4
1438		64.17	10/4
1439		94.00	3/4
1440		72.45	10/4
1441		1,051.95	24/4
1442		45.77	3/4
1443		86.25	24/4
1444		187.97	10/4
1445		173.28	10/4
1446		147.48	10/4
1447		4,548.02	6/4
1448		1,666.35	10/4
1451		31.13	24/4
1452		14.38	13/5
1453		91.63	10/4
1454		84.00	11/5
1455		57.50	10/4
1456		142.19	6/4
1457		149.50	28/5
1458		268.80	3/6
1459		33,994.62	6/4
1460		4,097.60	7/4
		51,035.78	

Cheque No	*Amount*	*Date cleared*
Bal b/f	51,035.78	
1462	65,188.40	3/4
1464	160.00	7/4
1465	133.02	7/4
1467	2,852.48	11/4
1472	186.87	13/4
1473	98.05	13/4
	119,654.60	K3.1
	v	

<u>Schedule of o/s bankings</u>

Date per PIB	*Amount £*	*Date per bank statement*
30/3	34.10	3/4
30/3	4,550.32	3/4
31/3	46.40	4/4
31/3	10,652.63	4/4
31/3	37.15	4/4
	15,320.60	K3.1
	v	

<u>Key</u>

v Casts checked.

Client		File No.	Ref.
Bright-a-Light Ltd			K3.3
Subject		Prepared by	Date
Verification of bank reconciliation		KM	9/6/95
		Reviewed by	Date
– Current Account		EAA	19/6/95
		Accounting Dates	31·3·95

Work done

A sample of items was selected from the cash book and agreed to the bank statements (8 receipts and 8 payments, selected at random from the last month of the year). If items had not been dealt with by the bank before the year end, these were also agreed to the bank reconciliation.

Receipts

	Received from	*Amount* £	*Date*	*Total per PIB*	*Date per PIB*	*Date per bank*	*Included in reconciliation*
1	Binns Motors	1,682.12	6.3.95	15,874.91	6.3.95	8.3.95	NO
2	Dorset Garages Ltd	5,212.91	13.3.95	7,143.12	13.3.95	16.3.95	NO
3	Parker Estates	729.00	16.3.95	12,486.93	16.3.95	20.3.95	NO
4	Taylors	1,022.40	20.3.95	1,982.12	20.3.95	23.3.95	NO
5	Woodland Crafts	796.95	23.3.95	8,821.93	23.3.95	27.3.95	NO
6	Mr & Mrs Roberts	250.00	27.3.95	697.12	27.3.95	30.3.95	NO
7	Morris Heating	1,128.76	30.3.95	4,550.32	30.3.95	3.4.95	√
8	Manns Garage	650.00	31.3.95	10,652.63	31.3.95	4.4.95	√

Payments

	Payee	*Amount* £	*Date*	*Cheque No*	*Date per bank*	*Included in reconciliation*
1	George Sanders	650.00	3.3.95	1406	9.3.95	NO
2	EC Fuels Ltd	125,32	3.3.95	1407	13.3.95	NO
3	Arthur Fuels Ltd	16,271.39	13.3.95	1410	21.3.95	NO
4	Fuel Supplies Ltd	8,992.12	13.3.95	1411	21.3.95	NO
5	Camping Supplies	4,548.02	16.3.95	1447	6.4.95	√
6	Fuel Supplies Ltd	33,994.62	27.3.95	1459	6.4.95	√
7	Arthur Fuels Ltd	65,188.40	27.3.95	1462	3.4.95	√
8	AJ Smith	2,852.48	27.3.95	1467	11.4.95	√

K4

Messrs Jones Watson & Co
Chartered Accountants
24 Barracks Square
Oldtown
Yorkshire

21 April 1995

CAPITAL BANK
17 Charter Way, Oldtown
Yorkshire
Tel (0772) 127843 Fax (0772) 127849

Dear Sirs

BRIGHT-A-LIGHT LTD

As requested, we give below the information, as at the close of business on 31 March 1995, relating to the above.

Bank accounts

1. Accounts held

Full title	*A/c type*	*Account no*	*Balance* £	
Bright-A-Light Ltd	Current	05212509	62,728.83 CR	K3.1
Bright-A-Light Ltd No 2	Business development loan	0465212509	40,000.00 DR	K6
Bright-A-Light Ltd No 3	Business development loan	0465212510	80,696.68 DR	K7
Bright-A-Light Ltd – Vehicle Loan	Business development loan	0465025517	2,827.08 DR	K8

2. Accounts closed during period

Full title	*A/c type*	*Account no*	*Date closed*
None			

3. Interest/charges accrued but not credited/charged as at above date
(a) Provisional charges: Accounts grouped therefore cannot specify
(b) Interest: Accounts grouped therefore cannot specify
Accrued interest has been calculated on the present CRT status of account.

4. Interest charged during period, of not specified separately in the bank statements
None

5. Set-off arrangements
The bank's form of security incorporates, *inter alia*, a right of set-off.

6a. Overdrafts and loans repayable on demand

Account/type of facility	*Agreed limit* £	*Review date* £
Overdraft	75,000	5/6/95

6b. *Overdrafts and loans other than those repayable on demand*

Account/type of facility/interest rate	*Agreed limit* £	*Review date*
Business development loan	44,000	5/6/95
Business development loan	83,177	5/6/95
Business development loan	3,493	5/6/95

6c. *Other facilities*
None

Customers assets

7. *Assets held as security (whether or not formally charged to the bank)*
4/5/93 – Mortgage debenture over fixed and floating assets.
4/5/93 – Mortgage over unit 12, Westend Industrial Estate, Oldtown, Yorkshire.

8. *Other assets held*
None

Contingent liabilities

9a. *Total of bills discounted with recourse*
None

9b. *Details of guarantees, bonds or indemnities given in favour of third parties*
None

9c. *Details of guarantees, bonds or indemnities given by bank on customer's behalf where there is recourse to customer*
None

9d. *Total of acceptances*
None

9e. *Total sterling equivalent of forward foreign exchange contracts*
None

9f. *Total of outstanding liabilities under documentary credits*
None

9g. *Other contingent liabilities*
None

Other information

10. None known

This reply is given solely for the purpose of your audit without any responsibility to you on the part of the bank, its employees or agents, but it is not to relieve you from any other enquiry or from the performance of any other duty.

Yours faithfully

____

(Authorised signatory) (Official stamp of bank)

Client		File No.	Ref.
Bright-a-Light Ltd			K6
Subject: Business Development Loan (A/C No. 0465212509)		Prepared by: KM	Date: 9/6/95
Bank Account No. 2		Reviewed by: EAA	Date: 19/6/95
		Accounting Dates	31·3·95

Repayments	W4.3	5,000.00	Balance b/f	✓ 45,000.00
Balance c/f	K1	✓̶ β 40,000.00		
		45,000.00		45,000.00
		ν		ν

ν Casts checked.
✓ Agreed to last year's working papers.
β Agreed to bank statement.
✓̶ Agreed to bank confirmation letter (K4).

(i) loan terms
Pay £5,000 p.a. in 5 equal instalments during each year. Interest calculated separately.

(ii) due within one year $5 \times £1{,}000 =$	£5,000		
(iii) due after one year	35,000	K1.1	
	£40,000		

Amounts due in 1–2 years	£5,000		K1.1
Amounts due in 3–5 years	£15,000	(3 @ £5,000)	K1.1
Amounts due after 5 years	£15,000	(3 @ £5,000)	K1.1
Due over 1 year as above.	£35,000		

Results and conclusion – see K1.

Client		File No.	Ref.
Bright-a-Light Ltd			K7
Subject: Business Development Loan (A/C No. 0465212510)		Prepared by: KM	Date: 9/6/95
Bank A/C No. 3		Reviewed by: EAA	Date: 19/6/95
		Accounting Dates	31·3·95

Repayments	W4.3	7,169.90	Balance b/fwd	√ 87,866.58
Balance c/fwd	K1	⊀ β 80,696.68		
		£87,866.58		£87,866.58
		ν		ν

Audit key

ν Casts checked.
√ Agreed to last year's working papers.
β Agreed to bank statement.
⊀ Agreed to bank confirmation letter (K4).

(i) Loan terms

10 year loan, £1,394.33 per month, principal £100,000. Repayment is split by the bank between interest and capital repayment, both being paid separately from the current account.

(ii) Split between amount due within one year and amount due after one year

Interest paid this year = £9,562.66 (average £796.84 pm)
Will fall next year as capital balance outstanding falls.

Repayments next year	12 × £1,394.33		16,731.96	
less estimated interest		say	(9,000.00)	
				7,731.96
Repayments between 1 and 2 years	12 × £1,394.33		16,731.96	
less estimated interest		say	(9,000.00)	
Capital liability due between 1 and 2 years			K1.1	7,731.96
Repayments between 3 and 5 years	36 × £1,394.33		50,195.88	
less estimated interest		say	(27,000.00)	
Capital liability due between 3 and 5 years			K1.1	23,195.88
Balance = capital liability due over 5 years			K1.1	42,036.88
				£80,696.68

Results and conclusions – see K1.

Client		File No.	Ref.
Bright-a-Light Ltd			K8
Subject		Prepared by	Date
Bank A/C: Vehicle Loan A/C No. 0465025517		KM	9/6/95
		Reviewed by	Date
		EAA	19/6/95
		Accounting Dates	31·3·95

Repayments	W4.3	1,714.62	Balance b/f	√ 4,541.70
Balance c/f	K1	∤β 2,827.08		
		4,541.70		4,541.70
		ν		ν

Audit key

- ν Casts checked.
- √ Agreed to last year's working papers.
- β Agreed to bank statements.
- ∤ Agreed to bank confirmation letter (K4).

(i) Loan terms

Monthly repayment £189.31, 3 yr loan, interest calculated by bank and paid separately from current account.

(ii) Split between amount due within and amount due after 1 year

Repayments next year	2,271.72	
Estimated interest (this year £557.10)	480.00	
Due within 1 year	1,791.72	
Due after 1 year (+ within 2 years)	1,035.36	
	2,827.08	K1.1

Results and conclusion

See K1.

L CREDITORS AND ACCRUALS

1	Lead schedule	✓
2	Audit programme	✓
3	List of creditor balances	✓
4	Accruals and provisions	
5	Directors' accounts: summary	✓
6	Hire purchase/finance leases	✓
7	Results of confirmation	
8	Certificates/confirmation replies	
9		
10		
11		

Client: Bright-a-Light Ltd		Prepared by:	Date:	Ref: **L**
Year/Period End: 31.3.95	File No:	Reviewed by:	Date:	

SUMMARY SHEET – CREDITORS AND ACCRUALS

Audit objectives	***Planning*** Number of tests which satisfy objective	Additional/ alternative tests to be carried out	***Final*** Are you satisfied that the objectives have been met?	Comments	Initials
1 To ensure that all liabilities exist and are supported by satisfactory independent evidence.	1, 2, ~~3~~, 4, 5, 6, 7, 8, 9, 10, ~~11~~, 12, 22		Yes/~~No~~		EAA
2 To ensure that trade creditors have been fully and accurately recorded.	1, 2, ~~3~~, 4, ~~11~~, 12, 22		Yes/~~No~~		EAA
3 To ensure that proper cut-off has been applied.	1, 2, ~~3~~, 4, 13, 14, ~~15~~, 22		Yes/~~No~~		EAA
4 To ensure that all hire purchase and finance leases have been accounted for in accordance with SSAP 21.	1, 2, ~~3~~, 4, 16, 22		Yes/~~No~~		EAA
5 To ensure that all material accruals, loans and other creditors have been accounted for.	1, 2, ~~3~~, 4, 17, 18, 19, 20, 21, 22		Yes/~~No~~		EAA
6 To ensure that expenditure has not been under recorded.	1, 2, ~~3~~, 4, 5, 6, 7, 8, 9, 10, ~~11~~, 12, 13, 14, ~~15~~, 22		Yes/~~No~~		EAA

Conclusion

From the audit work carried out I confirm that:

- nothing has occurred to necessitate changing the audit plan* ~~or the audit plan has been updated~~.*
- nothing has occurred to necessitate revising the risk assessment* ~~or the risk assessment has been revised~~.*
- nothing has occurred to necessitate revising the materiality level* ~~or the materiality has been revised~~.*
- ~~adjustments to the plan, risk assessment and materiality have been detailed on **B5** or **B8**~~.*
- the work has been performed in accordance with the audit programme.
- the work performed and the results obtained have been adequately documented.
- all necessary information has been collected for the preparation of the statutory accounts.
- in my opinion (~~subject to the matters highlighted on **B5** or **B8**~~)* creditors and accruals are fairly stated.

Prepared by EA Arbuthnott Date 22.6.95

Reviewed by DGW Date 3.7.95

* Delete if not applicable.

Alternative conclusion (*ANY* alternative conclusion *MUST* be referred to on **B5** or **B8**)

Prepared by__________ Date__________

Reviewed by__________ Date__________

Client: Bright-a-Light Ltd	File No.	Ref. L1
Subject: Creditors falling due within one year	Prepared by: EAA	Date: 16/6/95
	Reviewed by: DGW	Date: 3/7/95
	Accounting Dates: 31·3·95	

	Ref.		1995		1994	
			£	£	£	£
Bank loans & overdrafts		K1		56,129		41,661 √ ⊬
Trade creditors	L3	W12	81,590			
add credit bals on s/l		J1	1,218			
				82,808		51,109 √ ⊬
Taxation and Social Security						
PAYE/NIC		W11	1,286		1,082 ⊬	
		W11	628			
Corporation Tax		P1	7,872		2,741 ⊬	
				9,786		3,823 √ ⊬
Other creditors						
Director's loan		L5.1	4,895		4,895 ⊬	
Loan from mother		L5.1	3,000			
Weekly wages		W11	302		3,000 ⊬	
				8,197		7,895 √ ⊬
Accruals						
Audit			β 2,285		1,585 ⊬	
Computer maintenance			—		439 ⊬	
				2,285		2,024 √ ⊬
Obligations under finance leases		L6		2,090		—
				£161,295		£106,512
				ν		ν√

Key

- ν Costs checked.
- √ Agreed to last years financial statements.
- ⊬ Agreed to last years working papers.
- β Accrual is £3,050 budgeted fee less payment in advance of £765.

See above references for detailed work.

Conclusion

Creditors due within 1 year are fairly stated.

Client: Bright-a-Light Ltd		Prepared by: EAA	Date: 19.6.95	Ref: **L2**
Year/Period End: 31.3.95	File No:	Reviewed by: DGW	Date: 3.7.95	

AUDIT PROGRAMME – CREDITORS AND ACCRUALS

Nature of test:	Test required Y/N	Covered by accountancy Y	Results satisfactory Y/N	Ref/ comments	Initials and date
General					
1 (a) Agree opening balances to last year's accounts.	Y	Y	Y	L1	EAA 19.6.95
(b) Obtain and check, or prepare, a lead schedule for the current year's figures.	Y	Y	Y	L1	EAA 19.6.95
(c) Enquire into and make notes of reasons for any major variations from expectations.	Y		Y	None	EAA 19.6.95
2 Assess whether the initial materiality and/ or risk assessment should be revised in view of the audit evidence obtained to date.	Y		Y	No revision needed	EAA 19.6.95
3 Undertake detailed analytical review procedures and determine whether the results enable us to reduce our sample size.	N		—	—	EAA 8.6.95
4 Review for large and unusual items and verify.	Y		Y	covered by test L3.2	EAA 19.6.95
Trade creditors					
5 Obtain or prepare a list of trade creditor balances. Check a sample to the underlying records and vice versa.	Y		Y	L3	EAA 19.6.95
6 Test the casts of the list.	Y		Y	L3	EAA 19.6.95
7 Agree the list to the control account. Obtain explanations for all material adjustments to the control account.	Y		Y	W12	EAA 19.6.95
8 List all debit balances over £500 and obtain explanations. Ensure they are correctly treated in the accounts.	Y		Y	None	EAA 19.6.95
9 Select a sample of accounts.					
(a) Ensure that it is made up of specific items.	Y		Y	L3.1	EAA 19.6.95
(b) Verify all contra entries.	Y		Y		
(c) Check casts.	Y		Y		
10 Compare the list of balances with the previous year and enquire into any major variations.	Y		Y	None	EAA 19.6.95

Client: Bright-a-Light LTD		Prepared by: EAA	Date: 19.6.95	Ref: **L2**
Year/Period End: 31.3.95	File No:	Reviewed by: DGW	Date: 3.7.95	

AUDIT PROGRAMME – CREDITORS AND ACCRUALS (*cont.*)

	Test required Y/N	Covered by accountancy Y	Results satisfactory Y/N	Ref/ comments	Initials and date
11 Perform a creditors circularisation. (a) Select a sample of accounts for confirmation from a complete list of balances (include nil and debit balances where applicable). Record the details on the standard working paper.	N		—		
(b) Confirm with client the creditors you wish to circularise. Obtain explanations where they do not want you to circularise.	N		—		
(c) Send the confirmation requests. Enclose a prepaid envelope for return to the firm. Ensure the reply part of the letter is properly referenced.	N		—		EAA 19.6.95
(d) Record replies on the control sheet.	N		—		
(e) Where replies are not received within a reasonable period send a follow-up letter.	N		—		
(f) Follow the alternative procedures for any unfavourable responses or where no response obtained.	N		—		
(g) Summarise the results and consider whether adequate audit comfort has been obtained for trade creditors.	N		—		
12 Where a circularisation is not carried out, or unsatisfactory results obtained, carry out alternative procedures to verify completeness of creditors. (a) Select a sample of supplier accounts and vouch the balances to supplier statements.	Y		Y	L3.2 to L3.4	EAA 19.6.95
(b) Review invoices and cash book in the new period to ensure all material amounts have been provided for.	Y		Y	L3.5	EAA 19.6.95
Cut-off 13 Review large returns to suppliers after the year end and consider whether they have been treated correctly.	Y		Y	L3.6	EAA 19.6.95

Client: Bright-a-Light Ltd		Prepared by: EAA	Date: 19.6.95	Ref: **L2**
Year/Period End: 31.3.95	File No:	Reviewed by: DGW	Date: 3.7.95	

AUDIT PROGRAMME – CREDITORS AND ACCRUALS (*cont.*)

	Test required Y/N	Covered by accountancy Y	Results satisfactory Y/N	Ref/ comments	Initials and date
14 If the company retains goods received records, examine the goods received/purchased records immediately before and after the year end and ensure that:					
(a) all goods delivered prior to the year end are included in stock, purchases and creditors where appropriate;	Y		Y	L3.6	EAA 19.6.95
(b) all goods delivered after the year end are excluded from stock, purchases and creditors where appropriate.	Y		Y	L3.6	EAA 19.6.95
15 If the company does not have goods received records, specify below the audit work to ensure that cut-off has been correctly applied.	N		—	—	EAA 8.6.95
Hire purchase					
16 Obtain details of all hire purchase and finance leases.					
(a) Examine new agreements and ensure that the treatment in the accounts is correct.	Y		Y	F6 & L6	EAA 16.6.95
(b) Ensure that only capital balances are carried forward.	Y		Y	L6	EAA 16.6.95
(c) Ensure that amounts carried forward are correctly classified as due within and without one year.	Y		Y	L6	EAA 16.6.95
Accruals					
17 Vouch all accruals over £2000 to supporting documentation, and verify.	Y	Y	Y	L1	EAA 16.6.95
Taxes					
18 Agree tax and VAT liabilities to the appropriate sections on the file.	Y	Y	Y	P1	EAA 22.6.95
19 Prepare or obtain a control account for PAYE and other deductions and ensure correct provision has been made.	Y	Y	Y	W11	EAA 22.6.95

Client: Bright-a-Light Ltd		Prepared by: EAA	Date: 16.6.95	Ref: **L2**
Year/Period End: 31.8.95	File No:	Reviewed by: DGW	Date: 3.7.95	

AUDIT PROGRAMME – CREDITORS AND ACCRUALS (*cont.*)

	Test required Y/N	Covered by accountancy Y	Results satisfactory Y/N	Ref/ comments	Initials and date
Provisions					
20 Review provisions.					
(a) Ensure basis of calculation is acceptable and consistent.	Y		Y	None	EAA 19.6.95
(b) Check the calculation of material items.	Y		Y	None	EAA 19.6.95
Other creditors					
21 Vouch any material other creditors to supporting documentation.	Y		Y	L5.1	EAA 19.6.95
Conclusion					
22 Consider whether there are any items which need to be included in a letter of representation or letter of comment and record on **A5** or **A6** as appropriate.	Y		Y	None	EAA 19.6.95
23 Other tests:	N	—	—	—	EAA 8.6.95

Client: Bright-a-Light Ltd		Prepared by:	Date:	Ref: L2.1
Year/Period End: 31.3.95	File No:	Reviewed by:	Date:	

SAMPLE SELECTION PLANNING – BALANCE SHEET

Objective: *To record the resources from which audit assurance has been obtained, and to assist in calculating sample sizes for tests of details.*

Audit area Trade creditors

Approximate number of transactions in year	

Inherent risk factor

Test of detail only = Table figure 1.2

OR

Test of detail and analytical review = Table figure × ⅔ ______

Tolerable error = $\frac{\text{Materiality}}{\text{Inherent risk factor}}$ $\frac{15,000}{1.2}$ = £12,500

Monetary value of population	(100%)	£ 81,590
Value of items above the tolerable error	(%)	£(77,307)
Value of scheduled other 'key' items	(%)	£(–)
Value of residual population	(%)	£ 4,283

Sample size =

$\frac{\text{Residual population} \times \text{Inherent risk factor}}{\text{Materiality}}$ $\frac{£\ 4,283}{£\ 15,000}$ × 1.2 = 1 say

Plus: Number of items above the tolerable error	=	2
Number of other 'key' items	=	–
Actual sample size		3

Conclusion

I am satisfied that the actual sample size will fairly test the population.

Prepared by EAA Date 8.6.95

Reviewed by DGW Date 3.7.95

BRIGHT-A-LIGHT LIMITED

TRADE CREDITORS
LIST OF BALANCES FROM PURCHASE LEDGER

		1995	*1994*
		£	£
Fuel Supplies Limited		22,298.13	12,482
EC Fuel Limited		131.98	242
Fitzgerald Joinery		57.50	—
Arthur Fuels Ltd		55,009.36	35,671
George Sanders & Sons		340.52	—
Primus Stoves Ltd		49.68	107
P W Saunders Limited		50.00	—
UBC Ltd		108.83	—
B T Warren		74.75	—
Camping Supplies		772.80	1,744
Heat Engineering Limited		91.85	—
Gimeg		509.88	863
Sureglow Heating Limited		1,985.82	—
A J Smith Haulage		108.66	—
	L1	£81,589.76	£51,109

W12

DGW
3.7.95

Client		File No.	Ref.
Bright-a-Light Ltd			L3.1
Subject		**Prepared by**	**Date**
Trade Creditors – validity		EAA	19/6/95
		Reviewed by	**Date**
– test 9		DGW	3/7/95
		Accounting Dates	31·3·95

Objective

To ensure that recorded liabilities are valid.

Work done

3 accounts were selected from the purchase ledger and the following tests carried out – from test 9 on L2. The 3 largest balances were selected.

9(a) Ensure that the balance is made up of specific items.
9(b) Verify all contra entries.
9(c) Check casts.

	9(a)	9(b)	9(c)
Fuel Supplies Ltd	√	√	√
Arthur Fuels Ltd	√	√	√
Sureglow Heating	√	√	√

Results

Satisfactory.

Conclusion

On the basis of the work performed, recorded liabilities are valid.

Client	File No.	Ref.
Bright-a-Light Ltd		L3.2

Subject	Prepared by	Date
Trade creditors – Supplies Statement testing	EAA	19/6/95
	Reviewed by DGW	Date 3/7/95
	Accounting Dates	31·3·95

Work done

A sample of 3 balances were selected for testing by reviewing the cash book and purchase ledger to identify the most likely trade creditors.

Balances in the ledger were agreed or reconciled to the supplier statements.

Supplier	*Balance per ledger* £	*Balance per statement* £	*Agreed*	*Reconciled*	*Reference*
Fuel Supplies Ltd	22,298.13	75,044.05	NO	√	L3.3
Arthur Fuels Ltd	55,009.36	130,018.88	NO	√	L3.4
Gimeg	509.88	509.88	√	N/A	N/A

Results

Satisfactory.

Conclusion

Supplier statement balances are properly recorded.

Client		File No.	Ref.
Bright-a-Light Ltd			L3.3
Subject		Prepared by	Date
Trade Creditors		EAA	19/6/95
		Reviewed by	Date
Reconciliation – Fuel Supplies Ltd		DGW	3/7/95
		Accounting Dates	31·3·95

					£	£
Balance per supplier statement						75,044.05√
Cheques not yet presented						
		no	*date written*	*date presented*		
		1459	28.3.95	6.4.95		(33,994.62)β
Items invoiced but not yet received						
	invoice no	*date*	*GRN no*	*GRN date*		
	12053	31.3.95	1063	3.4.95	✓ 198.24	
	12161	31.3.95	1064	3.4.95	✓ 2,679.81	
	12164	31.3.95	1071	4.4.95	✓15,873.25	
						(18,751.30)
Balance per purchase ledger						£22,298.13
						ν

ν Casts checked.
√ Agreed to supplier statement.
β Cheque shown as unpresented (K3.2).
✓ Delivery details agreed to GRN.

Client		File No.	Ref.
Bright-a-Light Ltd			L3.4
Subject: Trade Creditor – Supplier		Prepared by: EAA	Date: 19/6/95
Statement testing – Arthur Fuels Ltd		Reviewed by: DGW	Date: 3/7/95
		Accounting Dates: 31·3·95	

					£
Balance per supplier statement					130,018.88✓
Cheque not yet presented					
		no	*date written*	*date presented*	
		1462	28.3.95	3.4.95	(65,188.40)β
Invoices not yet received					
	invoice no	*date*	*GRN*	*GRN date*	
	68778	30.3.95	1068	3.4.95	(9,821.12)✓̶
Balance per purchase ledger					£55,009.36
					ν

ν Casts checked.
✓ Agreed to supplier statement.
✓̶ Delivery details agreed to GRN.
β Cheque shown as unpresented (K3.2).

Client		File No.	Ref.
Bright-a-Light Ltd			L3.5
Subject Trade Creditors – Post year end payments review		Prepared by EAA	Date 19/6/95
		Reviewed by DGW	Date 3/7/95
		Accounting Dates	31·3·95

Work done

(a) Major cheque payments per the bank statements were reviewed for 1 month after the year end. The supporting invoices etc were traced to ensure that items relating to the y/e 31.3.95 were included in creditors or accruals.

date per bank	*cheque no*	*amount £*	*payee*	*trade cred/accrual*	*unpresented cheque* K3.2	*1995/96 payment*
3.4.95	1462	65,188.40	Arthur Fuels Ltd	N/A	√	N/A
6.4.95	1459	33,994.62	Fuel Supplies Ltd	N/A	√	N/A
6.4.95	1447	4,548.02	Steetley Minerals	N/A	√	N/A
6.4.95	1474	2,241.75	HMIT – Corp. Tax	√	N/A	N/A

(b) Also reviewed invoices received after the year end for $2\frac{1}{2}$ months to see if any relate to the period before the year end and should be accrued.

Results

No additional accruals found.

Conclusion

Trade creditors and accruals are not materially mis-stated.

Client Bright-a-Light Ltd	File No.	Ref. L3.6
Subject Cut off – Goods Received Notes	Prepared by EAA	Date 19/6/95
– Credit Notes/Returns	Reviewed by DGW	Date 3/7/95
	Accounting Dates 31·3·95	

Work done

Six GRN details were extracted from the warehouse records (3 before the year end and 3 afterwards) and the following tests performed:

(a) delivered before the year end
- agree to stocktake records and stock ageing
- agree to purchase ledger before year end
- agree to creditors *or* trace payment if paid before year end.

(b) delivered after the year end
- trace to purchase ledger after year end
- trace to stock cards after year end and stock ageing.

	GRN no	*date*	*details*	*in P/L*	*in YE creditors*	*in YE stock*	*correctly treated*
(a)	1062	31.3.95	40 × 25 kg bags Coalite from Fuel Supplies Ltd	31.3.95	√	√	√
	1061	31.3.95	50 × 25 kg Maxibrite from Fuel Supplies Ltd	31.3.95	√	√	√
	1060	31.3.95	Valiant water from Sureglow Heating Ltd	31.3.95	√	√	√
(b)	1063	3.4.95	50 × 25 kg Sunbrite from Fuel Supplies Ltd	3.4.95	NO	NO	√
	1064	3.4.95	425 × 5.5 kg Shellgas refill – Fuel Supplies Ltd	3.4.95	NO	NO	√
	1065	3.4.95	Primus refills – Primus Stoves Ltd	3.4.95	NO	NO	√

GDN after the year end were reviewed for large returns to suppliers. None found.

Conclusion

Cut off on goods received has been correctly applied.

Client	File No.	Ref.
Bright-a-Light Ltd		L5.1
Subject	**Prepared by**	**Date**
Other creditors	EAA	19/6/95
	Reviewed by	**Date**
	DGW	3/7/95
	Accounting Dates	31·3·95

		1995	*1994*
		£	£
Director's Loan – Mr K Strike, interest free and no net repayment in year	L1 L5.2	√4,895	4,895
Other loan – from Mr Strike's mother, interest free and no repayment in year	L1 L5.2	√3,000	3,000
		7,895	7,895
		ν	ν

Work

ν Casts checked.
√ Agreed to confirmation – see reference.

Conclusion

Other creditors are not materially mis-stated.

BRIGHT-A-LIGHT LIMITED

LOANS AT YEAR END 31 MARCH 1995

I confirm that the balance of the loan outstanding to me at 31 March 1995 was £4,895.00.

I have not received any net repayment in the year.

The loan is unsecured and repayable on demand. Interest is not charged on the outstanding balance.

____

MR K STRIKE
DIRECTOR

I confirm that the balance of the loan outstanding to me at 31 March 1995 was £3,000.00.

I have not received any net repayment in the year.

The loan is unsecured and repayable on demand. Interest is not charged on the outstanding balance.

____

MRS J STRIKE

Client		File No.	Ref.
Bright-a-Light Ltd			L6
Subject		Prepared by	Date
		EAA	16/6/95
Hire purchase/finance leases		Reviewed by	Date
		DGW	3/7/95
		Accounting Dates	31·3·95

Capital at 19.6.94		8,995.00	
Repayments in year	£728.34 initial + 9 @ £242.78	(2,913.36)	F6
Interest		1,055.03	F6
Capital balance at 31.3.95		7,136.67	
Due within one year	12 @ £242.78	2,913.36	
	less interest YE 3.3.96	(823.93)	F6
		2,089.43	L1
Balance due after one year and within five years		5,047.24	M1
		7,136.67	
Balance due after one year and within five years		5,047.24	
Due within 1–2 years	2,913.36		
less interest	(341.63)		F6
Balance due 1–2 years		2,571.73	
Balance due 3–5 years		2,475.51	

M LONG-TERM LOANS AND DEFERRED INCOME

1 Lead schedule ☑

2 Audit programme ☑

3 Confirmation certificates ☐

4 ☐

5 ☐

6 ☐

Client: Bright-a-Light Ltd		Prepared by:	Date:	Ref: **M**
Year/Period End: 31.3.95	File No:	Reviewed by:	Date:	

SUMMARY SHEET – LONG-TERM LOANS AND DEFERRED INCOME

Audit objectives	***Planning*** Number of tests which satisfy objective	Additional/ alternative tests to be carried out	***Final*** Are you satisfied that the objectives have been met?	Comments	Initials
1 To ensure that all material loans have been correctly accounted for.	1, 2, ~~3~~, 4, 5, 6, 7, 9		Yes/~~No~~		EAA
2 To ensure that deferred income has been correctly accounted for.	1, 2, ~~3~~, 4, ~~8~~, 9		Yes/~~No~~		EAA

Conclusion

From the audit work carried out I confirm that:

- nothing has occurred to necessitate changing the audit plan* ~~or the audit plan has been updated.*~~
- nothing has occurred to necessitate revising the risk assessment* ~~or the risk assessment has been revised.*~~
- nothing has occurred to necessitate revising the materiality level* ~~or the materiality has been revised.*~~
- ~~adjustments to the plan, risk assessment and materiality have been detailed on **B5** or **B8**.*~~
- the work has been performed in accordance with the audit programme.
- the work performed and the results obtained have been adequately documented.
- all necessary information has been collected for the preparation of the statutory accounts.
- in my opinion ~~(subject to the matters highlighted on **B5** or **B8**)~~* long-term loans and deferred income are fairly stated.

Prepared by EA Arbuthnott Date 22.6.95

Reviewed by DGW Date 3.7.95

* Delete if not applicable.

Alternative conclusion (*ANY* alternative conclusion *MUST* be referred to on **B5** or **B8**)

Prepared by__________ Date__________

Reviewed by__________ Date__________

Client	File No.	Ref.
Bright-a-Light Ltd		M1
Subject: Long term loans	Prepared by: EAA	Date: 22/6/95
	Reviewed by: DGW	Date: 3/7/95
	Accounting Dates: 31·3·95	

		1995	*1994*
		£	*£*
Business development loans	K1.1	109,000	77,687 √
Finance leases	L6	5,047	—
		114,047	77,687
		v	v

Audit work

√ Agreed to 1994 accounts and working papers.
v Casts checked.

(a) Business development loan – see K1.1.

(b) Finance leases – 1995 only.

Conclusion

I am satisfied that long term loans are fairly stated.

Client: Bright-a-Light Ltd		Prepared by: EAA	Date: 22.6.95	Ref: **M2**
Year/Period End: 31.3.95	File No:	Reviewed by: DGW	Date: 3.7.95	

AUDIT PROGRAMME – LONG-TERM LOANS AND DEFERRED INCOME

Nature of test:	Test required Y/N	Covered by accountancy Y	Results satisfactory Y/N	Ref/ comments	Initials and date
General					
1 (a) Agree opening balances to last year's accounts.	Y	Y	Y	M1	EAA 22.6.95
(b) Obtain and check, or prepare, a lead schedule for the current year's figures.	Y		Y	M1	EAA 22.6.95
(c) Enquire into and make notes of reasons for any major variations from expectations.	Y		Y	None	EAA 22.6.95
2 Assess whether the initial materiality and/ or risk assessment should be revised in view of the audit evidence obtained to date.	Y		Y	No revision needed	EAA 22.6.95
3 Undertake detailed analytical review procedures and determine whether the results enable us to reduce our sample size.	N		—	—	EAA 8.6.95
4 Review for large and unusual items and verify.	Y		Y	None	EAA 22.6.95
Loans					
5 Obtain third-party verification for all material loans.	Y		Y	K4	EAA 22.6.95
6 Review loan agreements and consider the implications of any breach of covenants.	Y		Y	Loan covenants not breached	EAA 22.6.95
7 Calculate the apportionment between long- and short-term loans.	Y		Y	L6 & K1.1	EAA 22.6.95
Deferred income					
8 Review the basis for deferring income and ensure that it is valid and has been correctly and consistently applied.	N		—	—	EAA 8.6.95
Conclusion					
9 Consider whether there are any items which need to be included in a letter of representation or letter of comment and record this on **A5** or **A6** as appropriate.	Y		Y	None	EAA 22.6.95
10 Other tests:	N	—	—	—	EAA 8.6.95

N PROVISIONS FOR LIABILITIES AND CHARGES, CONTINGENT LIABILITIES AND FINANCIAL COMMITMENTS

1	Lead schedule	✓
2	Audit programme	✓
3	Details of contingent liabilities	✓
4	Capital expenditure authorised/contracts placed	
5	Operating lease commitments	
6		
7		
8		

Client: Bright-a-Light Ltd		Prepared by:	Date:	Ref: **N**
Year/Period End: 31.3.95	File No:	Reviewed by:	Date:	

SUMMARY SHEET – PROVISIONS FOR LIABILITIES AND CHARGES, CONTINGENT LIABILITIES AND FINANCIAL COMMITMENTS

Audit objectives	***Planning*** Number of tests which satisfy objective	Additional/ alternative tests to be carried out	***Final*** Are you satisfied that the objectives have been met?	Comments	Initials
1 To ensure that full provision has been made for all liabilities or losses which are likely to be incurred, or certain to be incurred, but uncertain as to the amount or date on which they will arise.	1, 2, 11		Yes/~~No~~		EAA
2 To ensure that all contingent liabilities have been identified and adequate provision made.	3, 4, 5, 6, 7, 8, 11		Yes/~~No~~		EAA
3 To ensure that capital and other commitments have been properly accounted for.	9, 10, 11		Yes/~~No~~		EAA

Conclusion

From the audit work carried out I confirm that:

- nothing has occurred to necessitate changing the audit plan* ~~or the audit plan has been updated~~.*
- nothing has occurred to necessitate revising the risk assessment* ~~or the risk assessment has been revised~~.*
- nothing has occurred to necessitate revising the materiality level* ~~or the materiality has been revised~~.*
- ~~adjustments to the plan, risk assessment and materiality have been detailed on **B5** or **B8**~~.*
- the work has been performed in accordance with the audit programme.
- the work performed and the results obtained have been adequately documented.
- all necessary information has been collected for the preparation of the statutory accounts.
- in my opinion (~~subject to the matters highlighted on **B5** or **B8**~~)* provisions for liabilities and charges, contingent liabilities and financial commitments are fairly stated.

Prepared by EA Arbuthnott Date 22.6.95

Reviewed by DGW Date 3.7.95

* Delete if not applicable.

Alternative conclusion (*ANY* alternative conclusion *MUST* be referred to on **B5** or **B8**)

Prepared by ______________________ Date ____________

Reviewed by ______________________ Date ____________

Client: Bright-a-Light Ltd		Prepared by: EAA	Date: 22.6.95	Ref: **N2**
Year/Period End: 31.3.95	File No:	Reviewed by: DGW	Date: 3.7.95	

AUDIT PROGRAMME – PROVISIONS FOR LIABILITIES AND CHARGES, CONTINGENT LIABILITIES AND FINANCIAL COMMITMENTS

Nature of test:	Test required Y/N	Covered by accountancy Y	Results satisfactory Y/N	Ref/ comments	Initials and date
Provisions for liabilities and charges					
1 Review obligations under pension schemes and ensure that adequate provision has been made.	Y		Y	N3	EAA 22.6.95
2 Obtain details of any other liabilities and charges and ensure that adequate provision has been made where necessary.	Y		Y	N3	EAA 22.6.95
Contingent liabilities					
3 Obtain or prepare a list of contingent liabilities. Review the list for any obvious omissions by reviewing: (a) the previous year's contingent liabilities;	Y		Y	N3	EAA 22.6.95
(b) items recorded on the bank certificate;	Y		Y	K4	
(c) minutes of meetings;	Y		Y	N3	
(d) major contracts; and	Y		Y	None	
(e) correspondence.	Y		Y	N3	
4 Discuss the list with the client and ensure that it is complete and that adequate provision has been made for likely losses.	Y		Y	N3	EAA 22.6.95
5 (a) Send a letter to the client's solicitor requesting details of all contingent liabilities known to them.	Y		Y	N3.1	EAA 22.6.95
(b) Review the reply and ensure that adequate provision is made for all items noted.	Y		Y	N3.1	EAA 22.6.95
6 Obtain or prepare a schedule of the major insurances maintained. The schedule should state the amount insured, premium payable, period covered and the date of last renewal.	Y		Y	N3.2	EAA 22.6.95
7 Obtain estimates of the current replacement value of major assets and the maximum potential losses under third party, employers' liability, loss of profits and other policies. Confirm that cover appears adequate and, if not, note on **B5** or **B8**.	Y		Y	N3.2	EAA 22.6.95

Client: Bright-a-Light Ltd		Prepared by: EAA	Date: 22.6.95	Ref: **N2**
Year/Period End: 31.3.95	File No:	Reviewed by: DGW	Date: 3.7.95	

AUDIT PROGRAMME – PROVISIONS FOR LIABILITIES AND CHARGES, CONTINGENT LIABILITIES AND FINANCIAL COMMITMENTS (*cont.*)

	Test required Y/N	Covered by accountancy Y	Results satisfactory Y/N	Ref/ comments	Initials and date
Law and regulations					
8 (a) Enquire of the directors as to the relevant laws and regulations which are central to the entity's ability to conduct its business.	Y		Y	Fire regulations re storage of gas	EAA 22.6.95
(b) Enquire of the directors whether they are on notice of any possible instances of non-compliance with such law or regulations.	Y		Y	None	EAA 22.6.95
(c) Update the permanent audit file for any changes.	Y		Y	PAF 1.4	EAA 22.6.95
(d) Review correspondence files of any relevant licensing or regulatory authorities for any indications of breaches of laws and regulations.	Y		Y	Reviewed fire inspectors file – no problem	EAA 22.6.95
(e) Draft specific representations for inclusion in the letter of representation.	Y		Y	A5	EAA 22.6.95
Capital and other commitments					
9 Review the management minutes and after date invoices and ensure that all material capital commitments have been identified.	Y		Y	None see L3.5	EAA 22.6.95
10 Obtain details of future commitments under operating leases and ensure they are correctly disclosed.	Y		Y	None per directors	EAA 22.6.95
Conclusion					
11 Consider whether there are any items (in addition to laws and regulations) which need to be included in a letter of representation or letter of comment and record on **A5** or **A6** as appropriate.	Y		Y	Contingent liabilities + capital commit. + law and regulations	EAA 22.6.95
12 Other tests:	N	—	—	—	EAA 8.6.95

Client Bright-a-Light Ltd	File No.	Ref. N3	
Subject Provisions	Prepared by EAA		Date 22/6/95
	Reviewed by DGW		Date 3/7/95
	Accounting Dates 31·3·95		

1. Pension scheme

Company runs a defined contribution scheme. The assets of the scheme are held in an independently administered fund. The pension charge to the profit and loss represents contributions payable by the company for the year. This treatment complies with SSAP 24 and no further provision is necessary.

2. Other provisions

Deferred tax – see section P

No other provisions expected.

3. Contingencies.

Secured liabilities – BDL and overdrafts secured by fixed and floating charge – see K4. Disclosed correctly in accounts.

No other contingencies shown in last year's accounts.

Client's correspondence file and minutes of meetings reviewed. These only indicate need to provide for J Austin. Distributors debt – see J4.2. Directors are not aware of need for any provisions.

Review of correspondence files to 22.6.95 – no other contingencies indicated.

Conclusion

No additional contingencies found.

HOWE WILLIAMS & CO

Solicitors

43 York Road, Oldtown, Yorkshire
Tel 01999 721325 Fax 01999 721350

Jones Watson & Co
Chartered Accountants
24 Barracks Square
Oldtown
Yorkshire

18 April 1995

Dear Sirs

BRIGHT-A-LIGHT LIMITED

Thank you for your letter of 20 March regarding the affairs of our mutual client, Bright-a-light Ltd.

We are pleased to supply the information requested, as follows:

1. We do not hold any deeds, leases, bonds, share certificates or any other documents of title.
2. This does not apply as we do not hold any documents of title.
3. We are not aware of any litigation, lawsuits, hearings or negotiations affecting the company.
4. We do not hold any deeds by way of security for advances.

Yours faithfully

Howe Williams & Co

Client Bright-a-Light Ltd	File No.	Ref. N3.2	
Subject Provisions & Insurance (test 6)	Prepared by KM		Date 22/6/95
	Reviewed by EAA		Date 22/6/95
	Accounting Dates 31·3·95		

Buildings insurance	£200,000
Motor vehicles insurance	£15,000
Stock insurance	£30,000
Employers liability	£1,000,000
Loss of profits	£200,000

Premiums total £442.85 pcm. April 94 – March 95
Last renewed 6.3.95 for year April 95 – March 96

Level of insurance appears reasonable in comparison with value of assets held.

Client: Bright-a-Light Ltd		Prepared by: EAA	Date: 22.6.95	Ref: PAF 1.4
Year/Period End:	File No:	Reviewed by: DAW	Date: 3.7.95	

REGISTER OF LAWS AND REGULATIONS

1 *Laws and regulations governing accounts*

Relevant laws (e.g., Companies Act, Charities Act) Companies Act 1985

Relevant regulations (e.g., specific SSAPs, FRSs) Normal SSAPs & FRSs

2 *General business laws and regulations*

Relevant laws (e.g., health and safety, employment law)

Fire regulations - in particular in relation to the storage of bottled gas and other flammable products.

Relevant regulations (e.g., planning)

None

3 *Other specific laws and regulations*

Relevant laws and regulations (e.g., Financial Services Act, food hygiene)

None

Relevant regulations (e.g., ABTA)

None

O CAPITAL, RESERVES AND STATUTORY RECORDS

1	Lead schedule	✓
2	Audit programme	✓
3	Extracts of registers and returns	
4	Extracts of current year minutes	
5	Prior period adjustments	
6		
7		
8		

Client: Bright-a-Light Ltd		Prepared by:	Date:	Ref: **O**
Year/Period End: 31.3.95	File No:	Reviewed by:	Date:	

SUMMARY SHEET – CAPITAL, RESERVES AND STATUTORY RECORDS

Audit objectives	***Planning*** Number of tests which satisfy objective	Additional/ alternative tests to be carried out	***Final*** Are you satisfied that the objectives have been met?	Comments	Initials
1 To ensure that the statutory records have been properly maintained and are up to date.	1, 3, 4, 5, 6, 7, 8, 9, 10, 11, 12, 13		Yes/~~No~~		KM
2 To ensure that any changes in share capital are supported by appropriate resolutions and are properly reflected in the accounts.	2, 4, 8, 12, 13		Yes/~~No~~		KM
3 To ensure that changes in reserves and other statutory information are properly reflected in the accounts.	2, 5, 8, 12, 13		Yes/~~No~~		KM

Conclusion

From the audit work carried out I confirm that:

- nothing has occurred to necessitate changing the audit plan* ~~or the audit plan has been updated~~.*
- nothing has occurred to necessitate revising the risk assessment* ~~or the risk assessment has been revised~~.*
- nothing has occurred to necessitate revising the materiality level* ~~or the materiality has been revised~~.*
- ~~adjustments to the plan, risk assessment and materiality have been detailed on **B5** or **B8**~~.*
- the work has been performed in accordance with the audit programme.
- the work performed and the results obtained have been adequately documented.
- all necessary information has been collected for the preparation of the statutory accounts.
- in my opinion ~~(subject to the matters highlighted on **B5** or **B8**)~~* capital, reserves and statutory records are fairly stated.

Prepared by K Martin Date 19.6.95

Reviewed by EA Arbuthnott Date 22.6.95

* Delete if not applicable.

Alternative conclusion (*ANY* alternative conclusion *MUST* be referred to on **B5** or **B8**)

Prepared by______________________ Date__________

Reviewed by______________________ Date__________

Client	File No.	Ref.	
Bright-a-Light Ltd		01	
Subject	Prepared by		Date
Share Capital and Reserves	KM		19/6/95
	Reviewed by		Date
	EAA		22/6/95
	Accounting Dates	31·3·95	

	1995		*1994*	
	No	*£*	*No*	*£*
Share capital				
Authorised – Ordinary £1 shares	10,000	10,000	10,000	10,000
Allotted, issued and fully paid – Ordinary £1 shares	10,000	10,000	10,000	10,000
Shareholdings:				
Mr K Strike	9,900			
Mrs B Strike	100			
	10,000			

Work done and conclusion

Reviewed statutory books: no changes in ownership of shares; no charges over assets recorded.
Only reserve is profit and loss account.
Share capital and reserves are fairly stated.

Client: Bright-a-Light Ltd		Prepared by: KM	Date: 19.6.95	Ref: **O2**
Year/Period End: 31.3.95	File No:	Reviewed by: EAA	Date: 22.6.95	

AUDIT PROGRAMME – CAPITAL, RESERVES AND STATUTORY RECORDS

Nature of test:	Test required Y/N	Covered by accountancy Y	Results satisfactory Y/N	Ref/ comments	Initials and date
1 Obtain copies of statutory records for this period. (This might entail carrying out a company search.)	Y		Y	No changes	KM 19.6.95
2 Record details of any changes in statutory information and reserves in this period and ensure that these have been properly reflected in the accounts.	Y		Y	O1	KM 19.6.95
3 Enquire as to whether all necessary documents have been filed, e.g., • annual return ✓ • share transfer form None • previous period's accounts ✓ • resolutions None • changes in directors/secretary. None	Y		Y		KM 19.6.95
4 Ensure that all relevant changes have been correctly minuted.	Y		Y	None	KM 19.6.95
5 Schedule all movements in reserves. (a) Ensure that transfers between reserves are correctly treated and authorised.	Y	Y	Y	None	KM 19.6.95
(b) Ensure that the treatment in the accounts is correct.	Y	Y	Y	—	KM 19.6.95
6 Ensure that any mortgages or charges created during the year have been entered into the register of mortgages and charges.	Y		Y	None	KM 19.6.95
7 Ensure that all changes in directors and secretaries and their interests in shares or debentures have been entered into the relevant register.	Y		Y	No changes	KM 19.6.95
8 Agree details in the share register to: (a) the accounts;	Y		Y		KM 19.6.95
(b) the annual return; and	Y		Y		KM 19.6.95
(c) the directors' report.	Y		Y		KM 19.6.95
9 Ensure that the company has not exceeded any restrictions on borrowing powers imposed in the Articles of Association or any loan agreement.	Y		Y	No restriction	KM 19.6.95

Client: Bright-a-Light Ltd		Prepared by: KM	Date: 19.6.95	Ref: **O2**
Year/Period End: 31.3.95	File No:	Reviewed by: EAA	Date: 22.6.95	

AUDIT PROGRAMME – CAPITAL, RESERVES AND STATUTORY RECORDS (*cont.*)

	Test required Y/N	Covered by accountancy Y	Results satisfactory Y/N	Ref/ comments	Initials and date
10 Where a dividend is proposed or has been paid in the period, consider whether the distribution is legal. If not, consider the effect on the audit report on **B6**.	Y		Y	No dividends	KM 19.6.95
11 Ensure that all changes have been properly reflected in the Permanent audit file.	Y		Y	No changes	KM 19.6.95
12 Review minutes of meetings and ensure that all relevant points are noted and cross-referenced to the relevant section of the file.	Y		Y	No relevant points	KM 19.6.95
Conclusion					
13 Consider whether there are any points which need to be included in a letter of representation or letter of comment and record on **A5** or **A6** as appropriate.	Y		Y	None	EAA 22.6.95
14 Other tests:	N	—	—	—	EAA 8.6.95

P TAXATION

1 Summary of taxation account ✓

2 Audit programme ✓

3 Corporation tax computation checklist

4 Reconciliation of tax charges ✓

5 Deferred taxation

6 Advance corporation tax

7 P11D information

8

9

10

Client: Bright-a-Light Ltd		Prepared by:	Date:	Ref: **P**
Year/Period End: 31.3.95	File No:	Reviewed by:	Date:	

SUMMARY SHEET – TAXATION

	Planning Number of tests which satisfy objective	Additional/ alternative tests to be carried out	***Final*** Are you satisfied that the objectives have been met?	Comments	Initials
Audit objectives					
1 To ensure that the taxation provision is adequate.	1, 2, 3, 4, 5, 6, 7, 8, ~~9~~, 11		Yes/~~No~~		EAA
2 To ensure that deferred taxation has been correctly accounted for.	10,11		Yes/~~No~~		EAA

Conclusion

From the audit work carried out I confirm that:

- nothing has occurred to necessitate changing the audit plan* ~~or the audit plan has been updated.*~~
- nothing has occurred to necessitate revising the risk assessment* ~~or the risk assessment has been revised.*~~
- nothing has occurred to necessitate revising the materiality level* ~~or the materiality has been revised.*~~
- ~~adjustments to the plan, risk assessment and materiality have been detailed on **B5** or **B8**.*~~
- the work has been performed in accordance with the audit programme.
- the work performed and the results obtained have been adequately documented.
- all necessary information has been collected for the preparation of the statutory accounts.
- in my opinion (~~subject to the matters highlighted on **B5** or **B8**~~)* taxation is fairly stated.

Prepared by EA Arbuthnott Date 23.6.95

Reviewed by DGW Date 3.7.95

* Delete if not applicable.

Alternative conclusion (*ANY* alternative conclusion *MUST* be referred to on **B5** or **B8**)

Prepared by__________ Date__________

Reviewed by__________ Date__________

Client		File No.	Ref.
Bright-a-Light Ltd			P1
Subject: Corporation Tax		Prepared by: EAA	Date: 23/6/95
		Reviewed by: DGW	Date: 3/7/95
		Accounting Dates	31·3·95

			£		£
Payment	W4.3		500.00		
				Bal b/fwd	2,741.75
Bal c/fwd 1994		2,241.75			
1995		5,630.25		Corpn tax charge for the year	5,630.25
	L1		7,872.00	A2	
			£8,372.00		£8,372.00

Balance re 1994 outstanding as not yet agreed with Inspector of Taxes. Interest will be accruing.

Due date:	31.12.94
Interest rate: say	10%
Date paid:	6.4.95

Interest to year end:
3/12 × 10% × 2,241.75 = £56.05

Balance re 1995 based on revised profit after post TB adjustments to include asset acquired on finance lease and write-off of bad debts – see A2 for detailed computation.

Client: Bright-a-Light Ltd		Prepared by: EAA	Date: 23.6.95	Ref: **P2**
Year/Period End:	File No:	Reviewed by: DGW	Date: 3.7.95	

AUDIT PROGRAMME – TAXATION

Nature of test:	Test required Y/N	Covered by accountancy Y	Results satisfactory Y/N	Ref/ comments	Initials and date
General					
1 Obtain and check, or prepare, draft tax computations, analysis of corporation tax account, and proof of tax/tax reconciliation.	Y	Y	Y	P1 & P4	EAA 23.6.95
2 Complete the corporation tax computation checklist on **P3**.	Y		Y	P3	EAA 23.6.95
3 Ensure profit before tax used in the computation agrees to draft profit and loss account.	Y	Y	Y	A2	EAA 23.6.95
4 (a) Review computation adjustments in comparison with last year for reasonableness.	Y	Y	Y	Additional adjustment re Peugeot lease	EAA 23.6.95
(b) Verify major adjustments.	Y	Y	Y	None	EAA 23.6.95
5 Agree closing CT liabilities to latest computations and CT200.	Y	Y	Y	A2	EAA 23.6.95
6 Verify movements on CT account to CT61's, CT200's, etc.	Y	Y	Y	P1	EAA 23.6.95
7 Review proof of tax for unusual items.	Y	Y	Y	P4	EAA 23.6.95
8 Verify arithmetical accuracy of computations.	Y	Y	Y	P1	EAA 23.6.95
ACT					
9 Where ACT paid or payable is being carried forward as a debtor, consider its ultimate recoverability and ensure that the treatment in the accounts correctly reflects this.	N		—		EAA 23.6.95
Deferred taxation					
10 Calculate the full potential deferred tax liability and consider what provision, if any, is necessary.	Y	Y	Y	Subject to provision	EAA 23.6.95
Conclusion					
11 Consider whether there are any items which need to be included in a letter of representation or letter of comment and record this on **A5** or **A6** as appropriate.	Y		Y	None	EAA 23.6.95
12 Other tests:	N	—	—		EAA 8.6.95

Client: Bright-a-Light Ltd		Prepared by: EAA	Date: 23.6.95	Ref: **P3**
Year/Period End: 31.3.95	File No:	Reviewed by: DGW	Date: 3.7.95	

CORPORATION TAX COMPUTATION CHECKLIST

Objective: *To ensure that any corporation tax liabilities or available losses are correctly reflected in the accounts.*

This checklist sets out the common points to be considered when preparing corporation tax computations – it is not exhaustive.

	Yes/No or N/A	Comments
1 *Pay and file*		
(a) Confirm that the company is not liable for any penalties for late filing of its corporation tax return.	Y	
(b) Confirm that the company is not liable for interest on the late payment of corporation tax.	N	P1
(c) Confirm that tax due under s419 ICTA 1988 in respect of directors' overdrawn loan accounts has been paid within 14 days of the end of the accounting period, and that no interest charge arises.	N/A	
(d) Confirm that notice of chargeability under s419 has been given to the Inland Revenue within 12 months of the end of the accounting period.	N/A	
2 *Schedule D Case I and II computation*		
2.1 Stock and work in progress		
(a) Confirm that the basis of valuation has not changed since the previous year.	Y	
(b) Confirm that there are no general provisions.	Y	
2.2 Advertising		
(a) Confirm that all business gifts or hospitality included in advertising are correctly treated as entertaining.	Y	
(b) Confirm advertising excludes all capital items (e.g., signs).	Y	
2.3 Entertaining		
(a) Confirm that all entertaining is disallowed, except staff entertaining and small promotional gifts (not food, drink or tobacco).	N/A	
(b) Confirm that staff subsistence, internal and board meeting expenses (also AGM expenses) are at reasonable levels or confirm disallowance.	N/A	
(c) Confirm 'round sum' general allowances do not relate to entertaining. (Beware P11D implications. Record details for employees PAYE.)	N/A	
2.4 Repairs and renewals		
(a) Confirm that the analysis excludes all capital items.	N/A	Not material
(b) Confirm that the analysis excludes all 'initial repairs' (see Law shipping).	N/A	

Client: Bright-a-Light Ltd		Prepared by: EAA	Date: 23.6.95	Ref: **P3**
Year/Period End: 31.8.95	File No:	Reviewed by: DGW	Date: 3.7.95	

CORPORATION TAX COMPUTATION CHECKLIST (*cont.*)

	Yes/No or N/A	Comments
2.5 Leasing		
(a) Confirm that the disallowable element of 'expensive car' leases are adjusted in the computation.	N/A	Below £12,000
(b) Confirm that the capital element of finance lease payments are allowed in the computation.	Y	Depreciation charge
2.6 Legal and professional charges		
(a) Confirm that the analysis excludes all capital items.	Y	
(b) Confirm that all disallowable revenue items are identified and adjusted in the computation.	N/A	None
2.7 Bad and doubtful debts		
(a) Confirm that all provisions are specific.	Y	
(b) Confirm that the file includes debtors' names and addresses for bad debts written off and provisions for individual doubtful debts.	Y	
(c) Confirm that any general provisions are accounted for separately from specific provisions.	N/A	
(d) Confirm that movements on the general provision are adjusted in the computation.	N/A	
2.8 Subscriptions and donations		
(a) Confirm that all disallowable items are adjusted in the computation.	N/A	
(b) Confirm that covenants are deducted as gross charges in the computation and that income tax deducted is paid over.	N/A	
(c) Confirm that all non-covenanted charitable donations covered by Gift Aid are claimed as charges and that the CT61 procedure has been followed, with income tax paid over.	N/A	
2.9 Sundry expenses		
(a) Confirm that the analysis highlights disallowable items (if not otherwise covered by this checklist).	Y	Miscellaneous exps. reviewed
(b) Confirm that all disallowable items are adjusted in the computation.	N/A	
2.10 Formation expenses		
Confirm that these are adjusted in the computation.	N/A	
2.11 Penalties		
Confirm that all disallowable penalties (e.g., VAT default surcharges) are identified and adjusted in the computation.	N/A	

Client: Bright-a-Light Ltd		Prepared by: EAA	Date: 23.6.95	Ref: **P3**
Year/Period End: 31.3.95	File No:	Reviewed by: DGW	Date: 3.7.95	

CORPORATION TAX COMPUTATION CHECKLIST (*cont.*)

	Yes/No or N/A	Comments
2.12 Directors' emoluments		
(a) Confirm that the schedule showing analysis of directors' remuneration and benefits is complete.	Y	Q7
(b) Confirm that bonuses have been 'paid' within nine months after year end. (If not, add back and deduct in year of payment.)	N/A	
2.13 Pension contributions		
(a) Confirm that the computation is adjusted for accruals.	N/A	None
(b) Confirm that the computation is adjusted for spreading of special contributions (see booklet IR12).	N/A	
2.14 Rent		
(a) Confirm that rents paid to persons resident outside the UK are disclosed separately in the computation.	N/A	
(b) Confirm that tax has been deducted from rents paid to non-residents.	N/A	
(c) Confirm that the deductible proportion of short lease premiums has been correctly claimed under s87 ICTA 1988.	N/A	
(d) Confirm that rents received are excluded from the computation but are included as Schedule A income in calculating the profits chargeable to corporation tax.	Y	
2.15 Interest and royalties paid		
(a) Confirm that a schedule has been prepared showing payees and dates, whether paid gross or net (and reason for paying gross, if applicable).	N	All normal bank/finance lease interest
(b) Confirm that 'annual payments' are excluded from the computation.	N/A	
(c) Confirm that amounts paid in respect of 'annual payments' are deducted as a gross charge in calculating the profits chargeable to corporation tax.	N/A	
(d) Confirm that income tax deducted is paid over and that CT61 returns are up to date and profit and loss account entries reconciled with CT61.	N/A	
2.16 Interest and royalties received		
(a) Confirm that the schedule identifies whether amounts received are gross or net of tax.	N/A	None
(b) Confirm that amounts are excluded from the computation, but are included as Case III or Unfranked Investment Income, in calculating the profits chargeable to corporation tax.	N/A	
(c) Confirm that income tax deducted at source from income is deducted from corporation tax payable (or identified as tax recoverable).	N/A	

Client: Bright-a-Light Ltd		Prepared by: EAA	Date: 23·6·95	Ref: **P3**
Year/Period End: 31.3.95	File No:	Reviewed by: DGW	Date: 3.7.95	

CORPORATION TAX COMPUTATION CHECKLIST (*cont.*)

	Yes/No or N/A	Comments
2.17 Dividends received		
(a) Confirm that they are excluded from the computation.	N/A	
(b) Confirm that they are grossed up in the accounts and tax credits form part of the tax charge (Franked Investment Income affects small companies' marginal rate computation).	N/A	
(c) Confirm that tax credits are only treated as recoverable where loss relief is available and a relevant election is made under s242 ICTA 1988.	N/A	
2.18 Dividends paid Confirm that ACT has been accounted for on all dividends paid since the last accounts.	N/A	
3 *Fixed assets*		
(a) Confirm that total additions per accounts reconcile with additions per capital allowance computation.	Y	A2 excludes finance lease
(b) Confirm that 40% first year allowance is being claimed for expenditure on plant and machinery from 1/11/92 until 31/10/93.	N/A	
(c) Confirm that 20% initial allowance is being claimed for expenditure on industrial or agricultural buildings.	N/A	
(d) Confirm that all available industrial or agricultural buildings allowances are claimed for property expenditure (and any disallowed repairs) from 1/11/92 until 31/10/93 brought into use by 31/12/94.	N/A	
(e) Confirm that any disposals with proceeds above cost are dealt with appropriately (i.e., proceeds for capital allowance purposes restricted to cost; proceeds above cost treated as chargeable gain).	N/A	
(f) Confirm that elections for short life assets under s37 CAA 1990, are made where appropriate (e.g., computers, vans, etc.).	N/A	None
(g) Confirm that writing down allowances have been restricted in accordance with the length of the accounting period.	N/A	12 months
(h) Confirm that writing down allowances have been restricted as appropriate on 'expensive' cars.	N/A	below £12K
(i) Confirm that all 'inexpensive' cars have been pooled for capital allowance purposes.	Y	
4 *Chargeable gains*		
4.1 Confirm computations have been prepared for disposals of:		
(a) Freehold/leasehold property.	N/A	
(b) Investments.	N/A	
(c) Goodwill.	N/A	

Client: Bright-a-Light Ltd		Prepared by: EAA	Date: 23.6.95	Ref: **P3**
Year/Period End: 31.3.95	File No:	Reviewed by: DGW	Date: 3.7.95	

CORPORATION TAX COMPUTATION CHECKLIST (*cont.*)

	Yes/No or N/A	Comments
4.2 Confirm computation shows:	N/A	
(a) Date of acquisition.		
(b) Cost of acquisition.		
(c) Cost of enhancements/improvements.		
(d) Amount of sale proceeds and expenses.		
(e) Values at 6/4/65 and 31/3/82 where relevant.		
5 Treatment of Case I or II losses	N/A	
5.1 Confirm that losses have been set off in the most effective way by consideration of the following possibilities:		
(a) Set off against other current year profits (including chargeable gains).		
(b) Carry back (against profits of previous three years).		
(c) Carry forward – only against Case I or II profits of the same business (take care not to offset losses brought forward against Case III, Schedule A income, etc.).		
(d) Confirm that losses carried forward are allowed for, as appropriate, in deferred tax calculations.		
6 Groups	N/A	
6.1 Inter-group dividends		
(a) Confirm that any dividends paid by one member of the group to another have been identified.		
(b) Confirm that an election has been made under s247 ICTA 1988 for dividends to be paid gross.		
(c) Confirm that any dividends have been paid in accordance with the s247 election.		
6.2 Inter-group charges on income		
(a) Confirm that an election has been made under s247 ICTA 1988.		
(b) Confirm that all relevant charges on income have been paid gross.		

Client: Bright-a-Light Ltd		Prepared by: EAA	Date: 23.6.95	Ref: **P3**
Year/Period End: 31.3.95	File No:	Reviewed by: DGW	Date: 3.7.95	

CORPORATION TAX COMPUTATION CHECKLIST (*cont.*)

	Yes/No or N/A	Comments
6.3 Inter-group transfer of assets		
(a) Confirm schedule prepared showing details of assets transferred and name of company to which transferred.	N/A	
(b) Confirm schedule shows details of when each asset was first acquired by the group.	N/A	
(c) Confirm schedule shows details of original cost to the group of each asset, and also value at 6/4/65 and 31/3/82 (where relevant).	N/A	
6.4 Group relief Confirm claims for surrender of loss relief to other group companies have been made in time for:	N/A	
(a) Trading losses.	N/A	
(b) Capital allowances.	N/A	
(c) Excess charges on income.	N/A	
(d) Excess management expenses.	N/A	

Conclusions

1 I consider that assistance from a taxation specialist ~~is~~/is not* required.

2 The computations do/~~do not~~* deal correctly with all material matters relating to corporation tax.

3 The accounts do/~~do not~~* include all material corporation tax liabilities.

4 Any corporation tax aspects which require bringing to the client's attention have been recorded on **B5** or **B8**.

Senior/Manager EA Arbuthnott Date 23.6.95

Reviewed by DGW Date 3.7.95

*Delete as appropriate.

Client		File No.	Ref.
Bright-a-Light Ltd			P4
Subject		Prepared by	Date
Proof of tax		EAA	23/6/95
		Reviewed by	Date
		DGW	3/7/95
		Accounting Dates	31·3·95

			£	£
Profit per accounts				17,320.00
@ 25%				4,330.00
Actual provision		P1		5,630.25
Difference				£1,300.25
Depreciation on building	5,223 @ 25%	F3.1		1,305.75
Movement on unprovided deferred tax	(£127 – £121)	P5		(6.00)
Small randing difference				0.50
				£1,300.25

Client		File No.	Ref.
Bright-a-Light Ltd			P5
Subject		Prepared by	Date
Deferred Tax Provision		EAA	23/6/95
		Reviewed by	Date
		DGW	3/7/95
		Accounting Dates	31·3·95

			1995	*1994*
		£	*£*	*£*
Net book value (F1)				
Plant			2,280.00	2,850.00
Motor vehicles			17,626.00	10,768.00
Fixtures			1,382.00	1,302.00
			21,288.00	14,920.00
less leased asset (F6)	(£8,995 – £2,998)		(5,997.00)	—
			15,291.00	14,920.00
Tax written down value (A2)				
Fixtures		3,016.00		(3,696.00)
Motor vehicles		11,765.00		(10,738.00)
			(14,781.00)	
Timing difference			£510.00	486.00
@ 25%			£127.50	£121.50

Client has not made a provision for deferred tax.
Transferred to schedule of unadjusted errors (B7) and points for partner.

Q INCOME

1	Turnover	
2	Dividend and interest received/receivable	
3	Rent received/receivable	
4	Management charges	
5		
6		

EXPENDITURE

7	Directors' emoluments	✓
8	Interest payable	
9	Subscriptions and donations	
10	Insurance (cover and premiums)	
11	Repairs and renewals None over £500	
12	Legal, professional and audit None over £500 except audit	
13	Entertaining	
14	Sundry None over £1000	
15		
16		

Client Bright-a-Light Ltd	File No.	Ref. Q7
Subject Benefits in kind	Prepared by EAA	Date 22/6/95
	Reviewed by DGW	Date 3/7/95
	Accounting Dates 31·3·95	

Mr K Strike

	£
Montego 1600cc MV £9,600 1.4.94 to 18.6.94	
$£9,600 \times 35\% \times \frac{2}{3} \times \frac{2.5}{12}$ months	467
Peugeot 405 1900cc MV £10,680 19.6.94 – 31.3.95	
$£10,680 \times 35\% \times \frac{2}{3} \times \frac{9.5}{12}$ months	1,973
Fuel	810
Mobile telephone	200
	£3,450

Mrs B Strike

	£
Renault 1605cc > 4 years old MV £8,250	
$£8,250 \times 35\% \times \frac{2}{3} \times \frac{2}{3}$	1,283
Fuel	810
	£5,543

NB: All car mileage between 2,500 and 18,000 miles per annum.

R PROFIT AND LOSS

1 Lead schedule ✓

2 Audit programme ✓

3 ~~Audit work summary~~ Audit work programme - PAYE & national insurance ✓

4 Audit work summary ✓

5

6

S CASH FLOW STATEMENTS

1 Lead schedule and explanations

2

3

4

Client: Bright-a-Light Ltd		Prepared by:	Date:	Ref: **R**
Year/Period End: 31.3.95	File No:	Reviewed by:	Date:	

SUMMARY SHEET – PROFIT AND LOSS

Audit objectives	***Planning*** Number of tests which satisfy objective	Additional/ alternative tests to be carried out	***Final*** Are you satisfied that the objectives have been met?	Comments	Initials
1 To ensure that income is not under stated and is correctly classified.	1, ~~2~~, 3, 4, 5, ~~6~~, 7, 8, 9, ~~10~~, 11, 12, 28		Yes/~~No~~		EAA
2 To ensure that expenditure is not over stated, is authorised and correctly classified.	1, ~~2~~, 3, ~~15~~, ~~16~~, 28		Yes/~~No~~		EAA
3 To ensure all items are processed in the correct period.	1, ~~2~~, 3, 5, 14, 28		Yes/~~No~~		EAA
4 To ensure that wages and salaries are correctly accounted for.	1, ~~2~~, 3, ~~18~~, 19, 20, 21, 22, 23, 28		Yes/~~No~~		EAA
5 To ensure that items requiring specific disclosure are correctly reported.	1, ~~2~~, 3, 11, 23, 28		Yes/~~No~~		EAA
6 To ensure the nominal ledger is correctly maintained.	1, ~~2~~, 3, 25, 26, 27, 28		Yes/~~No~~		EAA

Conclusion

From the audit work carried out I confirm that:

- nothing has occurred to necessitate changing the audit plan* ~~or the audit plan has been updated~~.*
- nothing has occurred to necessitate revising the risk assessment* ~~or the risk assessment has been revised.~~*
- nothing has occurred to necessitate revising the materiality level* ~~or the materiality has been revised~~.*
- ~~adjustments to the plan, risk assessment and materiality have been detailed on **B5** or **B8**~~.*
- the work has been performed in accordance with the audit programme.
- the work performed and the results obtained have been adequately documented.
- all necessary information has been collected for the preparation of the statutory accounts.
- in my opinion (~~subject to the matters highlighted on **B5** or **B8**~~)* the profit and loss account is fairly stated.

Prepared by EA Arbuthnott Date 22.6.95

Reviewed by DG Watson Date 3.7.95

*Delete if not applicable.

Alternative conclusion (*ANY* alternative conclusion *MUST* be referred to on **B5** or **B8**)

Prepared by ______________________ Date __________

Reviewed by ______________________ Date __________

Client: Bright-a-Light Ltd		Prepared by: KM	Date: 15.6.95	Ref: **R2**
Year/Period End: 31.3.95	File No:	Reviewed by: EAA	Date: 22.6.95	

AUDIT PROGRAMME – PROFIT AND LOSS ACCOUNT

Nature of test:	Test required Y/N	Covered by accountancy Y	Results satisfactory Y/N	Ref/ comments	Initials and date
General					
1 Assess whether the initial materiality and/or risk assessment should be revised in view of the audit evidence obtained to date.	Y		Y	No revision needed	KM 15.6.95
2 Undertake detailed analytical review procedures and determine whether the results enable us to reduce our sample sizes.	N		—	—	EAA 8.6.95
3 Review for large and unusual items and verify.	Y		Y	None	KM 15.6.95
Income					
4 Identify all material sources of income and specify how each source has been audited (either by standard tests below or a tailored programme).	Y		Y	C7	KM 15.6.95
5 Where available, select a sample of goods despatched notes, including a number of items around the year end and vouch to supporting documentation. (a) Vouch details to invoice.	Y		Y	R4.1	KM 15.6.95
(b) Agree invoices through to day book, sales ledger, nominal ledger and cash book.	Y		Y	R4.1	KM 15.6.95
(c) Ensure item accounted for in the correct period.	Y		Y	R4.1	KM 15.6.95
6 Where goods despatched notes are not used/ retained, specify below the audit work to ensure that all sales made are invoiced:	N		—	—	EAA 8.6.95

Client: Bright-a-Light Ltd		Prepared by: KM	Date: 15.6.95	Ref: **R2**
Year/Period End: 31.3.95	File No:	Reviewed by: EAA	Date: 22.6.95	

AUDIT PROGRAMME – PROFIT AND LOSS ACCOUNT (*cont.*)

	Test required Y/N	Covered by accountancy Y	Results satisfactory Y/N	Ref/ comments	Initials and date
7 Where pre-numbered invoices are used check the sequence and investigate missing items.	Y		Y	R4.3	KM 15.6.95
Cash sales					
8 Check to ensure that cash sales are banked regularly.	Y		Y	R5	KM 15.6.95
9 Select a sample of till rolls or sales dockets, and vouch to supporting documentation.	Y		Y	R5	KM 15.6.95
(a) Check the additions.					
(b) Check the numerical sequence and investigate any missing items.	Y		Y	R5	KM 15.6.95
(c) Check the pricing.	Y		Y	R5	KM 15.6.95
(d) For till rolls, ensure that the level of 'no sales' is acceptable.	Y		Y	R5	KM 15.6.95
(e) Check total cash sales to the cash book.	Y		Y	R5	KM 15.6.95
Sales returns					
10 Review sales returns and, where material, select a sample and vouch to supporting documentation.	N		—	Not Material	EAA 8.6.95
(a) Ensure the details agree to the original invoice.					
(b) Check the quantity and description on the credit note to a goods returned note or other documentary proof of receipt of goods.	N		—		
(c) Vouch posting to sales ledger.	N	—	—		
(d) Vouch posting, via sales day book, to the nominal ledger.	N	—	—		
Other income					
11 Check that, prima facie, all grants to which the client is entitled have been claimed.	Y		Y	None	EAA 8.6.95
12 Vouch any material other income to supporting documentation and ensure that it is correctly described.	Y		Y	R6	EAA 12.6.95

Client: Bright-a-Light Ltd		Prepared by: KM	Date: 15.6.95	Ref: **R2**
Year/Period End: 31.3.95	File No:	Reviewed by: EAA	Date: 22.6.95	

AUDIT PROGRAMME – PROFIT AND LOSS ACCOUNT (*cont.*)

	Test required Y/N	Covered by accountancy Y	Results satisfactory Y/N	Ref/ comments	Initials and date
13 Other tests:	N	—	—	—	EAA 8.6.95
Expenditure					
14 Select a sample of payments and vouch to supporting documentation. (a) Ensure the invoice is properly authorised.	Y		Y	R7.1	KM 15.6.95
(b) Ensure the invoice is correctly classified.	Y		Y		
(c) Ensure the invoice is properly addressed.	Y		Y		
(d) Check the casts and cross casts.	Y		Y		
(e) Ensure discount is taken where appropriate.	Y		Y		
(f) Trace details to goods received notes and orders.	Y		Y		
(g) Trace the invoice and payment to the purchase ledger.	Y		Y		
(h) Inspect the paid cheque and ensure that it: (i) is payable to the person or company specified on the invoice; (ii) has not been altered; and (iii) is signed by an authorised signatory.	Y		Y		
Cash expenditure					
15 Select a sample of cash purchases and vouch to supporting documentation. (a) Ensure the invoice is properly authorised.	N		—	None	EAA 8.6.95
(b) Ensure the invoice is correctly classified.	N	—	—		
(c) Ensure the invoice is properly addressed.	N	—	—		
(d) Check the casts and cross casts.	N	—	—		
(e) Trace details to goods received notes and orders.	N		—		
(f) Trace to the nominal ledger.	N	—	—		

Client: Bright-a-Light Ltd		Prepared by: KM	Date: 15.6.95	Ref: **R2**
Year/Period End: 31.3.95	File No:	Reviewed by: EAA	Date: 22.6.95	

AUDIT PROGRAMME – PROFIT AND LOSS ACCOUNT *(cont.)*

	Test required Y/N	Covered by accountancy Y	Results satisfactory Y/N	Ref/ comments	Initials and date
Purchase returns					
16 Review purchase returns and, where material, select a sample and vouch to supporting documentation. (a) Vouch details to original invoice.	N		—	Not material	EAA 8.6.95
(b) Agree details to credit note.	N		—		
(c) Vouch posting to purchase ledger.	N	—	—		
(d) Vouch posting, via the day book, to the nominal ledger.	N	—	—		
17 Other tests:	N	—	—	—	EAA 8.6.95
Wages and salaries					
18 Prepare a summary of wages and salaries and number of employees (month by month). Explain any material fluctuations from expectations.	N		—	Low numbers covered by 19 & 20	EAA 8.6.95
19 Select a sample of payrolls. (a) Check the casts and cross casts.	Y	Y	Y	R8.1 & R8.2	KM 16.6.95
(b) Check the postings to the nominal ledger.	N	—	—	No N/L	EAA 8.6.95
(c) Check the total net to the cash book.	Y	Y	Y	R8.1	KM 16.6.95
(d) Ensure that payroll is authorised by a responsible official.	Y		Y	cheques signed by director	KM 16.6.95
(e) Ensure that the PAYE/NI is paid over properly.	Y	Y	Y	R8.1 & R8.2	KM 16.6.95
20 Select a sample of employees and vouch. (a) Agree employee details to personnel records.	Y		Y	R8.1 + R8.2	KM 16.6.95
(b) Check rates of pay to authorisation.	Y		Y		
(c) Where applicable check hours to time records.	Y		Y		
(d) Where applicable check production to piecework records.	N		—	—	EAA 8.6.95
(e) Ensure all overtime has been authorised.	Y		Y	R8.1 + R8.2	KM 16.6.95
(f) Check the calculation of gross pay, deductions and net pay.	Y		Y		

Client: Bright-a-Light Ltd		Prepared by: KM	Date: 5.6.95	Ref: **R2**
Year/Period End: 31.3.95	File No:	Reviewed by: EAA	Date: 22.6.95	

AUDIT PROGRAMME – PROFIT AND LOSS ACCOUNT (*cont.*)

	Test required Y/N	Covered by accountancy Y	Results satisfactory Y/N	Ref/ comments	Initials and date
21 Enquire into unclaimed wages and verify.	Y		Y	None	KM 16.6.95
22 Complete the PAYE and National Insurance audit programme on **R3**.	Y		Y	R3	EAA 22.6.95
23 Obtain details of directors' emoluments paid and payable, including benefits-in-kind.	Y		Y	Q7	EAA 22.6.95
24 Other tests:	N	—	—	—	EAA 8.6.95
Other					
25 (a) Enquire of the directors whether the company has entered into any transactions in which one or more of the directors have an interest.	Y		Y	None	EAA 22.6.95
(b) Consider whether any such transactions need to be disclosed in the accounts.	Y		Y	N/A	EAA 22.6.95
26 (a) Check the casts and cross casts of the cash book, sales day book and purchase day book.	Y	Y	Y		KM 9.6.95
(b) Check casts of a sample of nominal ledger accounts.	N	—	—	No N/L	EAA 8.6.95
(c) Check postings to the nominal ledger.	N	—	—	No N/L	EAA 8.6.95
(d) Check extraction of final trial balances.	N	—	—	No N/L	EAA 8.6.95
(e) Check the cast of the trial balance.	Y	Y	Y		EAA 22.6.95
(f) Ensure all adjustments to the accounts are recorded in the books of the company.	N	—	—	NO N/L	EAA 8.6.95
(g) Agree the closing balances to the accounts.	Y	Y	Y		KM 5.7.95
27 Analyse for tax and/or disclosure purposes the following: (Specify): Legal fees	Y		Y	Q12	KM 9.6.95
Rental income	Y		Y	R6	EAA 22.6.95

Client: Bright-a-Light Ltd		Prepared by: KM	Date: 15.6.95	Ref: **R2**
Year/Period End: 31.8.95	File No:	Reviewed by: EAA	Date: 22.6.95	

AUDIT PROGRAMME – PROFIT AND LOSS ACCOUNT (*cont.*)

Conclusion

	Test required Y/N	Covered by accountancy Y	Results satisfactory Y/N	Ref/ comments	Initials and date
28 Consider whether there are any points which need to be included in a letter of representation or letter of comment and record on **A5** or **A6** as appropriate.	Y		Y	None	EAA 22.6.95
29 Other tests:	N	—	—	—	EAA 8.6.95

Client: Bright-a-Light Ltd		Prepared by: EAA	Date: 22.6.95	Ref: **R3**
Year/Period End: 31.3.95	File No:	Reviewed by: DGW	Date: 3.7.95	

AUDIT PROGRAMME – PAYE AND NATIONAL INSURANCE

Nature of test:	Test required Y/N	Covered by accountancy Y	Results satisfactory Y/N	Ref/ comments	Initials and date
1 Enquire into the system for reimbursing expenditure incurred by employees. Is it fully documented?	Y		Y	No expenses claimed	EAA 22.6.95
2 Review end of year returns – P35s/P38As, etc.: (a) confirm that they were submitted on time; and	Y		Y		EAA 22.6.95
(b) confirm that copies are held.	Y		Y		EAA 22.6.95
3 Review the cash book for any unusual payments, e.g., round sums, private bills, etc. Confirm that they are correctly treated for PAYE/NIC purposes.	Y		Y	None	EAA 22.6.95
4 Review P11Ds/P9Ds to ensure that: (a) there are no apparent omissions; and	Y		Y	None	EAA 22.6.95
(b) any dispensations are still valid.	Y		Y	None	EAA 22.6.95
5 Complete the following checklists: (a) PAYE and NI on **R3.1**.	N		—	—	EAA 22.6.95
(b) P11D on **R3.2**.	N		—	—	EAA 22.6.95
Conclusion 6 Do the checklists highlight any outstanding liabilities?	Y		Y	None. very simple system	EAA 22.6.95
7 Other tests:	N	—	—	—	EAA 22.6.95

Client Bright-a-Light Ltd	File No.	Ref. R4.1
Subject Credit sales	Prepared by KM	Date 15/6/95
Completeness – GDN testing (test 5)	Reviewed by EAA	Date 22/6/95
	Accounting Dates 31·3·95	

Sample size – low inherent risk – factor = 1.2

Credit sales population = £748,100
No 'high value' items
Sample size $= \frac{£748,100}{£15,000} \times 1.2 \times \frac{1}{2} = 30$

Tolerable error $= \frac{15,000}{1.2} = £12,500$

Audit work

A sample of 30 goods despatch notes (GDN) was taken throughout the year from the file maintained in the warehouse. The first GDN number was selected at random, and then every 39th GDN was selected. The following tests were carried out:

(a) Agree details (customer, goods & date) to invoice.
(b) Agree despatch of item to stock card.
(c) Casts and pricing of invoice checked.
(d) Invoice traced to sales day book & sales ledger.
(e) Trace payment of invoice, agree to cash book and bank statements or ensure included in debtors.
(f) Ensure invoice in correct period.

Results

(a) see R4.2 – one debtor has not paid because he went bust, owes £295.89.

Conclusion

Subject to above, I am satisfied that income is not understated.

NB Manager review – debtor has been provided for.
See J4.2.

Client	File No.	Ref.
Bright-a-Light Ltd		R4.2

Subject	Prepared by	Date
Sales – GDN testing (test 5)	KM	15/6/95
	Reviewed by	**Date**
	EAA	22/6/95
	Accounting Dates	31·3·95

	GDN no & date	*Invoice no & date*	*Customer*	*Goods*	*Payment date*	*Tests* (a)	(b)	(c)	(d)	(e)	(f)	*Tests satisfactory*
(1)	2196 4.4.94	910462 4.4.94	Mr George	5 × 10 kg Coalite	5.6.94	√	√	√	√	√	√	√
(2)	2235 18.4.94	910476 18.4.94	A J Spratts	10 × 10 kg Warmacite	— Bad debt	√	√	√	√	(a)	√	(a)
(3)	2274 3.5.94	910600 3.5.94	Binns Motors	20 × 15 kg Shellgas	3.6.94	√	√	√	√	√	√	√
(4)	2313 20.5.94	910670 20.5.94	Edwards Garage	30 × 15 kg Shellgas	29.7.94	√	√	√	√	√	√	√
(5)	2352 3.6.94	910759 3.6.94	DEF Plumbing	Valiant Water Heater	30.9.94	√	√	√	√	√	√	√
(6)	2391 20.6.94	910787 20.6.94	Dorset Garages	20 × 46 kg Shellgas	29.8.94	√	√	√	√	√	√	√
(7)	2430 8.7.94	910815 8.7.94	Freds Coals	20 × 25 kg Maxibrite	2.9.94	√	√	√	√	√	√	√
(8)	2469 29.7.94	910863 29.7.94	Mr R Hall	6 × 3 kg Charcoal	1.8.94	√	√	√	√	√	√	√
(9)	2508 8.8.94	910869 8.8.94	Newtown Stores	20 × 10 kg Peat blocks	2.9.94	√	√	√	√	√	√	√
(10)	2547 23.8.94	910929 23.8.94	Mr M. Skinner	10 × 25 kg Coalite	16.9.94	√	√	√	√	√	√	√
(11)	2586 2.9.94	910965 2.9.94	ABC Solid Fuels	50 × 25 kg DSLN	4.11.94	√	√	√	√	√	√	√
(12)	2625 30.9.94	911040 30.9.94	Mr T Smith	5 × 10 kg Coalite	30.9.94	√	√	√	√	√	√	√
(13)	2664 4.10.94	911089 4.10.94	Mr A Morris	2 × 46 kg Shellgas	4.10.94	√	√	√	√	√	√	√
(14)	2703 18.10.94	911142 18.10.94	P Kingdom Ltd	4 × 46 kg Shellgas	2.12.94	√	√	√	√	√	√	√
(15)	2742 21.10.94	911151 21.10.94	Mr Stackhouse	2 × 46 kg Shellgas	31.10.94	√	√	√	√	√	√	√
(16)	2781 31.10.94	911171 31.10.94	A O'Kane	5 × 10 kg Housecoal C	8.11.94	√	√	√	√	√	√	√
(17)	2820 4.11.94	911248 4.11.94	Mrs Mills	5 × 10 kg Housecoal B	2.12.94	√	√	√	√	√	√	√
(18)	2859 11.11.94	911260 14.11.94	A B Oldfield Ltd	20 × 10 kg Lumpwood charcoal	6.1.95	√	√	√	√	√	√	√
(19)	2898 21.11.94	911344 21.11.94	Geo. Stone Ltd	4 × 46 kg Shellgas	3.2.95	√	√	√	√	√	√	√
(20)	2937 29.11.94	911389 2.12.94	Westway Filling Station	20 × 15 kg Shellgas	3.2.95	√	√	√	√	√	√	√
(21)	2976 5.12.94	911433 5.12.94	Dorset Garages	30 × 15 kg Shellgas	6.2.95	√	√	√	√	√	√	√
(22)	3015 23.12.94	911486 23.12.94	Supa Fuel Ltd	20 × 25 kg Fireglo	3.3.95	√	√	√	√	√	√	√
(23)	3054 30.12.94	911527 30.12.94	Bow Garage	30 × 10 kg Housecoal B	10.3.95	√	√	√	√	√	√	√
(24)	3093 6.1.95	920008 6.1.95	Dorset Garages	30 × 10 kg Coalite	17.3.95	√	√	√	√	√	√	√

Client		File No.	Ref.
Bright-a-Light Ltd			R4.2
Subject: Sales – GDN testing (test 5)		Prepared by: KM	Date: 15/6/95
		Reviewed by: EAA	Date: 22/6/95
		Accounting Dates: 31·3·95	

	GDN no & date	*Invoice no & date*	*Customer*	*Goods*	*Payment date*	*Tests* (a)	(b)	(c)	(d)	(e)	(f)	*Tests satisfactory*
(25)	3132 23.1.95	920093 23.1.95	Mr K Palmer	5 × 10 kg Housecoal B	27.2.95	√	√	√	√	√	√	√
(26)	3171 1.2.95	920174 3.2.95	I Rush	2 × 46 kg Shellgas	4.5.95	√	√	√	√	√	√	√
(27)	3210 14.2.95	920237 14.2.95	Wilson Motors	10 × 15 kg Shellgas	6.4.95	√	√	√	√	√	√	√
(28)	3249 28.2.95	920273 28.2.95	Slaters Garage	10 × 46 kg Shellgas	14.4.95	√	√	√	√	√	√	√
(29)	3288 9.3.95	920313 10.3.95	Newtown Stores	50 × 10 kg Coalite	1.5.95	√	√	√	√	√	√	√
(30)	3327 17.3.95	920354 17.3.95	A O'Kane	50 × 25 kg Housecoal	5.5.95	√	√	√	√	√	√	√

(a) See R4.1.

Client Bright-a-Light Ltd	File No.	Ref. R4.3
Subject Credit sales – sequence testing (test 7)	Prepared by KM	Date 15/6/95
	Reviewed by EAA	Date 22/6/95
	Accounting Dates 31·3·95	

Work done

The numerical sequence of invoices and GDNs was checked for completeness. Where gaps in the sequence were found, the cancelled copy documents were checked. These are kept by the client to ensure completeness of the sequence.

Sequences tested and found to be complete.

Sales invoices	January 95	nos	920001–920173
	Sept 94	nos	910963–911042
GDN	Feb 95	nos	3170–3250
	June 94	nos	2350–2412

Conclusion

Income is not understated by the omission of sales invoices or GDNs.

Client		File No.	Ref.
Bright-a-Light Ltd			R5
Subject		**Prepared by**	**Date**
Cash Sales – completeness		KM	16/6/95
		Reviewed by	**Date**
– test 9		EAA	22/6/95
		Accounting Dates	31·3·95

Sample size – low inherent risk – factor = 1.2

Cash sales population = £113,317
No 'high value' items
Sample size $= \frac{£113,317}{£15,000} \times 1.2 \times \frac{1}{2} = 5$

Tolerable error $= \frac{15,000}{1.2} = £12,500$

Audit work

Five days were selected for testing. The 15th of every other month was selected (or nearest working day), except March, and the following tests carried out:

(a) agreed to daily cash sheet.
(b) agreed to cash book.
(c) casts of cash book and cash sheet checked.
(d) agreed to banking – any unusual delays were investigated.
(e) level of 'no sales' reviewed for reasonableness

	till roll date	*total £*	*banking date*	*agrees to cash sheet*	*agrees to cash book*	*casts OK*	*agrees to banking*	*level of 'no sales' reasonable*
(1)	16.5.94	352-12	17.5.94	√	√	√	√	√
(2)	15.7.94	309.91	18.7.94	√	√	√	√	√
(3)	16.9.94	382-12	19.9.94	√	√	√	√	√
(4)	15.11.94	513.08	16.11.94	√	√	√	√	√
(5)	16.1.95	521-98	17.1.95	√	√	√	√	√

Conclusions

Cash sales are not materially mis-stated.

NOTE

Cash sales are banked on the next working day. The takings for Friday and Saturday mornings are banked on the following Monday. This was reviewed during the above tests and no indication of any unusual delays were seen.

The till roll totals are entered onto daily cash sheets. These also show sales ledger cheques received, and back up the amounts banked.

Numerical sequence of till rolls checked for July, December and March – no missing days.

Client		File No.	Ref.
Bright-a-Light Ltd			R6
Subject Rental Income		Prepared by EAA	Date 19/6/95
		Reviewed by DGW	Date 3/7/95
		Accounting Dates 31·3·95	

Audit work

Client rents out the following buildings on its site at Westend Industrial Estate. Rental income was estimated using the rental agreements kept by Mr Strike, and then compared with the actual figure. Any discrepancies were investigated.

Building	*Tenant*	*Annual rent*	*Occupation*	*Expected rent*
		£		£
Store 1	J Austin Distribution	7,250	Full Year	7,250
2	Duchy Supply Ltd	5,250	4 months	1,750
3	ABC Cleaning Services	1,500	Full year	1,500
4	Mr Dodger	260	Full year	260
	Expected income			10,760
	Actual rent			10,530
	Difference			£230

Difference arises because J Austin Distribution not billed in full for March 95 – rent reduced from £604.16 pcm to £375 pcm. J Austin Distribution is run by Mr Strike's brother-in-law and was having cash flow problems (see also Debtors).

File No.		Ref	R7.1
Prepared by:	KM	Date	13/6/95
Reviewed by:	EAA	Date	22/6/95
Accounting Dates P/E			31/3/95

Client **Bright-a-light Limited**

PURCHASES – Test 14

Payments per R7.2	756,303	Fuel Supplies & Arthur Fuels are the two major suppliers. These have been tested as follows:
less Fuel Supplies/Arthur Fuels	529,021	– Statements are retained for both suppliers – the year end statements will be reconciled – See L3.3 & L3.4
Other payments	£227,282	– Statements reviewed throughout the year – no unusual items – Invoices only paid when matched with supporting GRN

Sample for other payments = (£227,282/£15,000) × 1.2 × $\frac{1}{2}$ = 9 items. First item on bank statement for the last day of the month selected, starting April, omitting August & Feb. & Mar.

No.	*Date*	*Amount £*	*Name*	*Agreed to authorised invoice*	*Invoice properly addressed*	*Cash book analysis agreed*	*Invoice cast*	*Discount taken if applicable*	*Agreed to GRN*	*Agreed to purchase ledger*	*Payment agreed to paid cheque*
1	29.4.94	328.88	Rosa Truck Haulage	√	√	√	√	N/A	N/A	√	√
2	31.5.94	70.46	J Stanley UK	√	√	√	√	√	N/A	√	√
3	30.6.94	10,801.84	Sheedy minerals	√	√	√	√	N/A	√	√	√
4	29.7.94	157.66	J Sanders Ltd	√	√	√	√	√	√	√	√
5	30.9.94	313.95	Coal Dust Ltd	√	√	√	√	√	√	√	√
6	31.10.94	4,612.91	Gimeg	√	√	√	√	√	√	√	√
7	30.11.94	6,324.13	E C Fuels	√	√	√	√	N/A	√	√	√
8	30.12.94	231.15	Rangewell Garages	√	√	√	√	N/A	N/A	√	√
9	31.1.95	118.30	BWE Electrics	√	√	√	√	N/A	N/A	√	√

Conclusion Purchases and other payments are not materially mis-stated.

Client	File No.	Ref.
Bright-a-Light Ltd		R7.2

Subject	Prepared by	Date
Purchases and expenses sample selection	KM	8/6/95
	Reviewed by EAA	Date 9/6/95
	Accounting Dates	31·3·95

Figures per original summary trial balance

		£	
Total debits for P & L		863,419	
less opening stock		(22,860)	
		840,559	
less items tested elsewhere:			
wages, National Insurance & pensions			
– delivery costs	16,048		
– yard establishment	6,760		
– management	21,361		
– finance	11,467		
		(55,636)	
Accountancy		(4,400)	
Depreciation		(5,705)	
Loan interest		(13,912)	
Bank charges and interest		(3,807)	
Legal fees		(388)	
Credit card charges		(408)	
		£756,303	R7.1

Client Bright-a-Light Ltd	File No.	Ref. R8.1
Subject Weekly wages testing – review of employees	Prepared by KM	Date 16/6/95
	Reviewed by EAA	Date 22/6/95
	Accounting Dates 31·3·95	

Population	=	£55,636 Total wages & salaries	–	28,738 monthly per R8.2	–	2,052 monthly pensions	=	£24,846 population

Sample size $= \frac{24{,}846}{15{,}000} \times 1.2 \times \frac{1}{2} = 0.99$, say 1

Name	*Gross pay* £	*Review personnel records for existence*
Delivery wages		
M Sargeant	7,601.35α	√
A Jeffries	2,673.25α	√
B Hill	3,111.48α	√
	13,386.08	
Yard wages		
D Flowers	5,778.70α	√

α Agreed to P35

Audit work

Wages are paid weekly and will vary depending on overtime etc. Therefore a detailed review of payments to individual employees has not been done.

The following payment to D Flowers was checked (see above – only one item needs testing in detail)

w/e 21.10.94	*Gross pay*	£106.00 (40 hours @ £2.65)
	PAYE	8.31
	EE NIC	6.04
	Cash paid	£91.65

(a) Gross Pay agreed to hourly rate per personnel file, 40 hours is normal working week.
(b) Calculation of PAYE & EE NIC checked, and agreed to P11.
(c) Casts and cross casts of weekly payroll checked.
(d) Net pay agreed to cash book.
(e) Payment of PAYE & NIC checked (to Yellow Book).

Conclusion

Weekly wages are fairly stated.

Client		File No.	Ref.
Bright-a-Light Ltd			R8.2
Subject		**Prepared by**	**Date**
Monthly salaries tesing		KM	16/6/95
		Reviewed by	**Date**
		EAA	22/6/95
		Accounting Dates	31·3·95

	Gross pay
K Strike	12,450α
Mrs B Strike	5,000α
	17,450
S Rideout	11,288α
	28,738

α = Agreed to P35

The monthly employees are all known by us, so that existence has been covered.
Directors' pay agreed to minutes of board mtg. S Rideout agreed to personnel records.
Deductions and net pay covered by control a/c, which balances.

March payslip for K Strike and S Rideout examined, and calculation of deductions and net pay checked.

Conclusion

Monthly salaries are fairly stated.

T POST BALANCE SHEET EVENTS

1 Lead schedule ☑

2 Final audit programme – post balance sheet events ☑

3 Audit programme – going concern ☑

4 Final programme – post balance sheet event ☑

5 ☐

6 ☐

Client: Bright-a-Light Ltd		Prepared by:	Date:	Ref: **T**
Year/Period End: 31.3.95	File No:	Reviewed by:	Date:	

SUMMARY SHEET – POST BALANCE SHEET EVENTS

Audit objectives	***Planning*** Number of tests which satisfy objective	Additional/ alternative tests to be carried out	***Final*** Are you satisfied that the objectives have been met?	Comments	Initials
1 To ensure that all material adjusting and non-adjusting post balance sheet events are identified and correctly treated in the accounts.	1, 2, ~~4~~, 5		Yes/~~No~~		EAA
2 To ensure that the going concern basis of accounting is appropriate.	3, 5		Yes/~~No~~		EAA

Conclusion

From the audit work carried out I confirm that:

- nothing has occurred to necessitate changing the audit plan* ~~or the audit plan has been updated.*~~
- nothing has occurred to necessitate revising the risk assessment* ~~or the risk assessment has been revised.*~~
- nothing has occurred to necessitate revising the materiality level* ~~or the materiality has been revised.*~~
- ~~adjustments to the plan, risk assessment and materiality have been detailed on **B5** or **B8**.*~~
- the work has been performed in accordance with the audit programme.
- the work performed and the results obtained have been adequately documented.
- all necessary information has been collected for the preparation of the statutory accounts.
- in my opinion (~~subject to the matters highlighted on **B5** or **B8**~~)* post balance sheet events are fairly stated.

Prepared by EA Arbuthnott Date 22.6.95

Reviewed by DGW Date 3.7.95

* Delete if not applicable.

Alternative conclusion (*ANY* alternative conclusion *MUST* be referred to on **B5** or **B8**)

Prepared by__________ Date__________

Reviewed by__________ Date__________

Client Bright-a-Light Ltd	File No.	Ref. T1
Subject Post balance sheet events	Prepared by EAA	Date 22/6/95
	Reviewed by DGW	Date 2/7/95
	Accounting Dates 31·3·95	

Audit work

(1) Review of cash book and invoices to 22.6.95 and bank statements to 31.5.95
– no post balance sheet events indicated

(2) Review of correspondence files to 22.6.95 and minutes to date
– no contingencies or PBSE indicated.

(3) Discussion of going concern with Mr Strike
– no problems envisaged. The company is expanding, and operates in a stable industry. Although budgets are not prepared there is no prospect of a problem within the next 12 months. Bank facilities renewed on 5.6.95.

(4) See also work done on contingencies N3.

Conclusion

No post balance sheet events have arisen and no disclosures are needed.

Client: Bright-a-Light Ltd		Prepared by: EAA	Date: 22.6.95	Ref: **T2**
Year/Period End: 31.3.95	File No:	Reviewed by: DGW	Date: 3.7.95	

AUDIT PROGRAMME – POST BALANCE SHEET EVENTS

Nature of test:	Test required Y/N	Covered by accountancy Y	Results satisfactory Y/N	Ref/ comments	Initials and date
1 Review the following to ensure that nothing has occurred since the year end which should be disclosed or provided for:					EAA 22.6.95
(a) management accounts;	N		—	—	
(b) cash book, invoices and bank statements;	Y		Y	T1	
(c) correspondence;	Y		Y	T1	
(d) minutes of meetings; and	Y		Y	T1	
(e) major contracts.	N		—	None	
2 Discuss with management and ensure that all material items have been identified.	Y		Y	T1	EAA 22.6.95
3 Complete the going concern audit programme on **T3**.	Y		Y	T3	EAA 22.6.95
4 Where there is a long delay between completing the field work and signing the audit report, complete programme **T4**.	N			Should be no delay in signing	EAA 22.6.95
Conclusion					
5 Consider whether there are any points which need to be included in a letter of representation or letter of comment and record this on **A5** or **A6** as appropriate.	Y		Y	Normal PBSE para	EAA 22.6.95
6 Other tests:	N	—	—	—	EAA 8.6.95

Client: Bright-a-Light Ltd		Prepared by: EAA	Date: 22.6.95	Ref: **T3**
Year/Period End: 31.3.95	File No:	Reviewed by: DGW	Date: 3.7.95	

AUDIT PROGRAMME – GOING CONCERN

Nature of test:	Test required Y/N	Covered by accountancy Y	Results satisfactory Y/N	Ref/ comments	Initials and date
1 Complete the going concern checklist on **T3.1** and consider what effect, if any, any 'yes' answers will have on the company's ability to continue trading as a going concern.	Y		Y	None	EAA 22.6.95
2 Where available obtain copies of cash flow forecasts and/or budgets and consider: (a) the applicability of the bases and assumptions used;	N		—	None	EAA 22.6.95
(b) whether they provide adequate evidence of the company's ability to continue as a going concern;	N		—		
(c) where a period of less than twelve months has been considered, what other evidence is available to support the company's ability to continue as a going concern.	N		—		
3 Where no cash flows or budgets are available, describe what evidence is available to support the company's ability to continue as a going concern.	Y		Y	T1	EAA 22.6.95
4 Where there is a significant level of concern about the company's ability to continue as a going concern, ensure the following items are adequately disclosed: (a) a statement that the accounts have been prepared on the going concern basis;	Y		Y	No concerns over going concern basis	EAA 22.6.95
(b) a statement of the pertinent facts;	Y		Y		
(c) the nature of the concern;	Y		Y		
(d) a statement of the assumptions adopted by the directors, which should be clearly distinguishable from the pertinent facts;	Y		Y		
(e) (where appropriate and practicable) a statement regarding the directors' plans for resolving the matters giving rise to the concern; and	Y		Y		
(f) details of any relevant actions by the directors.	Y		Y		
5 Complete the conclusion on **T3.1**.	Y		Y	T3.1	EAA 22.6.95

Client: Bright-a-Light Ltd		Prepared by: EAA	Date: 22.6.95	Ref: **T3.1**
Year/Period End: 31.3.95	File No:	Reviewed by: DGW	Date: 3.7.95	

GOING CONCERN – CHECKLIST

1 Financial

1.1	Does the company have net liabilities or net current liabilities? Not a major problem position is improving	YES/~~NO~~*
1.2	Has the company failed to negotiate finance to cover its borrowing requirements? (E.g., is it trading over its overdraft facility or is it having difficulty negotiating a time extension on its overdraft?)	~~YES~~/NO*
1.3	Has the company defaulted on any loan agreement or breached any covenant?	~~YES~~/NO*
1.4	Does the company have serious liquidity or cash flow problems?	~~YES~~/NO*
1.5	Has the company sustained major losses or experienced cash flow problems since the period end which could threaten the company's continued existence?	~~YES~~/NO*
1.6	Has the company sold a substantial number of fixed assets which it is not intending to replace?	~~YES~~/NO*
1.7	Is the company seeking a major restructuring of its debt?	~~YES~~/NO*
1.8	Has the company experienced problems in obtaining and/or retaining normal terms of trade credit by suppliers?	~~YES~~/NO*
1.9	Does the company have major debt repayments which are due or are about to fall due where refinancing is necessary to meet the obligation?	~~YES~~/NO*
1.10	Is the company experiencing problems paying debts as they fall due?	~~YES~~/NO*

2 *Operational*

2.1	Have there been any fundamental changes in the market or technology to which the entity is unable to adapt adequately?	~~YES~~/NO*
2.2	Have there been any externally forced reductions in operations (for example, as a result of legislation or regulatory action?)	~~YES~~/NO*
2.3	Has the company lost any key management or staff?	~~YES~~/NO*
2.4	Is the company experiencing any labour difficulties?	~~YES~~/NO*
2.5	Is the company relying on a few product lines and operating in a depressed market?	~~YES~~/NO*
2.6	Has the company lost any key suppliers or customers or have there been technical developments which could render a key product obsolete?	~~YES~~/NO*

3 *Other*

3.1	Is the company involved in any major litigation in which an adverse judgement could imperil the entity's continued existence?	~~YES~~/NO*
3.2	Are there any issues which involve a range of possible outcomes so wide that an unfavourable result could affect the appropriateness of the going concern basis?	~~YES~~/NO*
3.3	Are there any other factors which could adversely affect the appropriateness of the going concern basis? If 'yes', specify:	~~YES~~/NO*

____

____

* Delete as appropriate.

Client: Bright-a-Light Ltd		Prepared by:	Date:	Ref: **T3.1**
Year/Period End: 31.3.95	File No:	Reviewed by:	Date:	

GOING CONCERN – CONCLUSION

1 Where going concern has been reviewed by the directors for a period of less than 12 months has this been disclosed in the accounts or in the audit report?	~~YES~~/N/A*
2 Where you have been unable to obtain all the information and evidence necessary to adequately assess the company's ability to continue as a going concern, has a suitably worded qualified audit report been drafted?	~~YES~~/N/A*
3 Where the accounts have not been drawn up on a going concern basis, either: (a) are you happy that the basis of preparation of the accounts is reasonable and that there is adequate disclosure in the accounts; or (b) has a suitably worded qualified audit report been drafted?	~~YES~~/N/A*
4 Where there is a significant level of concern about the company's ability to continue as a going concern, either: (a) have adequate disclosures been made in the accounts and the explanatory paragraph in the audit report; or (b) has a suitably worded qualified audit report been drafted?	~~YES~~/N/A*

Prepared by EA Arbuthnott Date 22.6.95

Reviewed by DGW Date 3.7.95

*Delete if not applicable.

Client: Bright-a-Light Ltd		Prepared by: EAA	Date: 19.7.95	Ref: **T4**
Year/Period End: 31.3.95	File No:	Reviewed by: DGW	Date: 19.7.95	

FINAL PROGRAMME – POST BALANCE SHEET EVENTS

Nature of test:	Test required Y/N	Covered by accountancy Y	Results satisfactory Y/N	Ref/ comments	Initials and date
1 Establish whether the management have effective procedures to ensure that subsequent events are identified.	Y		Y	Directors heavily involved in business	EAA 19.7.95
2 Read the management minutes held since the final audit and enquire about matters discussed at meetings for which minutes are not yet available.	Y		Y	None	EAA 19.7.95
3 Review any available accounting records and identify whether anything needs to be reflected in the accounts.	N		—	—	EAA 19.7.95
4 Enquire with management whether any subsequent events have occurred which might affect the accounts. Cover specifically: (a) the current status of items involving subjective judgement or which were accounted for on the basis of preliminary data: specify:	Y		Y	Spoke to Director. J Austin Distrib. still not paid – unlikely to survive	EAA 19.7.95
(b) whether new commitments, borrowings or guarantees have been entered into;	Y		Y	None	EAA 19.7.95 (items (b)–5)
(c) whether sales of assets have occurred or are planned;	Y		Y	None	
(d) whether the issue of new shares or debentures, or an agreement to merge or to liquidate, has been made or is planned;	Y		Y	None	
(e) whether any assets have been destroyed;	Y		Y	None	
(f) whether there have been any developments regarding risk areas and contingencies;	Y		Y	None	
(g) whether any unusual accounting adjustments have been made or are contemplated;	Y		Y	None	
(h) whether any events have occurred or are likely to occur which might bring into question the appropriateness of the accounting policies.	Y		Y	None	
5 Consider, where appropriate, the validity of the going concern basis of accounting.	Y		Y	None	

U VALUE ADDED TAX

1 VAT account/reconciliation ☑

2 Audit programme ☑

3 VAT compliance checklist ☑

4 Analysis of VAT account ☐

5 ☐

6 ☐

7 ☐

Client: Bright-a-Light Ltd		Prepared by:	Date:	Ref: **U**
Year/Period End: 31.3.95	File No:	Reviewed by:	Date:	

SUMMARY SHEET – VALUE ADDED TAX

Audit objectives	***Planning*** Number of tests which satisfy objective	Additional/ alternative tests to be carried out	***Final*** Are you satisfied that the objectives have been met?	Comments	Initials
1 To ensure that VAT has been correctly accounted for.	1, 2, 4, ~~5~~, 7, 8		Yes/~~No~~		KM
2 To ensure any potential liabilities have been identified.	1, 2, 3, 4, ~~5~~, 6, 7, 8		Yes/~~No~~		KM

Conclusion

From the audit work carried out I confirm that:

- nothing has occurred to necessitate changing the audit plan* ~~or the audit plan has been updated.~~*
- nothing has occurred to necessitate revising the risk assessment* ~~or the risk assessment has been revised.~~*
- nothing has occurred to necessitate revising the materiality level* ~~or the materiality has been revised.~~*
- ~~adjustments to the plan, risk assessment and materiality have been detailed on **B5** or **B8**.~~*
- the work has been performed in accordance with the audit programme.
- the work performed and the results obtained have been adequately documented.
- all necessary information has been collected for the preparation of the statutory accounts.
- in my opinion (~~subject to the matters highlighted on **B5** or **B8**~~)* value added tax is fairly stated.

Prepared by K Martin Date 12.6.95

Reviewed by EA Arbuthnott Date 22.6.95

* Delete if not applicable.

Alternative conclusion (*ANY* alternative conclusion *MUST* be referred to on **B5** or **B8**)

Prepared by ______________________ Date ______________

Reviewed by ______________________ Date ______________

Client	Bright-a-Light Ltd	File No.	Ref. U1
Subject	VAT Control	Prepared by KM	Date 12/6/95
		Reviewed by EAA	Date 22/6/95
		Accounting Dates	31·3·95

		Dr			Cr
Op balance			Output VAT – Cash Sales	W13.2	15,147.56
Feb	837.44				
Mar	103.28		– SDB	W13.2	97,351.79
	J1	940.72			
Input VAT			VAT repaid	W2	12,729.92
– cash book	W4.1	8,016.04			
– petty cash	W9	71.83	Fuel scale charges		238.32
– PD B	W12	122,023.72			
			VAT receipt wrongly analysed in SDB column	W13.1	940.72
VAT paid	W4.3	129.21			
			Closing debtor		
			Feb	2,635.06	
			Mar	2,138.15	
				J1	4,773.21
		£131,181.52			£131,181.52

√ = Agreed to VAT returns

Conclusion

VAT debtor is fairly stated.

Client		File No.	Ref.
Bright-a-Light Ltd			U1.1
Subject		**Prepared by**	**Date**
VAT – Turnover reconciliation		KM	12/6/95
		Reviewed by	**Date**
		EAA	22/6/95
		Accounting Dates	31·3·95

			£
(a)	Outputs per returns agreed to turnover		
	Outputs per VAT returns/calculations		859,935
	less: fuel scales charges (net output)		1,360
			858,575
	Turnover per accounts		858,901
	Difference – immaterial		£326
(b)	VAT on turnover		
	Turnover – per sales ledger		
	Gas equipment	£15,015 @ 17½%	2,627
	Bottle hire	£35,930 @ 17½%	6,287
	Leisure products	£141,663 @ 17½%	24,791
	Gas, fuel etc.	£273,109 @ 17½%	47,794
		£393,010 @ 8%	31,440
			112,939
	Outputs per A/c U1		112,498
	Difference – immaterial		£441

Client: Bright-a-Light Ltd		Prepared by: KM	Date: 12.6.95	Ref: **U2**
Year/Period End: 31.3.95	File No:	Reviewed by: EAA	Date: 22.6.95	

AUDIT PROGRAMME – VALUE ADDED TAX

Nature of test:	Test required Y/N	Covered by accountancy Y	Results satisfactory Y/N	Ref/ comments	Initials and date
General					
1 Obtain and check, or prepare, a VAT control account. Confirm the VAT creditor or repayment due.	Y	Y	Y	U1	KM 12.6.95
2 Vouch the entries on the VAT control account to the VAT returns.	Y		Y	U1 + U1.1	KM 12.6.95
3 Reconcile the turnover per the accounts to the outputs recorded on the VAT returns.	Y	Y	Y	U1.1	KM 12.6.95
4 Reconcile the potential VAT on the turnover per the accounts to the outputs on the VAT control account.	Y	Y	Y	U1.1	KM 12.6.95
5 Complete the VAT checklist on **U3**.	N		—		EAA 8.6.95
6 Review the client's VAT affairs, including any correspondence, and ensure that adequate provision is made for any possible penalties and interest on under-declarations.	Y		Y	None	KM 12.6.95
7 Check that VAT on private proportions, including car fuel, has been properly accounted for.	Y	Y	Y	U1	KM 12.6.95
Conclusion					
8 Consider whether there are any points which need to be included in a letter of representation or letter of comment and record on **A5** or **A6**, as appropriate.	Y		Y	None	EAA 22.6.95
9 Other tests:	N	—	—	—	EAA 8.6.95

W ACCOUNTS WORKING PAPERS

1	**Bank account**	✓
2	Analysis of receipts	✓
3	Unrecorded receipts	
4	Analysis of payments	✓
5	Unrecorded payments	
6	**Cash account**	
7	Analysis of receipts	
8	Analysis of payments	
9	**Petty cash account**	✓
10	Summary receipts/payments	
11	**Wages PAYE etc., summary**	✓
12	**Creditors control account**	✓
13	**Debtors control account**	✓
14		
15		
16		

X RECORDS RECEIVED

1	Summary of items	
2		
3		
4		

Client		File No.	Ref.
Bright-a-Light Ltd			W1
Subject		**Prepared by**	**Date**
Bank control account		KM	9/6/95
		Reviewed by	**Date**
		EAA	19/6/95
		Accounting Dates	31·3·95

Bankings	W2	961,423.24	Balance b/fwd	K1	27,775.39
Balance c/fwd	K1	41,605.17	Cheque payments	W4	975,253.02
		£1,003,028.41			£1,003,028.41

Client		File No.	Ref.
Bright-a-Light Ltd			W2
Subject		Prepared by KM	Date 9/6/95
Schedule of Bankings		Reviewed by EAA	Date 22/6/95
		Accounting Dates	31·3·95

Month	*Shop sales*	*Sales ledger*	*VAT*	*Sundry*	*Total*
April	8,945.63	54,368.21			63,313.84
May	9,143.63	51,667.51	71.43		60,882.57
June	9,442.81	48,306.21		01	57,749.03
July	8,113.35	47,209.58			55,322.93
August	7,239.61	58,476.65	1,002.66		60,718.92
Sept	8,071.09	47,941.66	1,724.32	877.61	58,614.68
Oct	11,663.25	48,340.52	1,764.60	3,402.50	65,170.87
Nov	12,584.17	61,956.76	1,924.20	612.22	77,077.35
Dec	10,921.73	68.699.64		24.52	79,645.89
Jan	8,073.42	108,176.98	2,799.10	3,598.08	122,647.58
Feb	9,872.12	120,319.89			130,192.01
March	9,246.31	111,397.65	3,443.61		124,087.57
	113,317.12	826,861.26	12,729.92	8,514.94	961,423.24
		W13.1	U1	W2.1	W1

Client	File No.	Ref.
Bright-a-Light Ltd		W2.1
Subject	**Prepared by**	**Date**
Schedule of Sundry Receipts	KM	9/6/95
	Reviewed by	**Date**
	EAA	22/6/95
	Accounting Dates	31·3·95

June			
Underbanking (Sales – Coal)			0.01
September			
RCF Re NCB Advertising		382.72	
Fuel Supplies – Rebate		20.50	
Fuel Supplies – Rebate		415.74	
McDonald – Solicitor	Q12	61.15	
			880.11
October			
Loan – Mrs J Strike (Senior) Repaid on W4.3	L5.2	3,000.00	
Sale of Ford Fiesta	F3.1	400.00	
			3,400.00
November			
Fuel Supplies – Rebate			612.22
December			
Fuel Supplies – Rebate			24.52
January			
K Strike loan A/c } Repaid on W4.3		1,500.00	
J Strike loan A/c } Repaid on W4.3		1,500.00	
Loyalty Rebate – Fuel Supplies		598.06	
Underbanking (Sales – Coal)		0.02	
			3,598.08
		W2	8,514.94

Client		File No.	Ref.
Bright-a-Light Ltd			W4
Subject		**Prepared by**	**Date**
Schedule of Payments		KM	9/6/95
		Reviewed by	**Date**
		EAA	22/6/95
		Accounting Dates	31·3·95

		£	
April		52,018.10	
May		62,933.18	
June		47,910.59	
July		49,557.06	
August		54,102.25	
September		68,340.75	
October		126,980.13	
November		63,495.41	
December		70,534.45	
January		84,341.88	
February		149,585.02	
March		143,052.50	
Returned cheques		1,873.80	W13.1
Adjustments		527.30	W4.4
Per bank A/c		£975,253.02	W1
Payments per W4.1		£972,851.92	W4.1
Returned cheques	SLC A/c	1,873.80	W13.1
Adjustments		527.30	W4.4
		£975,253.02	W1

Client		File No.	Ref.
Bright-a-Light Ltd			W4.1
Subject		**Prepared by**	**Date**
Analysis of payments per cashbook		KM	9/6/95
		Reviewed by	**Date**
		EAA	22/6/95
		Accounting Dates	31·3·95

Category		£	
	VAT	√8,016.04√	U1
Delivery	Wages	14,168.06	W4.2
	NIC & Pension	1,798.27	W4.2
	Petrol/Diesel	√6,352.86	
	Tyres & Repairs	√7,823.60	
	RFL & insurance	√2,637.25	
	Misc.	√2,707.36	
Yard	Wages	5,778.70	W4.2
	NIC & Pension	772.88	W4.2
	Plant Maintenance	√5,481.13	
	Depot Maintenance	√5,815.00	
	Services	√1,321.58	
	Rates	5,701.31	
	Insurance	2,860.26	
	Misc.	103.46	
Management	Salary	28,823.67	W4.2
	NIC & Pension	3,787.24	W4.2
	Travel Expenses	1,522.23	
	Motor Expenses	4,482.70	
	Agents Commission	1,874.11	
	Misc.	1,209.33	
Office	Printing	1,336.67	
	Computer	2,213.37	
	Telephone	2,623.63	
	Postage	1,300.00	
	Advertising	3,260.95	
	Repairs	75.19	
	Misc.	646.11	
	Audit & Legal	57,912.07	W4.3
	Petty cash	1,625.39	W9
	Ledger (purchase ledger)	788,821.50	W12
		£972,851.92	W4

Client		File No.	Ref.
Bright-a-Light Ltd			W4.2
Subject Wages/salaries		**Prepared by** KM	**Date** 9/6/95
Analysis of cash book payments		**Reviewed by** EAA	**Date** 22/6/95
		Accounting Dates 31·3·95	

	Total	Net	PAYE/NIC control PAYE	NIC	Pension	Other deductions
	£	£	£	£	£	£
Delivery	14,168.06	11,741.16	1,626.72		674.33	125.85
Delivery NIC	1,798.27			1,798.27		
Yard	5,778.70	5,488.70	290.00			
Yard NIC	772.88			772.88		
Management	28,823.67	21,526.20	4,792.25		2,505.22	
NIC	3,787.24			3,787.24		
	55,128.82	38,756.06	6,708.97	6,358.39	3,179.55	125.85

See W4.1

Client: Bright-a-Light Ltd	File No.	Ref. W4.3
Subject: Audit & Legal – analysis of CB column	Prepared by: KM	Date: 9/6/95
£57,912.07	Reviewed by: EAA	Date: 22/6/95
	Accounting Dates: 31·3·95	

	£	£	
Accountancy/audit (Jones Watson & Co)		3,700.00	
Credit card charges		408.20	
BDL interest – Vehicle loan	557.10		
– No 3	9,562.06		
– No 2	3,792.80		
		13,911.96	
BDL repayments – Vehicle loan	1,714.62		K8
– No 3	7,169.90		K7
– No 2	5,000.00		K6
		13,884.52	
Bank charges and interest		3,807.12	
VAT paid		129.21	U1
Legal		522.05	
Capital expenditure – Display	326.49		F3
– Lorry D446JAB	2,600.00		
– D872JRM	4,750.00		
Initial base payment for car		7,676.49	
S/L refund		728.34	F6
Registrar of Companies		6,372.31	W13.1
Loans		18.00	
Corporation tax		6,000.00	P1
Contract cleaning		500.00	
		253.87	
		£57,912.07	W4.1

Client		File No.	Ref.
Bright-a-Light Ltd			W4.4
Subject: Schedule of Bank A/C Adjustments		Prepared by: KM	Date: 9/6/95
		Reviewed by: EAA	Date: 22/6/95
		Accounting Dates	31·3·95

Date	*Detail*		*Amount* £	£	
June	Lost cheque			250.00	
August	Returned cheque	Cheques included in receipts but later bounced	(165.60)		
Nov	Returned cheque		(133.00)		
Dec	Returned cheque		(158.70)		
Jan	Returned cheque		(170.00)		
Feb	Returned cheque		(150.00)		
				(777.30)	W13.1
				£(527.30)	W4

Client	File No.	Ref.	
Bright-a-Light Ltd		W9	
Subject	**Prepared by**		**Date**
Petty cash	KM		12/6/95
	Reviewed by		**Date**
	EAA		22/6/95
	Accounting Dates	31·3·95	

		£	£
Balance B. Fwd		122.74	
Payments (analysis below)			1,287.28
Receipts from Bank	W4.1	1,625.39	
Balance C. Fwd	K1		460.85
		1,748.13	1,748.13

Analysis of petty cash expenditure:

		£	Code
Petrol & diesel		12.06	152
Repairs & maintenance		144.07	160
Miscellaneous		106.83	190
Repairs & maintenance		253.50	202
Travelling		130.06	255
Motor expenses		23.52	256
Miscellaneous		22.75	257
Printing & stationery		6.48	270
Postage		236.37	275
Advertising		14.34	280
Repairs & maintenance		49.21	285
Miscellaneous		216.26	290
VAT	U1	71.83	960
		1,287.28	

Client		File No.	Ref.
Bright-a-Light Ltd			W11
Subject		Prepared by	Date
PAYE/Wages Control		KM	9/6/95
		Reviewed by	Date
		EAA	22/6/95
		Accounting Dates	31·3·95

		Dr		Cr
		£		£
			Balance b/fwd	478.00
			NIC E'ees	327.85
Payments per summary	W4.2		NIC E'ers	275.87
				1,081.72
Net pay		38,756.06		
PAYE		6,708.97		
NIC		6,358.39	Gross Pay	
			Monthly	28,738.00
			Weekly	20,990.11
Pension – E'ees contributions			E'ers NIC	
Monthly		466.78	Monthly	2,051.64
Weekly		249.99	Weekly	1,395.10
Other deductions – weekly		125.85		
			E'ers Class 1A NIC	627.61
Difference		2.23		
Bal c/fwd				
M. PAYE/NIC	√862.93			
W.	√423.09			
		1,286.02	L1	
Wages week 53		√302.28	L1	
Class 1A NIC		627.61	L1	
		£54,884.18		£54,884.18

Conclusion

Difference not material ⇒ Not investigated.
√ = agreed to payrolls – month 12 and weeks 49 to 53.

Client	File No.	Ref.
Bright-a-Light Ltd		W12

Subject	Prepared by	Date
Purchase Ledger Control	KM	9/6/95
	Reviewed by EAA	Date 22/6/95
	Accounting Dates	31·3·95

		Dr £	*Cr* £
Balance b.f.	L1		51,109.15
Purchases – see below			819,302.11
Payments	W4.1	788,821.50	
Balance c.f.	L1	81,589.76	
		£870,411.26	£870,411.26

Analysis of purchases.

	Solid Fuel £	*Packed gas* £	*Bulk gas* £	*Gas equip.* £	*Leisure* £	*VAT* £	*Total* £
A	8,322.11	8,959.16	20,002.51	274.19	15,218.78	9,235.93	62,012.68
M	6,623.48	4,148.43	7,119.06	559.59	13,332.91	5,562.10	37,345.57
J	12,892.64	3,667.84	5,240.77	645.74	21,044.85	7,611.07	51,102.91
J	19,539.40	4,902.62	8,567.06	424.72	22,066.75	9,712.59	65,213.14
A	32,024.99	16,555.46	5,408.02	1,038.63	14,178.02	12,110.90	81,316.02
S	18,486.20	6,166.93	13,175.28	748.61	4,342.95	7,510.99	50,430.96
O	3,869.01	12,950.96	25,525.06	2,595.79	2,887.75	8,369.99	56,198.56
N	7,386.52	9,275.04	20,041.90	442.37	1,183.78	6,707.69	45,037.30
D	18,975.03	12,481.96	28,575.33	958.03	5,024.51	11,552.61	77,567.47
J	33,460.49	17,090.75	41,620.84	1,122.51	5,195.20	17,235.72	115,725.51
F	30,965.12	25,727.35	37,690.70	496.16	7,470.52	17,911.23	120,261.08
M	11,315.55	9,032.45	24,347.85	638.88	3,253.28	8,502.90	57,090.91
	203,860.54	130,958.95	237,314.38	9,945.22	115,199.30	122,023.72	819,302.11
						U1	

Client		File No.	Ref.
Bright-a-Light Ltd			W13.1
Subject		Prepared by	Date
Sales Ledger Control Account		KM	12/6/95
		Reviewed by	Date
		EAA	22/6/95
		Accounting Dates	31·3·95

		Dr £			*Cr* £
Opening balance	J1	73,195.70			
Sales	W13.2	868,442.66	Ledger receipts	W2	826,861.26
Non sales ledger receipts incl. in S/L column					
Sale of Montego	F3.1	2,000.00√			
Insurance claim		,256.91 √	Difference – written off to sales (coal)		19.82
Legal fees recovered		20.59√			
Legal fees recovered		52.77√			
Loyalty rebate – Fuel Supplies		656.96√			
Loyalty rebate – Fuel Supplies		689.28√			
VAT Receipts	U1	940.72√			
Sales ledger refunds	W4.3	6,372.31 √	Balance c.f.	J1	√ 128,397.92
Returned cheques	W4.4	777.30			
Returned cheques	W4	1,873.80			
		£955,279.00			£955,279.00
		ν			ν

Key

ν Casts checked
√ Agreed to list of sales ledger balances at 31.3.95

Client	File No.	Ref.
Bright-a-Light Ltd – Sales ledger		W13.2

Subject	Prepared by	Date
Sales summary	KM	12/6/95
	Reviewed by	**Date**
	EAA	22/6/95
	Accounting Dates	31·3·95

Credit sales		£	*Code*
Solid fuel		238,105.35	001
Gas packed		136,067.33	020
Gas hire charges (for bottle)		35,930.12	020
Gas bulk		280,158.36	020
Leisure products		70,299.71	030
Rent		10,530.00	105
VAT	U1	97,351.79	960
	W13.1	£868,442.66	

Cash sales		£	*Code*
Gas equipment		15,014.53	020
Solid fuel		11,792.74	001
Leisure products		71,362.98	030
VAT	U1	15,147.56	
		£113,317.81	

Y COMPUTER REPORTS

1 Year end trial balance NOT SHOWN ☑

2 Journals ☑

3 Nominal ledger printouts NOT SHOWN ☑

4 Posting summary/data entry ☐

5 Opening trial balance ☐

6 ☐

7 ☐

8 ☐

9 ☐

Z OBSOLETE WORKING PAPERS

1 ☐

2 ☐

3 ☐

4 ☐

Client	File No.	Ref.
Bright-a-Light Ltd		Y2

Subject	Prepared by	Date
Post TB adjustments	EAA	16/6/95
	Reviewed by DGW	Date 3/7/95
	Accounting Dates	31·3·95

		Dr £	*Cr* £
(1)	Dr Motor Vehicle – cost	8,995.00	
	Cr Finance lease liability <1 yr		8,995.00
(2)	Dr Depreciation – P & L	2,998.00	
	Cr Motor vehicle depreciation		2,998.00
(3)	Dr Finance lease liability <1 yr	1,858.33	
	Dr Finance lease interest	1,055.03	
	Cr Repairs & Maintenance – yard		2,913.36
(4)	Dr Finance lease liability <1 yr	5,047.24	
	Cr Finance lease due >1 year		5,047.24

Being: adjustments to record Peugeot 405 and associated finance lease F6

(5)	Dr Bad debts – profit & loss	2,501.16	
	Cr Trade debtors		2,501.16

Being: Provision against bad debts J4.2

(6)	Dr Depreciation – buildings (P & L)	4,263.00	
	Cr Buildings depreciation		4,263.00

Being: Increase in provision due to change in useful economic life of buildings F7

(7)	Dr Motor vehicle depreciation – Balance sheet	52.00	
	Cr Depreciation – P & L		52.00

Being: adjustment to depreciation calculation on motor vehicle pool F3.1

(8)	Dr Trade debtors	1,218.19	
	Cr Trade creditors		1,218.19

Being: Credit balances on sales ledger J1

(9)	DrBDL No 3	35,000.00	
	BDL No 2	72,965.00	
	Vehicle loan	1,035.00	
	Cr Creditors >1 year		109,000.00

Being: Amounts due >1 year for loans (2) K1.1

Client	File No.	Ref.
Bright-a-Light Ltd		Y2
Subject	**Prepared by**	**Date**
Post TB adjustments	EAA	3/7/95
	Reviewed by	**Date**
	DGW	3/7/95
	Accounting Dates	31·3·95

		Dr £	*Cr* £
(10)	Bad debts (P & L)	5,923.43	
	Cr Trade debtors		5,923.43
Being:	provision for bad debt post partner review J4.2		
(11)	Tax charge	5,863.00	
	Cr Corporation tax		5,863.00
Being:	Corporation tax charge for the year A2		
(12)	Motor expenses	627.61	
	Wages control		627.61
Being:	Class IA NIC for the year W11		